Springer Texts in Social Sciences

This textbook series delivers high-quality instructional content for graduates and advanced graduates in the social sciences. It comprises self-contained edited or authored books with comprehensive international coverage that are suitable for class as well as for individual self-study and professional development. The series covers core concepts, key methodological approaches, and important issues within key social science disciplines and also across these disciplines. All texts are authored by established experts in their fields and offer a solid methodological background, accompanied by pedagogical materials to serve students, such as practical examples, exercises, case studies etc. Textbooks published in this series are aimed at graduate and advanced graduate students, but are also valuable to early career and established researchers as important resources for their education, knowledge and teaching.

The books in this series may come under, but are not limited to, these fields:

– Sociology
– Anthropology
– Population studies
– Migration studies
– Quality of life and wellbeing research

Merrill Singer

The Anthropology of Human and Planetary Health

An Ecosyndemic Approach

Merrill Singer
Department of Anthropology
University of Connecticut
Storrs, CT, USA

ISSN 2730-6135 ISSN 2730-6143 (electronic)
Springer Texts in Social Sciences
ISBN 978-3-031-83673-2 ISBN 978-3-031-83674-9 (eBook)
https://doi.org/10.1007/978-3-031-83674-9

© The Editor(s) (if applicable) and The Author(s), under exclusive license to Springer Nature Switzerland AG 2025

This work is subject to copyright. All rights are solely and exclusively licensed by the Publisher, whether the whole or part of the material is concerned, specifically the rights of translation, reprinting, reuse of illustrations, recitation, broadcasting, reproduction on microfilms or in any other physical way, and transmission or information storage and retrieval, electronic adaptation, computer software, or by similar or dissimilar methodology now known or hereafter developed.
The use of general descriptive names, registered names, trademarks, service marks, etc. in this publication does not imply, even in the absence of a specific statement, that such names are exempt from the relevant protective laws and regulations and therefore free for general use.
The publisher, the authors and the editors are safe to assume that the advice and information in this book are believed to be true and accurate at the date of publication. Neither the publisher nor the authors or the editors give a warranty, expressed or implied, with respect to the material contained herein or for any errors or omissions that may have been made. The publisher remains neutral with regard to jurisdictional claims in published maps and institutional affiliations.

This Springer imprint is published by the registered company Springer Nature Switzerland AG
The registered company address is: Gewerbestrasse 11, 6330 Cham, Switzerland

If disposing of this product, please recycle the paper.

This book is dedicated to my granddaughter, Zoey Olivia Singer, in hopes that her world is the best of all scenarios.

Acknowledgments

I thank Lani Davison for reading and commenting on this book.

Introduction

This book has a simple goal but getting there is a complicated task. The aim is to introduce undergraduate students in health or environment-related classes to the mounting crisis of syndemics through the illuminating lens of planetary health. These terms may not be familiar. Just a few years ago, a staff writer at Smithsonian Magazine, the popular and colorful periodical that covers the many subjects researched and exhibited at the Smithsonian Institution in Washington, D.C., called syndemics "a little-known buzzword" although it added that the concept well "describes our troubled times" (Daley, 2019). In fact, the concept is not new, nor has it proven to be a fleeting participant in the ever innovative language of popular culture. In fact, it has gained growing traction in the lexicon of the health and social sciences. In turn, the term planetary health, which is of recent coinage, might at first glance seem to refer to the well-being of Earth, the sole astronomical body known (at this time) to harbor life. This is in part true, but, as we shall see, the concept encompasses much more and it too has gained a widening adherence in health-related thinking and research. Indeed, both concepts of central concern to this book have been applauded as thought-provoking, solutions-oriented approaches to what are, undeniably, troubled times.

The concept of syndemics, developed by the author about 30 years ago and now in wide use across multiple health-related disciplines, focuses attention on the adverse synergistic interaction of two or more diseases or other health conditions promoted or facilitated by social and/or environmental conditions. Highlighting the added health challenges of simultaneous and interconnected epidemics (e.g., cases like COVID-19 and diabetes; HIV/AIDS and tuberculosis; polysubstance abuse and depression), a syndemics approach is rooted in a critical biosocial understanding of health. As Maria Rico and Laura Pautass (2023) observe in the book From Crisis to Catastrophe, a syndemic approach "reveals the convergence of risks that affect a society at a specific time in history. Unless such risks are handled together, the effects of a syndemic multiply and increase vulnerability for large sectors of the population." Given the sweeping health-altering changes occurring across the world as a result of human actions, this book addresses paramount issues facing all Earthlings, human and non-human alike.

The syndemic approach has generated growing interest among health researchers around the world. The evidence of this is in the numbers. In a meta-analysis of the literature published on syndemics between 2001 and 2020, Mahbub Hossain and colleagues (2022), for example, found a total of 830 articles authored by 3025 authors; some articles, of course, have multiple authors. Publications on syndemics, they note, have gradually increased since 2003, with rapid development since 2013. This pattern has continued through to the present with over 200 scholarly articles on syndemics published in 2023, indicating that the field of syndemics remains a continuously growing focus of academic scholarship and researcher interest. The syndemics concept has proved to have appeal because it provides a useful and easily graspable framework for organizing what health researchers are seeing as they grapple with the complexities and mounting challenges of human health, including the epidemiological burden in populations suffering multiple health problems and associated adverse socio-environmental factors in local and regional contexts.

The syndemics approach highlights three key points: (1) diseases are not evenly dispersed across populations but rather tend to cluster in disadvantaged groups that suffer elevated rates of multimorbidity; (2) such clustering increases opportunities for adverse disease interactions across various biological and psychological pathways; and (3) macro/microlevel contextual factors from oppression to pollution facilitate interaction and increase overall vulnerability and disease burden. The term ecosyndemics specifically references cases in which the impact of social factors is mediated by anthropogenic disruptions of the climate/environment (e.g., the role of the fossil fuel industry in air pollution and the development of lung disease-involved syndemics). The eocosyndemics concept provides a direct connection to the issues of primary concern to the field of planetary health.

The planetary health framework, which was developed initially within biomedicine, is a holistic rethinking of our understanding of what makes health—yours, mine, and that of all other living beings. This approach resonates with the insight of the prolific writer and environmental activist Wendell Berry (1969) who noted: "We have lived our lives by the assumption that what was good for us would be good for the world. We have been wrong. We must change our lives so that it will be possible to live by the contrary assumption, what is good for the world will be good for us. And that requires that we make the effort to know the world and learn what is good for it."

Adopted as a transdisciplinary research paradigm planetary health seeks to identify the safe environmental limits within which humanity and other species can flourish on our increasingly imperiled planet. Adherents of the planetary health paradigm recognize that the natural systems that have enabled human and other life on Earth are beginning to collapse. At this moment in history, we are faced with a dangerous confluence of environmental crises. The accelerating pace of climate change and other critical environmental disruptions pose a grave but still preventable threat to the global population of humans and, indeed, all forms of life. As a result of this threat, we cannot engage in siloed thinking about human health, animal/plant health, and environmental health; we need an interconnected, multispecies, and animate/inanimate view on these ever more crucial issues. A planetary health perspective was developed in order to create a unified field and social movement designed to safeguard human health and the health of all life on Earth before it is too late (Horton 2013).

Introduction

By uniting ecosyndemics and planetary health theory, this book provides students in introductory medical anthropology, medical sociology, environmental health, public health, health psychology, and related courses with a conceptual framework for better understanding the grave risks—ranging from climate change to COVID-19 and from outdoor air contaminants to chemicals in consumer products—that now threaten our lives and world, while offering concrete directions for achieving a safe, equitable, and sustainable future.

The complicated task of this book involves overcoming a number of hurdles. One of the biggest challenges is simply grasping the complexity of our global crisis. There is a lot going on. Just fully getting one's head around one issue, say climate change, can keep a person up at night. But our planet is facing multiple threats, most of our own making, and what some call the doomsday clock is always ticking. A starting point is remembering, as botanist Frank Egler (quoted in Niering, 1998) explained, the world we live in is entwined and thus "ecosystems are not only more complex than we think but more complex than we can think." Their simplification or unraveling produces unforeseen but almost always dismal outcomes.

This point is illustrated by looking at the role of bats in the link between human and environmental health. Environmental economist Eyal Frank (2024) has shown that in counties in the USA with outbreaks of white nose syndrome, an infectious disease that kills bats, the rate of infant mortality goes up by 7.9% in comparison with counties without the disease. The explanation of this surprising finding is that after the onset of bat die-offs, farmers increase their use of insecticides by an average of 31.1%. This increase reflects the fact that bats eat agricultural pests like moths and loss of bats means there are more pests eating agricultural crops. As a result of these changes, newborns are exposed to more pesticides, chemicals known to be harmful to babies. Contaminated water and air probably serve as pathways for the pesticides to enter infant's bodies. This finding is not unique. A study by found Raynor et al. (2021) found that reintroducing grey wolves in Wisconsin reduced vehicle collisions with deer by 24%. The reason is that the reintroduced wolves established hunting patrols along highways which they also use as travel corridors. As a result, deer learn to stay clear of highways resulting in fewer accidents and related injuries and deaths. In Costa Rica and Panama in Central America, declines in amphibians and snakes caused by a fungal disease led to significant increases in cases of human malaria infections (Springborn et al., 2022). The decline in species that prey on mosquitos allowed mosquito populations to thrive unchecked, including mosquitos infected with malaria. In the case of Central America, climate change and increased rainfall also contributed to the proliferation of mosquitos. In an experimental study, Young and co-workers (2014) excluded large wildlife like zebras from parts of a savanna ecosystem in East Africa. They found that this emptied environment was then occupied by an increase in the number of rodents feeding on the grasslands. Because rodent and, consequently, flea abundance doubled following the removal of large mammals, the density of infected rodents and fleas carrying *Bartonella* bacteria was about two times higher in sites experimental areas compared with unaltered control areas. This change put humans living in the area at heightened risk of contracting bartonellosis, a disease that causes swollen lymph nodes, fever, headache, fatigue, poor appetite, and skin pustules.

Second, it means pouring into one holistic conceptual model data from diverse domains. For example, it is no small feat to link the structure of societies, including built-in social and economic inequality, with diverse human behaviors, the environmental impacts of these behaviors, the health consequences of these impacts, and the pathways, mechanics, and outcomes of disease interaction. Fortunately, there is a large body of research to draw upon to address the linkages of interest, and hence this book references numerous studies.

Third, our task involves demonstrating specific environmental influences on specific health outcomes in a complex world. With multiple factors always at play, identifying specific causal linkages presents researchers with weighty methodological challenges. As Hans Keune (2012) explains, "the interaction of all relevant elements, both pollutants and health parameters, as well as a wide range of intervening variables such as lifestyle and genetic factors, create a very complex interplay that is hardly possible to conceive in all its complexity, let alone fully measure, describe, and comprehend." One solution to this dilemma has been to move beyond studying the effects of exposure to single pollutants or toxins and instead to study how cocktails of pollutants and toxins create consequences that surpass the effect of single environmental risks. This has been called the study of ecocrises interactions. This term also applies to other adverse environmental interactions, like the interaction between overfishing the oceans and marine pollution in diminishing the fish populations in the seas.

Fourth, it necessitates addressing stormy public disputes over health effects and even the validity of scientific findings about those health outcomes. All public health issues are political, environmental health especially so. There are well-heeled vested interests in obscuring the causes (and causers) of environmental problems and their health consequences. A telling example of this pattern is seen in the "dirty air" campaign mounted by polluting industries and their political allies. Using fear mongering and an endless list of falsehoods, lobbyists try to sell the idea that the compliance costs for industry to clean up its own air pollution are too great, pollution is not that bad, and the Environmental Protection Agency is causing an energy crisis. One of the chief characteristics of this campaign is that its strategies and tactics derive from the tobacco industry playbook, the disinformation effort devised by the tobacco industry during the 1950s to protect profits in the face of the mounting evidence linking tobacco smoke and lethal diseases, especially cancer (Oreskes & Conway, 2010).

Finally, while the broader syndemic literature is now substantial, the portion that targets the role of the environment in ecosyndemic production is, thus far, limited. Indeed, an objective of this book is to promote and develop an interest in syndemics among students with a concern about the environment and health, including the ways disruptions we cause in the environment rebound on us and our well-being. For example, most of us drive cars; indeed, unless you are studying online, the college or university you are attending has been built to accommodate a large number of vehicles. In the USA, in particular, it is hard, if not impossible, to get around in most parts of the country without a vehicle. Yet, we know that cars and trucks pollute the air and that air pollution is a major and multifaceted threat to our health. It has been linked to over 700 diseases. Society is structured in a way that all but compels us to be complicit in creating health risks. And there are very wealthy and well-connected sectors of society that are deeply committed to retaining and even expanding our fossil fuel-dependent economy. Every day, advertisers entice us with carefully crafted media messages intended to get us to buy more, consume more, and drive more. Yet, an ecosyndemic/planetary health approach, as described in this book, is designed to empower us to swim upstream and challenge prevailing frames of reference and action in our world. Given the current state of our world, characterized by the threat of abrupt ecological change, this effort is propelled by a deep sense of urgency.

This book is organized in five chapters. The first considers many of the key indicators of the advancing environmental and climate crisis and the implications of the changes that are occurring on health. Also of keen concern are the underlying social structural causes of Earth's contemporary ecocrises, including species extinction and loss of biodiversity. On this foundation, Chap. 2 examines the emergence and scope of the planetary health perspective and further explores the role of the environment in health and health equity. It also assesses the health of animals, plants, and their shared environments. Also of concern in the chapter are Indigenous voices commenting on the planetary health approach. The next chapter focuses on ecosyndemics in light of the planetary health perspective. Further, it explores known and potential ecosyndemics, pathways of environmental and other disease interaction, and health impacts across disparate populations. Having laid out the severe challenges that threaten the sustainability of many species, including our own, Chap. 4 addresses grassroots efforts to build an effective and united fightback against the growing ecocrises that are occurring globally. The last chapter weaves together the diverse materials presented in the book to affirm the value of a reorientation to health that is informed by a unified syndemics and planetary health framework.

Contents

1	**Multiple Signs of the Advancing Environmental/Climate Health Crisis**	1
	How Has Earth and Our Understanding of It Changed in the Last 25 Years?	1
	An Anthropologist Studies the Ecosyndemics of Development in the Amazon...	3
	Becoming a Biocultural Anthropologist......................	3
	Impacts of the Southern Interoceanic Highway	5
	Costs and Benefits of Damming the Xengu	5
	Toward a Critical Health Anthropology	7
	Telltale Signs of the Environmental/Climate Health Crisis	11
	Heatwaves and Health..	12
	Melting, Ocean Rise, and Vulnerable Populations	14
	Deforestation and Disease.....................................	17
	Disruptions and Destruction of Sea Life.........................	18
	Climate Change and Deoxygenation	19
	Plastic Oceans..	21
	Overfishing..	23
	Desertification, Drought, and Malnutrition.......................	24
	Hurricanes and Disasters......................................	26
	The Spread of Infectious Diseases	29
	Infrastructure Maladaptation...................................	30
	Where Are We Headed?	31
	What Does "Us" Mean? The Lesson of Forever Chemicals...........	32
2	**The Shift to Planetary Health in the Twenty-First Century**	37
	Eliminating Disease	37
	How Epidemics End...	40
	Worldwide Equity...	41
	Safe Environmental Limits Within Which Humanity Can Flourish.....	43
	Ecocrises Interaction...	47
	Climate Change → Biodiversity.............................	48
	Biodiversity → Climate Change.............................	48
	Biodiversity → Infectious Disease	48

	Infectious Disease → Biodiversity	49
	Climate Change → Infectious Disease	50
	Infectious Disease → Climate Change	51
	The Social Context of Planetary Health	51
	Birth of Planetary Health	54
	One Health	58
	Formal Organization of Planetary Health	58
	The Colonial Roots of Public Health	66
	Applying Indigenous Knowledge	70
	Archaeogenetics and the Indigenous Struggle for Recognition in Argentina	76
	Planetary Health 2.0	77
	Reflections on the Challenges of Collaboration	86
3	**The Making of Ecosyndemics**	91
	The Changing Environment and Ecosyndemics	96
	The Lungs: A Key Interface with the Environment	96
	The Heart in Ecosyndemics	101
	A COVID-19 Ecosyndemic in Latin America	104
	The Elder Health Ecosyndemics in the USA	106
	Adverse Pathogen–Pathogen Interaction in Ecosyndemics	109
	Legionnaires' Disease	110
	HIV/HCV Co-infection	112
	Tick-Borne Diseases	113
	Malaria and Intestinal Parasites	118
	The Ecosyndemics of Childhood Diarrhea	122
	Antimicrobial Resistance Syndemic	126
4	**Fighting Back: Uniting the Health and Environment Movements**	135
	Planetary Health, Ecosyndemics, and Activism	135
	Prelude to Activism	137
	Bottom-Up: Grassroots Heath Activism	142
	AIDS Activism	143
	Disability Mobilizing	145
	Breast Cancer Activism	149
	Syringe Exchange and Harm Reduction	150
	Reproductive Rights and the Women's Health Movement	152
	Long COVID	155
	ME/CSF and Encumbered Activism	158
	Assessing Health Activism	160
	From Love Canal to the Environmental Health Movement	161
	Coupling Environmental and Health Activism: From Alberta, Canada to Flint, Michigan to Bergama, Turkey	165
	Learning from COVID-19	171
	Solidarity in a Big Tent	175

5	**Conclusion**	179
	In the Year 2050	179
	Worst Case	180
	Best Case	182
	Activist Momentum	185
	Centering Equity and Inclusion	186
	Health and Ecological Balance	187
	On the Precipice	189

References 191

Multiple Signs of the Advancing Environmental/Climate Health Crisis

1

Abstract

Beginning with a review of how Earth and our understanding of it have changed over the last 25 years, this chapter considers many of the key indicators of the advancing environmental and climate crisis and the health implications of the changes that are occurring. Also of keen concern are the underlying social structural causes of Earth's contemporary ecocrises, including species extinction and loss of biodiversity. The chapter highlights the ecosyndemics research of anthropologist Paula Skye Tallman. The chapter locates the study of ecosyndemics in critical health anthropology theory.

Keywords

Critical health anthropology · Heatwaves · Ocean rise · Deforestation · Threats to marine life · Drought · Extreme weather events · Infectious disease · Forever chemicals

How Has Earth and Our Understanding of It Changed in the Last 25 Years?

Twenty-five years (9125 days) does not seem like a long time, against say, the age of Earth (4.543 billion years), or the emergence of our species Homo sapiens (about 300,000 years ago), or even since the invention of telephones (over 100 years ago). In fact, November 1, 2000, about 25 years ago, was the last time all living humans were physically on Earth, since then there have always been a few people living on the International Space Station approximately 25 miles (40 km) above the planet. What else has changed in the world since then? Of course, there are a lot more people on Earth now than in 2000, almost 2 billion more, and that number is growing. The UN estimates there will be a global population of 9.7 billion people by

2050. While the world's human population continues to increase, the pace is actually slowing. With declines in fertility, the overall global population of our species has witnessed unprecedented aging. With increased age, human frailties increase as does multimorbidity (suffering from several serious diseases at the same time). Additionally, people are on the move. International migration has risen since the beginning of the twenty-first century. One expression of this mobility is that the human world is rapidly urbanizing, with substantial increases in rural-to-urban migration. The UN estimates that by the year 2050, two-thirds of the world's population will be living in cities. At the same time, we have witnessed a massive global proliferation of Internet-accessible mobile devices beginning in the early 2010s. More than half of the world's population obtained access to the Internet by 2018. Some have linked these and other technology changes to global rises in depression and anxiety during the last two and a half decades. All of these modifications in the lived experience of humans have implications for other species and for the planet's ecosystems and climate on which we depend. Some other dramatic developments thus far the first century of the third millennium include:

- *Over the last 25 years, global carbon dioxide emissions have increased by nearly 50%.*

Over the last 25 years, the planet has moved from having sea ice at both poles in summer to the likelihood in 2025 of what is called a Double Ocean Blue Event. This term labels the virtual disappearance (one million km^2 or less) of both Antarctic and Arctic sea ice. Temperatures are rising most rapidly in the Arctic, which contributes to the occurrence of more extreme weather events. Low winter temperatures in the Arctic are essential to building up ice thickness, thereby preserving sea ice as the melting season starts. Yet Arctic temperature hit a record high (for the time of year) on December 15, 2023. Melting sea ice means rising oceans and coastal flooding. Almost 3.6 billion people live in coastal areas or within 90 miles (145 km) of coastal waters. This includes about 66% of the world's total human population. Long a source of the resources that support life, the oceans are becoming an increasing threat to those who live along its shores and quite a ways inland.

- *The Slide toward a Runaway Greenhouse Effect has accelerated over the last 25 years.*

The advance toward a state of uncontrollable runaway greenhouse gas impact is now much closer than it was a quarter of a century ago. An increase of only a few tens of degrees of average planetary temperature would be sufficient to trigger an irreversible cascade that would make our planet as inhospitable as our neighboring planet, Venus. This fateful threshold, some research suggests, is closer at hand than people realize, although other climate scientists stress there is still time to avoid catastrophe. The average daily global temperature briefly passed 2.6 °Farenheit (2 °Celcius) above average pre-industrial levels for the first time in 2023. This small-sounding-but-actually-enormous jump marks the passing of a fateful milestone in Earth's escalating climate crisis. Passing still another 1.8 °F (1 °C) would unleash catastrophic consequences, including the displacement of over a billion people.

- *The COVID-19 Global Pandemic*

There were about 6–7 million COVID deaths reported worldwide between January 1, 2020, and December 31, 2021, although some estimate a far higher toll (over 18.2 million) over that period. Millions more fell sick, and even those who no longer test positive may suffer from the debilitating symptoms of long COVID. COVID-19, however devastating, was not the only infectious disease pandemic during the last 25 years. Eighty-six countries and territories reported evidence of mosquito-transmitted Zika infection during 2015–16. Also, thus far in this century, there have been pandemics of SARS, Ebola, and Mpox (formerly known as monkeypox), among others. These ever more frequent emerging infectious disease pandemics, which have been linked to disrupted environments and a changing climate, pose grave risks to human health and even species sustainability.

Human facilitated changes like climate change or global infectious disease outbreaks create the environmental and social conditions that foster ecosyndemics, a growing threat in our ever more disrupted world.

An Anthropologist Studies the Ecosyndemics of Development in the Amazon

Becoming a Biocultural Anthropologist

Paula Skye Tallman is a biocultural anthropologist at Loyola University Chicago since 2021—where she teaches courses such as "Sex, Science, and Anthropological Inquiry" and "Anthropology and Global Health." She is also a research associate at the famous Field Museum of Natural History in Chicago. Born in New Orleans, Paula grew up in Florida. When she was nine, she visited her mother's homeland of South Africa. When she was 15, her mother asked her to go with her to hear a talk on shamanism. The speaker, who worked for the World Bank, brought up the Shuar people and their struggle with encroaching oil companies. The speaker was planning a trip to visit the Shuar and Paula got her parents' permission to go along. So after she turned 16, she visited a Shuar (previously known as Jivaro) community in the Ecuadorian Amazon.

The Shuar people, who are small farmers and hunters, have been desperately fighting for decades to protect their land and means of survival from encroachment by cattle ranchers, loggers, miners, and oil companies, as well as government-sponsored infrastructural penetration of forest lands. During Paula's visit, Indigenous community members shared with her that that they were becoming worried about their health and well-being due to the highways that were being built on the edge of their rainforest home, part of a development effort for wealthy outsiders to gain profit from the forest. Community members expressed that the loss of the forest was impacting their ability to eat traditional foods and degrading their cultural practices, which were deeply entwined with the local rainforest ecology—creating significant psychological stress for the Shuar.

This experience had an existential impact on Paula and helped shape her life work. Beginning as an undergraduate, she started investigating stress biology at Johns Hopkins University, from which she graduated with a B.A. in 2008. That year, she was awarded a grant from the Johns Hopkins Program in Latin American studies to carry out a project designed to identify common health issues found in Indigenous communities in the southern Peruvian Amazon and the local medicinal plants people used to treat these conditions. This interest in ethnobotany and Indigenous health led Paula to enroll in the anthropology Ph.D. program at Northwestern University in 2009, which she completed in 2015. Her commitment to integrating her research with an environmental justice approach led Paula to undertake a postdoctoral fellowship at the Field Museum of Natural History in Chicago.

In 2022, Paula and her colleagues brought their interest in the health impacts of development projects to an ecosyndemic re-analysis of data collected during prior research on two Amazonian mega-development projects completed during the last 25 years, the Southern Interoceanic highway in Peru and the Belo Monte hydroelectric dam in Brazil (Tallman et al., 2022). They were motivated in this decision by their awareness that whatever the economic or other benefits of development projects, they often have steep costs, including destructive impacts on food, water, health, and sociocultural systems. The ecosyndemics framework importantly allowed the team to think of the potentially synergistic effects of chronic psychological stress, sexually transmitted infections, and vector-borne diseases that increase with the construction of dams and highways in highly biodiverse areas such as the Amazon rainforest. Finally, the concept of ecosyndemics supported these researchers in identifying relevant "health-based environmental indicators," which could be measured in social and environmental impact assessments of mega-development projects—connecting research to conservation action (Paula Tallman, personal communication).

Indeed, research shows that about 95% of the deforestation that has taken place in the Amazon has occurred within 3½ miles (5.5 km) of roads or about half a mile of navigable rivers. These zones of economic and infrastructural expansion and deforestation are often accompanied by rises in levels of violence, corruption, and drug trafficking. Limited government enforcement of regulations in these disrupted areas can trigger disputes that tear the social fabric of local communities. Moreover, sex work may also emerge to service the men who travel via river or road to work on development projects, exacerbating the spread of sexually transmitted infections, including HIV. Further, roads and ecologically fragmented areas are linked with increases in vector-borne diseases like malaria because of increases in standing pools of water and the disruption of existing ecosystems. Similarly, dams have been associated with an increased prevalence of parasitic infections like schistosomiasis, also known as "snail fever."

Impacts of the Southern Interoceanic Highway

The $2 billion Southern Interoceanic highway in Peru, completed in 2013, is a 1600-mile international route connecting Peru to Brazil. The highway was promoted as an initiative needed to bring economic development to local communities by enabling the export of Peruvian products to Acre, Brazil, and to the world, through Atlantic Coast seaports. Promoters of the costly project claimed that 30–40 long haul trucks would use the Interoceanic highway each daily, transporting products and providing a significant boost to the local economy. A decade later, few if any of these touted benefits have been realized. Rather, most of the trucks using the road haul lumber that was felled, mostly illegally, from the forests on both sides of the road. Minivans used the road to transport loggers to clear the forest or settlers from the Andes who claimed land from Indigenous communities through armed violence. Indeed, the Interoceanic has been called the most corrupt highway in the world. The giant Brazilian construction company, Odebrecht SA, admitted paying $800 million in bribes to gain construction bids. The scandal involved a number of high-level Peruvian officials and several former presidents, including Pedro Pablo Kuczynski, who was forced to resign as President of Peru in March 2018 due to his illegal financial ties to Odebrecht.

Costs and Benefits of Damming the Xengu

The Belo Monte hydroelectric dam in Brazil, which opened in 2016, is the fifth largest dam in the world. The dam was constructed on the northern section of the "Big Bend" of the Xingu River (see Fig. 1.1). Local Indigenous communities were provided with little information about the project and its potential impact on their lives. They soon began to oppose construction of the dam by organizing what they called the *I Encontro das Nações Indígenas do Xingu* (First Encounter of the Indigenous Nations of the Xingu). Additionally, a number of environmental and human rights organizations (e.g., the UN Human Rights Council) have criticized the project. Despite various legal and other hurdles, the project continued until it was completed in 2019.

Over the years, the dam has caused significant socio-environmental harm to the Xingu River and to the Indigenous and traditional peoples living along it. In part because of climate change it appears the dam cannot produce the amount of electricity promised by its builders. Climate change-induced droughts are decreasing Xingu River flows, thereby diminishing the dam's turbine electricity generating capacity. Many who live near the dam do not call it Belo Monte (Beautiful Hill) but rather Belo Monstro (Beautiful Monster). One cause of this was the appearance of a massive gathering of mosquitos. At times the bites of mosquitos drove farmers from their field and children became prisoners in their homes. Additionally, fishing in the river, a source of protein, became far less productive.

In both Amazonian case studies, Paula Skye Tallman and co-workers found that mega-development projects had telling influence on people's health through

Fig. 1.1 Xengu River

ecological, biological, and social pathways, and potentially created conditions that facilitated the clustering of sexually transmitted and vector-borne infections (especially HIV and dengue) among individuals who were psychologically stressed by rapid changes in their eco-social worlds. These changes included the rapid in-migration of large numbers of outside workers and illegal gold miners (primarily men who were separated from their families and partners), and accompanying commercial sex work and illicit drug use. People reported these changes threatened community cohesion and local tradition. While people impacted by the highway also saw benefits (e.g., availability of more diverse nutrition, better access to healthcare, and new economic opportunities), they also were highly concerned about its negative impacts. As they emphasized to Tallman's team, "multiple webs of interaction between humans and natural landscapes [were] altered in the context of the rapid changes ignited by mega-development projects in tropical ecosystems, with substantial potential for ecosyndemic interactions occurring between psychological stress and a variety of sexually-transmitted and vector-borne infections" (Tallman et al., 2022). These webs of interaction include (1) the role of psychological stress in dysregulation and disruption of the body's immune system; (2) the ability of vector-borne infections to facilitate sexually transmitted infections; and (3) the impact of HIV as a known syndemic generator (Singer et al., 2017). While these researchers were not able to demonstrate definitively the development of an ecosyndemic, the data they present offers strong support for this occurrence. Further, their work underlines the ecosyndemic risks of top-down development that ignores bottom/up input and approval, such as the needs and perspectives of Indigenous peoples.

Toward a Critical Health Anthropology

The syndemics approach emerged within the subfield of anthropology originally known as critical medical anthropology (today called critical health anthropology). Anthropology's take on environmental health was also influenced by a critical approach to scientific understanding. This raises the question: what does critical mean? In his blog, The Critical Turkey, Edinburgh University sociologist Martin Booker (2021) observes:

> In everyday common-sense language 'critical' usually means that we question someone's statement or opinion, and are, well, critical of it. We point out the weaknesses in an argument, probe its validity, and generally don't trust anything anyone says… And if we do this systematically… The point here is … to examine an argument, to look at the different sides of it, and then come to an *informed conclusion*… Critical engagement starts with critical reading. The point here is to not just passively take in and absorb and accept whatever someone is telling you (this would be uncritical reading), but to enter into an active internal dialogue with the text.

This approach, by the way, would encourage you to read this book from a critical vantage point and develop your own informed conclusions. For researchers in the social sciences—those that study humanity in all of its diverse aspects—the word critical has a somewhat special meaning. Continues Booker:

> Th[e] social-science-proper understanding of 'critical' is about examining what kinds of power dynamics, hierarchies and interests are connected to a specific social phenomenon. What produced the phenomenon and keeps it in place? And how does the phenomenon itself then (re-)produce hierarchies and power structures?

To unite these two understandings, it can be said that critical social scientists, anthropologists among them, are critical of (i.e., see the fault in) analyses of human behavior that fail to attend to the influences of power and social inequality. For example, critical social scientists would criticize social analyses of contemporary life in the USA that minimize the role colonial history plays in contemporary racism, or the intersection of race and class in the making and reproduction of poverty.

Critical approaches derive from and build upon the writings of two famous (or infamous, depending on your perspective) German political philosophers: Karl Marx and Frederick Engels. Of special importance is their joint book *German Ideology* (written in 1846) and Engels' volume *The Condition of the Working Class in England* (originally published in 1845), a product of Engels' 1842–1844 stay in Manchester, England. Also of note is the work of Rudolf Virchow, a German physician, writer, editor, and politician, who penned the often cited aphorism: "Medicine is a social science, and politics is nothing else but medicine on a large scale."

Learning from Marx, of course, does not mean you are a Marxist, or communist, a pejorative label in Western society. Ironically, even Marx denied he was a Marxist, as the term took on meanings he did not embrace. What is important is recognizing that power is not equally shared in society and that inequality is a significant determinant of health. Research by scientists from around the globe affirms that many health outcomes—everything from life expectancy to infant mortality and from obesity to infectious disease—are linked to the level of social and economic inequality in a society. The greater the economic inequality in society the worse the health outcomes for those on the lower rungs of the social hierarchy.

In their big-picture analyses, these nineteenth-century thinkers argued that the organization of any society, its culture, beliefs, and norms, as well as its distribution of health problems, even its land use practices, is strongly influenced, if not determined, by the reigning structures of power, and by the social classes that dominate in that society. The ruling ideas in society, as Marx and Engels asserted, are the ideas developed by and thus favor the interests of the ruling classes. For example, there is the idea of private property (especially of land and productive resources and facilities), a foundational concept in capitalism. It is a notion that is embraced (perhaps to varying degrees) at all social levels but one best reflects and serves the interests of the wealthiest property owners. Indeed, the notion of private ownership of what is called "real property" is justified by its adherents on the grounds that it encourages work effort and planning, enabling not only individual wealth creation but the generation of wealth for the whole society. A perusal of the relevant writings of John Locke, an influential seventeenth-century English philosopher, indicates that property ownership is a "natural right" that God bestowed upon people (and not just on the King). He further claimed that property is a product of labor that improved upon nature. As this suggests, our earliest Western conceptualizations of property as something that can be owned privately (initially by individuals but ultimately by corporations) are bound up with our ideas about the environment (nature) and our obligation to improve (change) it as a social good. Everyone (presumably) benefits! Never fully addressed in such dreamy assertions is the fact that private ownership was a foreign concept for most of human history. Until the rise of cities and empires, property was a communal asset, available to all. In other words, private property has a history; it only emerged as an acceptable idea under particular social and historical conditions when it was particularly beneficial for would-be dominant social classes. In the modern capitalist world, as sociologist Ray Elling (1988: 770) comments, "There is nothing more jealously guarded by the capitalist sector than control over the means and processes of production" (i.e., property like factories, mines, agricultural fields).

Also ignored in most discussions of property are the social barriers (e.g., racial discrimination in housing, education, and policing or the language and enforcement of tax codes) to acquire and retain private property. Dominant ideas, however, are those that help to enforce a status quo of inequality, a state of affairs that tends to hide the violence and exploitation that helps keep a disempowered group down. There are endless examples, old and new, to support this assertion but a notable and tragic case is the 1921 Tulsa race massacre, during which as many as 300 Black residents of the Greenwood District in Tulsa, Oklahoma, were murdered and their property destroyed by masked white rioters who were aided and abetted by the National Guard. Greenwood, known as America's Black Wall Street, was a vibrant neighborhood of grocery stores, hotels, nightclubs, billiard halls, theaters, doctor's offices, churches, and family homes. All of it was destroyed in 24 h. The anger that motivated white rioters reflected prevailing racist attitudes as well as a heightened level of white jealousy over the financial successes of some Black Tulsans. After the massacre, state and federal policy makers, as well as the private sector, quickly labeled the event a "race riot," which was likely a pretext that insurance companies used to avoid paying out the compensation that property owners were due. Local officials quickly announced they would help rebuild the shattered community. Instead, they destroyed available documentation and spent the next five decades pretending nothing of note had happened. The message was clear: Private ownership of property is cherished and defended for some but not all. Indeed slavery, the embodiment of racial inequality, not only denied property ownership to some, but it also made some people, including the ancestors of Greenwood residents, property owned by others.

In recognition of this tortured historic pathway, critical health anthropology (CHA) emerged during the 1980s as part of a movement formed in the shadow of the US war in Vietnam as an effort to go beyond microlevel accounts and explanations of health-related beliefs and practices and their interface with local ecologies, cultural configurations, and human psychology. The focus of CHA, instead, is on the vertical linkages that connect social groups, particular behaviors, and population health patterns to encompassing political and economic structures, as well as on the social relationships they help produce and reproduce over time within specific environmental contexts. Studies done within a CHA framework seek to understand the social determinants of health, including issues like the biology of poverty, the health consequences of discrimination, the role of power, control, oppression, social inequality in the making of health and disease, poverty (See Fig. 1.2), and forms of resistance to these forces. In short, CHA seeks to plot a "new way" of doing things, for overcoming the limits of traditional practice, and to broaden the framework of conventional research by health anthropologists. From the critical health anthropology perspective, the causal explanations traditionally offered for environmental influences on health were often too narrow, and linked the emergence of disease to issues like poor adaptation to the environment, with little focus on how unequal power relations and sociopolitical and historical factors channel human–environment interactions, thereby negatively impacting health. CHA approaches health issues in light of the larger political-economic forces—such as the dominant mode of production—that pattern everyday interpersonal relationships, shape social behavior, generate shared meaning, and mold people's collective experience. While a critical perspective asserts the ultimate priority of international and national political-economic processes and structures in setting the parameters of social life, it maintains also that a thorough understanding of any particular health issue requires a full exploration of on-the-ground activities and patterns, as well as social history. In other words, the critical approach avoids the false dichotomy between the

Fig. 1.2 Child Poverty in Belize

micro- and macrolevels, in that neither is seen as the essential level of social reality. It is the view of CHA that the local is embedded in the macrolevel (national and international structures), while the macrolevel is the embodiment of the microlevel but never reducible to it. However, there is no real empirical separation between the two levels of action. Rather, a useful division is made for the purpose of initiating detailed examination of the connection between unique social configurations and general crosscutting processes.

As a scholarly discipline, anthropology has a research commitment to close encounters with local populations and their lifeways, systems of meaning, motivations for action, and daily experiences. It also has a commitment to understanding the encompassing political economy. In other words, while it is necessary to describe, for example, how multinational corporations have penetrated and now dominate health-related activities around the world, and that the primary mission of these institutions is profit-making, this is only the starting point for CHA. Thus, we know that capitalist relations of production and distribution have spawned differing patterns of health, health care, and health-related behavior "worldwide, including contrasts among the crowded shantytowns of Lima, Peru, the peasant communities perilously perched on eroding hillsides in Haiti, the bustling streets of Singapore, the wealthy suburbs of Westchester County, New York, and the small farmer communities of Toledo District, Belize. Elucidating the nature and causes of this kind of variation across local settings (including diverse local treatment systems, health and disease beliefs, provider–patient relationships, illness behaviors, and dietary practices), while never losing sight of the overarching market and political forces that bind Lima to Singapore and Haiti to Westchester County, and all of these to the dynamics and contradictions of macrolevel structures, is a central mission of CHA.

It is within this approach to health that the syndemics concept developed. It began during the height of the AIDS epidemic. At the time, the author headed an action research program in a community-based institute in Hartford, CT. The author's research team had been funded to carry out various ethnographic and mixed method studies of HIV risk and prevention in low-income urban populations, especially in communities of color. Much of this work focused on people who inject drugs illicitly, especially heroin and cocaine. In the course of this research, study participants—active drug users—reported suffering from multiple serious health problems, a finding that triggered consideration of the effects of coterminous disease interaction. Does HIV infection cause other diseases to get worse, or vice versa? This line of thinking and the information being reported about their health by people who inject or otherwise consume psychoactive drugs led to the formation of the syndemics concept. The SAVA (an acronym for substance abuse, violence, and AIDS) syndemic, the first described syndemic, was defined as a set of closely intertwined and mutual enhancing epidemics including substance abuse, various expressions of violence, and AIDS that are reciprocally influenced and sustained by a larger risk environment and set of power relations in society shaped by axes of gender, ethnicity, and class. These intimately linked epidemics, researchers concluded, were synergistically reinforced by multiple behavioral, biological, and structural factors. In response to growing awareness of climate change impacts on health, as well as the multiple deleterious effects of other anthropogenic disruptions of the environment, the ecosyndemics concept was developed. A subtype of syndemics, in ecosyndemics unequal and oppressive social relations are mediated by the environment. For example, a disproportional percentage of Black Americans live near an unregulated toxic waste facility, a pattern that has been aptly called "environmental racism."

Telltale Signs of the Environmental/Climate Health Crisis

The scientific evidence for rapid climate and other environmental change is compelling: global temperatures are rising, the oceans are getting warmer, corals and other marine species are suffering, the ice sheets of the north and south are melting, and glaciers are retreating. Also, forests are being cleared of their tree cover, the sea level is rising, extreme weather events are increasing in frequency and severity, and pollution of the air, land, and water is advancing. All of these changes, alone and in eco-crisis interaction, are already having significant repercussions on health, as discussed below.

Heatwaves and Health

The term climate change is usually used to refer to what have become dramatic and enduring changes in ambient temperature and the related consequences of the seasonal shift we are all experiencing. Such change is not new, however, and has been going on for all of Earth's history. These alterations occur in varying degrees at the local, regional, and global levels. At one extreme, there are ice ages, which involve extensive cooling and result in the expansion of continental and polar ice sheets, as well as alpine glaciers. Geophysicists have determined that there have been at least five major ice ages since the formation of our planet. Between these frigid periods, there have been times when Earth appears to have been ice-free even in high latitude regions. Based on the analysis of core samples extracted during the Arctic Coring Expedition from more than 1000 feet below the Arctic Ocean floor, the last time this occurred was 55 million years ago, during the Eocene Epoch. At the time, the Arctic was as warm as Miami, Florida, with an average temperature of 74 °Fahrenheit (23 °C). The ancestors of modern alligators, ancient primate-like mammals, and sequoia, cypress, and palm trees were part of a northern swampy ecosystem characterized by numerous large freshwater lakes. It was also a time when the amount of carbon dioxide in the atmosphere was very high.

It is generally agreed among climatologists that currently Earth is in a comparatively mild ice age that is scientifically named the Holocene. But things are changing once again. We are experiencing a period of increasingly intense global warming. While noting a long slow rise in planetary temperatures since humans first evolved, climate scientists point to the Industrial Revolution and to social changes that began in the eighteenth century as the key turning point toward a significant upward shift in Earth's global temperature. Since the Industrial Revolution, which began around 1760 in Britain and accelerated during the 1830s and 1840s, and quickly spread to other parts of the world, the average global annual temperature has increased by a little more than 2 °F (about 1 °C). In the 100 years between 1880, the year that accurate climate recordkeeping began, and 1980, average temperatures on Earth increased every ten years by 0.13 °F (0.07 °C). Since 1981, it is of note that the rate of increase has more than doubled. Each new year, headlines and websites announce that temperature records are being broken around the world. Until recently, nine of the ten hottest years that have been recorded since 1880 occurred since 2005, and all of the five warmest years have occurred since 2015. The year 2023 was the hottest year, thus far, on record. But the impact of ambient temperature rise is not evenly distributed. Temperatures increase at different speeds at various locations around the planet. The strongest warming is occurring in the Arctic during its cool seasons and at mid-latitude regions during the warm season (Baer & Singer, 2024). Surface temperatures on Earth actually mask the true extent of global warming because the oceans have absorbed about 90% of the solar heat being trapped by greenhouse gases. Measurements over the last six decades show that every layer of the oceans, top to bottom, is heating up.

With rising temperatures have come killer heat waves. While heatwaves have occurred in the past, research indicates the risk of a high magnitude heat wave has tripled since 1960 due to global warming. In the USA, the average number of heatwaves each year has increased from two during the 1960s to six in the 2010s and 2020s. And these waves of roasting temperatures are lingering for longer periods of time than in the past. Extreme heat is more deadly than other kinds of disasters, killing more than twice as many people per year in the USA as hurricanes and tornadoes combined. High temperatures cause deadly illnesses like heat exhaustion and heat stroke, and can lead to electrolyte imbalance, kidney problems, and even heart attacks. These conditions developed for many people during the Chicago heatwave of 1995. Author Eric Klinenberg, who wrote a book about the event called *Heat Wave: A Social Autopsy in Chicago* (2022a), reports:

> Chicago felt tropical, like Fiji or Guam but with an added layer of polluted city air trapping the heat. On the first day of the heat wave, Thursday, July 13, the temperature hit 106 degrees, and the heat index—a combination of heat and humidity that measures the temperature a typical person would feel—rose above 120. For a week, the heat persisted, running between the 90s and low 100s. The night temperatures, in the low to mid-80s, were unusually high and didn't provide much relief. Chicago's houses and apartment buildings baked like ovens. Air-conditioning helped, of course, if you were fortunate enough to have it. But many people only had fans and open windows, which just recirculated the hot air… The heat made the city's roads buckle. Train rails warped, causing long commuter and freight delays. City workers watered bridges to prevent them from locking when the plates expanded. Children riding in school buses became so dehydrated and nauseous that they had to be hosed down by the Fire Department. Hundreds of young people were hospitalized with heat-related illnesses. But the elderly, and especially the elderly who lived alone, were most vulnerable to the heat wave (Klinenberg, 2022b):

Other noteworthy heatwaves also have occurred within the last 25 years. In 2003, Europe was hit by a heatwave that is considered one of the worst in modern history. The number of victims exceeded 70,000. France suffered the heaviest losses, with 14,000 deaths being recorded. There were so many deaths in a short time that it was not possible to bury all the bodies soon after death and they had to be stored in refrigerated trucks. In 2022, about 60,000 died because of another set of extreme heatwaves in Western Europe. Hardest hit were France in June, the UK in July, and both Spain and France in August. As a result, droughts in the region were widespread, with excess death (beyond what would be expected in a normal year) in the tens of thousands. In 2010, Russia experienced a devastating heatwave with temperatures peaking at 108 °F (42 °C). The inflicted areas spanned a wide stretch of western Russia, Belorussia, the Ukraine, and the Baltic nations. These conditions caused an estimated 55,000 deaths, a 25% drop in agricultural production, and an economic loss of over $15 billion. Analyses indicated that the 2010 Russian heatwave involved a number of natural factors and anthropogenic impacts. It is estimated that 1400 people died across Oregon, Washington, and British Columbia during the 2021 heat dome (a weather condition involving hot ocean heat air that is trapped by the atmosphere). The extreme heat ignited numerous, large wildfires, some reaching hundreds of square miles in size, with widespread destruction including over 650,000 farm animals. The human death toll exceeded 1400.

The impacts of recent heatwaves have not been limited to the Global North. It is estimated that thousands of people have died in the heatwaves that have hit the Global South in recent years. During the 2022 India–Pakistan heatwave, the Pakistani city of Nawabshah recorded a high temperature of 121 °F (49.5 °C). An earlier heatwave that occurred in 2015 caused the deaths of at least 2500 people across India.

Melting, Ocean Rise, and Vulnerable Populations

The term cryosphere refers to all the ice on Earth, including ice on rivers and lakes, sea ice, snow cover, glaciers, ice caps, ice sheets, and water that is frozen in soil known as permafrost. Most of the permanent ice in the world, over 99%, is locked up as land-based ice sheets and glaciers, especially in polar regions.

An ice sheet is defined as a mass of ice that is over 19,000 miles (over 30,000 km) in circumference (about 50,000 km^2). At one time, during the Pleistocene epoch, much of North America was covered by the Laurentide ice sheet. It is responsible for gouging out the basins of the Great Lakes. Today, there are only two ice sheets: one in Greenland and the other in Antarctica. These massive fields of ice form during the winter as snow builds up and then melts to some degree over the summer. The slightly melted snow gets harder and slowly compresses under newly fallen snow. During this process, the buried snow changes texture from a fluffy powder into a hard block of round, dense pellets called "firn." Over the years, layers of firn build up on top of each other. When the ice grows thick enough—about 165 feet (50 m)—the firn particles fuse into a huge mass of solid ice.

A second major component of the cryosphere are glaciers, which are large, perennial accumulations of ice, snow, rock, and sediment that originate on land and move slowly over time down a mountain slope under the influence of their own weight and the pull of gravity. Glaciers are found on mountains on every continent besides Australia. Because water molecules absorb other colors better than they do blue, glaciers appear to be blue. Most glaciers today are remnants of the massive ice sheets that covered Earth more than 10,000 years ago. Outside the Antarctic, the largest glaciers on Earth are the Malaspina-Seward Glacier in Alaska, the Wykeham Glacier South in the Canadian Arctic, and the Bering Glacier in Alaska.

Sea ice forms as seawater freezes and floats because ice is not as dense as water. Primarily, sea ice is found in the Artic and Southern Oceans. The bright, shiny surface of the ice helps cool polar temperatures stay cool by reflecting back into the atmosphere much of the sunlight that hits it. Also, sea ice helps propel ocean currents, which in turn contribute to the regulation of global climate by counteracting the uneven distribution of solar heat reaching Earth's surface. Moreover, sea ice provides an ecosystem for various species, especially seals, walruses, penguins, and polar bears.

As opposed to seasonally frozen ground or intermittently frozen ground, permafrost is a permanently frozen layer that lies beneath Earth's surface. It is the coldest land-based biome and is characterized by extremely low temperatures, low levels of precipitation, poor soil nutrients, and short growing seasons of only 50–60 days a year. The average winter temperature is −30 °F (−34 °C). It is made up of dead organic material in the form of nitrogen and phosphorus, soil, gravel, and sand, bound together by ice. Permafrost can be found on land but also below the ocean floor in areas where temperatures rarely rise above freezing. Land that has underlying permafrost is called *tundra*. It is common to Arctic regions including Greenland, the US state of Alaska, and Russia, China, Scandinavia, and parts of Eastern Europe. The thickness of permafrost can range from about three feet (1 m) to over 3000 feet (1000 m). Numerous human communities and even whole cities are built on permafrost, although this can be a tricky endeavor. A building raises the temperature of the ground beneath it, which can thaw permafrost causing the building to sink. This is avoided by building structures on top of wood piles or on thick gravel pads, among other strategies.

With global warming the cryosphere is changing as Earth experiences an extensive and increasingly rapid ice melt. The ice sheet in Greenland has been losing mass for more than 25 years. Recent estimates suggest that between 2012 and 2016 it lost about 250 gigatonnes (i.e., 1 billion tons or over 900,000,000 metric tons) per year of ice volume. While 60% of the ice that has been lost is through discharge across its ocean-facing front, 40% is from surface melt. Additionally, the massive tongues of ice, some 50 miles (80 km) in length, that extended off Greenland into surrounding ocean waters are melting from below. Overall loss is estimated to average 33 tons (30 metric tons) per hour. Ice that is discharged into the ocean far surpasses the snow that accumulates on the surface of the ice sheet each winter. These increases in ice mass losses from Greenland are directly tied to rising winter and summer air temperatures.

Ice melt is also occurring at the other end of the planet in Antarctica. As global temperatures increase, seawater is gnawing away at the underside of the Antarctic ice sheet that covers the ocean, speeding the decline of Antarctica's ice cover. Antarctica is losing ice mass at an average rate of about 150 billion tons (136 billion metric tons) per year, especially in western Antarctica. This is the site of the Thwaites Glacier, an unusually broad and vast stretch of ice. Its nickname is the "Doomsday Glacier" because its collapse—which may occur in a few years—would increase sea levels by as much as several feet, flooding numerous coastal communities and low-lying island nations and other inhabited islands around the world.

Old photographs reveal that glaciers have significantly melted in mountain regions worldwide, and in some cases have disappeared altogether. Erin Christine Pettit, who began her working life designing and building parts for hybrid electric cars, is now a glaciologist at Oregon State University. She has been studying the changes in glaciers that are due to climate change, including at Thwaites Glacier. She observes and measures the flow, fracture, and retreat of glaciers and then uses this information to determine how much water enters the oceans from melting glaciers. She participated in a study using optical (ASTER and Landsat) and radar (ERS-1 and ERS-2) satellite imagery to document changes in the Prince Gustav Ice Shelf, Antarctic Peninsula, and its tributary glaciers before and after the January 1995 collapse of the ice shelf. Pre-1995 images show that the central ice shelf was fed primarily by both Sjögren and Röhss Glaciers. After the ice shelf collapsed, Röhss Glacier retreated rapidly.

Sea ice is also melting. As its surface area shrinks, the size of its reflective surface drops, causing Earth to absorb more of the Sun's heat. As the ice melts it lowers heat reflection causing more heat to be absorbed by Earth and further increasing the amount of melting ice in a dangerous feedback loop. The melting of sea ice can spark a cycle of ice shrinking and warming temperatures, a transformative potential that makes the polar regions the most vulnerable sector of the Cryosphere. The melting of sea ice and the loss of habitat for walruses and seals endanger Indigenous communities that depend on these animals, both for food and as reaffirmation of their cultural identities.

As ice-free seasons grow longer, coastal Arctic communities are subject to extreme erosion from pounding waves during storms. Indigenous homes and other structures located near the advancing erosion are at risk of collapsing into the ocean. This dangerous process has made coastal communities highly vulnerable, leading some to uproot and move to new locations, an economically and emotionally burdensome decision. Kivalina, Alaska, at the forefront of this transformation, lies about 70 miles (112 km) above the Arctic Circle and 1000 (1600) miles from Anchorage, the state's largest city. Life in this small community of around 450 Iñupiat Indigenous people has become desperately uncertain. Few locations in the world have been hit as hard by the effects of climate change. Arctic sea ice has dissipated by half since 1979 and the state's glaciers lose 75 billion tons (68 billion metric tons) of ice every year. Powerful storms are swallowing the community's coastline and disrupting centuries-old Indigenous cultural practices like Bowhead whaling. The people of Kivalina, facing a future as climate refugees, have been forced to seek a new site for their beleaguered community, and soon.

Global warming is also causing a rapid melting of permafrost, transfiguring large areas of formerly frozen ground into mud, silt, and peat while releasing high levels of climate-warming greenhouse gases like methane, carbon dioxide, and nitrous oxide that have been sequestered in the permafrost for millennia. As permafrost melts, previously dormant microorganisms begin to break down exposed organic matter, which allows methane and carbon to be released in the atmosphere. Thawing also opens up pathways that release methane from reservoirs deep in the ground, causing it to rise to the surface. For residents of cities like Norilska, a nickel-producing city of 177,000 people in western Russia, the consequences are immediate. Sixty percent of all buildings in the city have been damaged by cracking walls and collapses. More than 100 residential apartment buildings have been vacated because of damage from thawing permafrost. On May 29, 2020, a fuel-storage tank cracked and spilled 21,000 tons (19,000 metric tons) of diesel fuel into nearby waterways and turned the local Ambarnaya River a metallic red. Many climatologists fear that as much as 2.5 million square miles of permafrost—which is 40% of the world's total—will melt by the close of this century.

It only takes a slight increase in temperature for an area to shift from frozen to thawed, and this change creates multiple overlapping health risks for people and other living things. Existing research indicates changes in the cryosphere, along with other associated environmental changes, which have already negatively impacted people living in high mountain areas have ushered in new challenges in securing water, energy, and food security while advancing ecosystem and environmental degradation. The effects of cryospheric changes tend to extend downstream to river basins where glacier melt contributes significantly to needed dry season river flows and supports irrigation, fisheries, and navigation, as well as water supply for many large cities.

Deforestation and Disease

Deforestation is the intentional anthropogenic clearing of forested land (defined as a large area primarily covered by trees and undergrowth). While extensive today, this is not a new practice. Throughout history forests have been cut down to create space for agriculture and animal grazing, as well as to obtain wood for fuel, manufacturing, and construction. During the seventeenth century, for example, English colonists, who poured into what came to be called New England, cut down forests of pine, oak, chestnut, maple, ash, birch, and beech. Further, they opened up fields for crops and orchards, meadows for grazing livestock, and wood stocks for building and heating, for fence rails, and for the damming of rivers to power grain and lumber mills. Over the first half-century of English occupation, the several thousand settlers in the Connecticut River Valley cut down so many trees that many towns began regulating the cutting and export of wood. By the 1870s, about half of the forests in the eastern part of North America were cut down. More broadly, deforestation has significantly altered landscapes all over the world. Two thousand years ago, 80% of Western Europe was forested; today this is true for only 34% of the region. China has lost enormous expanses of forests and now only about 20% of the country is still forested. An especially egregious example of deforestation occurred in Haiti, beginning under French colonial rule. To make a profit from their colonial possession, French landowners brought in African slaves to clear upland forests and replace them with vast coffee plantations. Even after the Haitian people successfully drove the French out in the second revolutionary war in the Americas, the Haitian government was forced to cut down and export huge tracks of timber to pay off the French for their loss of real estate and slaves.

This process has continued today especially in tropical rainforests, assisted by extensive road construction that extends human reach deep into regions that were once all but inaccessible to nonresidents. Every day, tropical forests are being cleared to make way for timber harvesting, cattle ranching, and monoculture oil palm and rubber tree plantations, especially for the export of products to overseas markets in wealthy countries. In 2022, the world lost more than 16 million acres of forest, an area somewhat larger than the US state of West Virginia. In the Amazon region, approximate 17% of the forest has been cut down over the last 50 years. Deforestation in this region is especially common near populated areas, roads, and rivers, but even quite remote areas have been penetrated following the discovery of gold and oil. Nigeria now has the world's highest deforestation rate of old-growth forests. Over the last five years, it lost more than half of its primary forest. Between 2001 and 2015, the combined global loss of forests was nearly the size of India, the seventh largest country in the world. If the current rate of deforestation continues, some scientists believe that Earth will be essentially denuded of rainforests by the end of the century.

Forests are home to most of the world's terrestrial life forms (90% of the world's species); the loss of forests does irrefutable damage to biodiversity and drives species extinction. Forests are also vital for human health, purifying both water and air and acting as a first line of defense against the spread of novel human infectious diseases. This is because, as noted earlier, the loss of forests can act as an incubator for insect-borne and other infectious diseases. In Borneo, for example, an island that is shared by the nations of Indonesia and Malaysia, some of the oldest tropical forests on the planet are being rapidly cleared and replaced with oil palm plantations. As a result, there has been a significant jump in cases of malaria. A study by Fornace and collaborators (Fornace et al., 2016) used satellite maps to discover why this was occurring. The satellite imagery showed that in areas where the forest had been cut down local monkeys (long- and pig-tailed macaques) concentrated in the remaining forest fragments. As humans worked on the new palm plantations, located close to the recently created forest edges, mosquitoes, which thrived in this new habitat, carried the disease from their traditional hosts, the macaques, to people. Other infectious diseases linked to deforestation include leptospirosis (a potentially fatal bacterial disease), onchocerciasis (river blindness), cutaneous leishmaniasis (which causes skin sores), dengue, SARS, Ebola, COVID-19, and HIV.

Additionally, because forests provide the food and fuel needed by billions of people, forest loss threatens food insecurity and malnutrition. Because they act as carbon sinks—soaking up carbon dioxide—forests also play a critical role in limiting climate change and its many risks to human health. When forests are chopped down, regional temperatures rise. The result is drying and subsequent pollution-causing forest fires, as has occurred in Brazil, California, Indonesia, Australia, and the Congo Basin countries of Central Africa. As Duffy (2020: 201) explains, future deforestation "will likely create new climate refugees as inhabitants are forced to leave their homes due to wildfires, erosion, landslides, lack of clean water, and other issues associated with deforestation and climate change. In this situation, the world's poor will inevitably be the hardest hit, exacerbating global inequality." Who most benefits? Research by Global Witness (2019) found that between 2013 and 2019 deforestation was financed by $44 billion from over 300 investment firms, banks, and pension funds headquartered across the globe, including JPMorgan Chase, Goldman Sachs, Bank of America, and Morgan Stanley.

Disruptions and Destruction of Sea Life

Without healthy oceans, many humans cannot survive long. It is estimated that 3.5 billion people, about 45% of the current population of the world, depend on the ocean as their primary source of food. Further, fish are the largest source of protein consumed by people each year. Additionally, oceans contribute invertebrates, plants, marine mammals, and seabirds to the global human diet. But what have been called "blue foods" are at grave risk. Also at risk are the many other products derived from the sea, from anticancer drugs (such as cytarabine and eribulin mesylate) to an ingredient (carrageenan) in peanut butter and ice cream. As discussed below, climate change and deoxygenation, chemical and plastic pollution, and overfishing are the primary threats to this fundamental resource. All of these threats are complex and adversely interrelated, meaning not only are they hard to solve but also magnified (Singer, 2021a, b).

Climate Change and Deoxygenation

The study of excavated rocks and fossils from past epochs when temperatures increased and oxygen levels fell reveals that huge areas of the seafloor became uninhabitable. In some areas, called dead zones, this is beginning to re-occur as the climate crisis worsens. Climate change is creating a major threat to ocean health globally. Several factors are involved.

First, since the beginning of industrialization, the oceans have absorbed over 90% of the heat associated with global warming. As greenhouse gases like CO_2 continue trapping increasing amounts of solar energy close to the planet, the average temperature of the ocean rises. The increase has been about 1.5 °F (0.84 °C) since 1901, which amounts to an average rate of 0.13 °F (0.07 °C) per decade. This notable level of increase began to be noticed in the 1950s and has continued ever since. Thus, average global ocean temperatures during 2023 were 0.45 °F (0.25 °C) warmer than in 2022. Sea surface temperatures also have gone up over the last 30 years, more so than at any other time since reliable measurements began during the latter part of the nineteenth century. Alarmingly, ocean warming is speeding up. The surface of the ocean down to 2300 feet (700 m) is warming about 24% faster than 25 years ago, and the rate of acceleration is likely to increase well into the future. The long-term trend of ever warmer seas is almost completely a result of human activities (NASA, 2023).

Second, the UN's Intergovernmental Panel on Climate Change (IPCC) (2019) issued a Special Report on the Ocean and Cryosphere in a Changing Climate based on an expert analysis of numerous studies. Participants on the panel concluded that from 1901 until 2018 the average global level of the planet's oceans rose by 6–10 inches (15–25 cm), reflecting a yearly average rise of 0.039–0.079 inches (1–2 mm) per year. But the pace began to accelerate in 2013 to 0.182 inches (4.62 mm) a year. While these numbers might seem small, they are actually cumulatively quite dramatic. Ocean rise is not uniform around the globe, but using computer models and the growing pool of available data from various sources, some climatologists predict that compared to 2005 levels, oceans will rise, on average, two feet higher by the year 2100. As climate change advances, some coastal communities, including major global cities like Tokyo, New York, Shanghai, Kolkata, Mumbai, Guangzhou, London, and Miami, may be facing an additional 4 inches of ocean rise every decade toward the end of the century. People living on island nations like Tuvalu in Polynesia are at risk of having their traditional homelands sink below the rising seas. Laments Tuvalu resident Leitu Frank: "The sea is eating all the sand... Before, the sand used to stretch out far, and when we swam we could see the sea floor, and the coral. Now, it is cloudy all the time, and the coral is dead. Tuvalu is sinking" (quoted in Roy, 2019). Adds António Guterres, Secretary-General of the UN, "Low-lying [island] communities and entire countries could disappear forever. We would witness a mass exodus of entire populations on a biblical scale" (quoted in Carrington, 2023).

This catastrophic change is a consequence of the loss of ice from the Greenland and Antarctic ice sheets combined with continued glacier melt and ocean heating caused by what climatologists refer to as "anthropogenic forcing," which is another way of saying "because of human actions." Contributing to ocean rise is the thermal expansion of the ocean. When water warms up it expands in volume. Warmer seawater takes up more space than cold seawater. Heat causes water molecules to move slightly farther apart from each other, which increases water volume.

Third, as the oceans absorb CO_2, they become more acidic and oxygen levels decrease. This significantly impacts ocean health and most marine species. For instance, coral reefs, which are critical marine ecosystems, are threatened by a trifecta of acidification, rising sea temperatures, and overfishing. But acidification is also a much broader issue since it disrupts carbon sequestration by other species including shellfish. Increases in ocean acidity make it difficult for shellfish to build their shells and for coral to develop their skeletal structures. Corals are also quite sensitive to ocean heating. Coral bleaching occurs when heat-stressed corals release the algae that live in their structures and provide their food source by converting sunlight into the sugar corals need for energy. When ocean temperatures remain elevated for too long, coral dies. For example, because of ocean heating, Australia's Great Barrier Reef has experienced seven mass bleaching events through 2023. Some predict that essentially all corals will be wiped out by the end of the century.

Fourth, ice melt is changing ocean currents, a transformation that threatens fish stocks and the communities that depend on ocean resources. Ocean currents are flows of water in the seas that are found at the ocean surface as well as in deep water below 984 feet meters (300 m). Currents act like aquatic conveyor belts and elevators moving marine ecosystems and are threatened by a trifecta of acidification, increasing sea temperatures, and ocean water both horizontally and vertically, in local settings and globally. A new study (Van Westen et al., 2024) suggests that the Atlantic Ocean's critical system of currents (called the Atlantic Meridional Overturning Circulation, or AMOC) may collapse in response to the melting ice sheet in Greenland, as portrayed in the movie *The Day After Tomorrow*. AMOC, acting like the planet's thermostat, moves ocean water and heat between Earth's poles, a dynamic process that helps shape weather and climate around the world. AMOC, for example, brings warm water from the Gulf of Mexico up to Europe, which is the reason why Western Europe has a relatively milder climate than the same latitude in North America. The disruption of AMOC could bring freezing and drying weather to Europe (e.g., producing sea ice around the UK) and deadly heat to the tropics and contribute to significant sea level rise in the North Atlantic.

All of these changes in the oceans portend major and overlapping impacts on human and planetary health.

Plastic Oceans

Plastic is a synthetic organic polymer made from petroleum. Plastic is used across almost every sector of society and the economy, including in construction, textiles, consumer goods, transportation, industrial machinery, insulation, and packaging. As a result of its many uses and the "throwaway" approach to its use (i.e., single-use plastic), plastic is now ubiquitous in oceans globally. Over 400 million tons (over 360 million metric tons) of plastic are produced every year and about 14 million tons (over 12 million metric tons) of it winds up in oceans. Studies show that as the amount of plastic increases in the oceans, fish populations dwindle. Not only do large pieces of plastic pose a direct threat to sea life, so too do microplastics (e.g., pieces of plastic smaller than a sesame seed) which are collecting in enormous quantities, even in parts of the ocean that are far from human activities. Notable is the case of Henderson Island, a remote and uninhabited atoll in the South Pacific Ocean. Henderson has white, sandy beaches, stunning limestone cliffs, and lush and almost undisturbed vegetation. It is the breeding ground for huge numbers of seabirds. In 1988, its special character earned it recognition as a UNESCO World Heritage Site. At the time, it was one of the few atolls in the world unspoiled by human activity. In 2017, however, researchers who surveyed the island's beaches found they contained the highest concentration of plastic trash ever recorded. Plastic comprises approximately 80% of all marine debris and is found from the surface of the ocean down to deep-sea sediments (Fig. 1.3).

Plastic washes up on the shorelines of every continent, especially in areas near popular tourist destinations and densely populated areas. It also lands on inhabited islands, destroying local fishing areas on which islanders depend. Examination of beach debris on Cocos (aka Keeling) Islands off the coast of northwestern Australia found numerous plastic items, including straws, bags, toothbrushes, bottles, rope, shoes, and nurdles or mermaid's tears (industrial resin pellets). Some fear that plastics will cover every beach in the world if the current rate of deposition continues. Moreover, degrading plastic releases greenhouse gases into the atmosphere, including about 84 tons (76 metric tons) of methane per year, thereby contributing to climate change.

Microplastics are created by the influence of solar UV radiation, wind, currents, and other natural forces that fragment plastic in the oceans. Not only do sea animals ingest microplastics, but they also become ensnared in larger pieces of plastic, often leading to their death. It is estimated by researchers that plastics injure, suffocate, or drown at least 100,000 marine animals every year. About 85% of microplastics contain substances that have been found to be toxic to marine animals. Seabirds mistake microplastics for food, and feed them to their offspring. The baby birds cannot

Fig. 1.3 Plastic in the ocean

digest the plastic pieces but they still feel full, which causes malnutrition and death of fledglings. In the ocean, microplastics act like sponges, absorbing toxic chemicals dumped or swept into the water, including pesticides, polychlorinated biphenyl, persistent organic pollutants, flame retardants, and heavy metals. Disturbingly, it is estimated that by 2050 there could be more plastic in the sea than fish. One way plastic contributes to declines in fish populations is through its presence in fish nurseries. In coastal Hawaiian waters, for example, there are fish nurseries covered by surface slicks populated by plankton, a food source for baby fish. But slicks have been found to also contain microplastics.

There is so much plastic in the oceans that it has been called the eighth continent. The Great Pacific Garbage Patch, referred to as one of the ocean's new "plastic islands," is a glaring sign of this environmental crisis. The Garbage Patch is composed of microplastics as well as lost or abandoned fishing gear, including fishing line, nets, and lobster and crab cages. Waste from ocean-going ships is a major contributor to this ecological disaster. As plastic particles and other discards hit rotating currents they clump together. The result is an enormous collection of human rubbish drifting halfway between Hawaii and California. With some of its contents dating to the 1970s, the Garbage Patch is a constantly growing collection measuring about 99,4193 sq. miles long (1.6 million km[2)] and containing as many as 80,000 tons (over 72,000 metric tons) of plastic (Lebreton et al., 2018). It is now the size of Alaska, or more than three times the size of France, with 94% of its total number of accumulated contents being minute fragments of plastic that have eroded from larger pieces.

Moving up the food chain, microscopic plastic ingested by fish and other species that we consume finds its way into human bodies. An assessment of the abundance and type of plastic in goatfish, sea mullet, paddle tail, and common coral trout caught and sold for human consumption in Australia and Fiji found that plastic was present in 61.6% of fish from Australia and 35.3% of fish from Fiji (Wootton et al., 2021). Scientists at the National University of Ireland (Wieczorek et al., 2018) collected over 200 fish specimens from a warm, circular current in the northwest Atlantic and found that 73% had digested microplastics. At this point, observes Laura Freyer, a dolphin researcher at Dalhousie University, "virtually no area of the world's oceans is untouched by human activity" (quoted in Taylor, 2024a, b). Through the action of sea spray, microplastics even enters the air we breathe. Microplastic inhalation can damage the lungs while ingestion is believed to have adverse impacts on the immune system, liver, energy metabolism, and reproduction. A recent study of heart patients (Marfella et al., 2024) found that patients with carotid artery plaque in which microplastics were identified had a higher risk of heart attacks, stroke, or death at 34 months follow-up than those without detected microplastics. While research on the negative effects of microplastics on human health is still limited, existing findings are deeply concerning.

Overfishing

As contrasted with traditional low-tech fishing in coastal waters, a practice that has existed for about 8000 years, the term industrial fish references the modern use of large, mechanically driven supertrawlers that make longer voyages, farther out to sea but also along coasts, and haul in enormous quantities of fish. Beginning in the mid-twentieth century, industrialization of fishing exploded and continued to expand thereafter. With huge fishing fleets that are subsidized by national governments (to the tune of $35 billion a year globally), weak or non-existent international regulations on fishing, and the flourishing of fishing piracy, the world's oceans are being emptied of their fish stocks. Especially at risk are sharks, rays, and chimaeras (cartilaginous fish known informally as ghost sharks). Government subsidies, including building new ports, offering tax breaks on fuel, providing assistance with the construction of bigger vessels or engines, or financing the updating of gear, allow fleets to fish cheaper with greater success. This technology has enabled trawlers to get to waters that previously were considered unsafe for vessels; GPS, fish finders, and acoustic cameras have allowed ships to more easily locate their prey; giant nets have been adopted to swoop up whole schools of fish; and habitat damaging bottom trawling with weighted nets that allow for the capture of otherwise hard to fish bottom-dwelling species. The biggest subsidizers are China, the European Union, Japan, South Korea, and Taiwan. Among those who have most immediately suffered the consequences of the industrialization of ocean fishing are Indigenous and other small-scale fishers. The Vezo (which means paddle or, alternately, those who struggle with the sea), for example, live in small villages along the coral-rich coastline of southwest Madagascar and make their living by fishing. Beyond providing food, fishing is central to the Vezo's cultural identity, conception of the world, and way of life. These traditional fishers carve outrigger canoes from a local softwood tree they call farafatsy (*Givotia madagascariensis*). These somewhat fragile vessels enable them to fish on the coral reef but also to travel in groups over longer distances. Thus, they have been called "semi-nomadic sailors." Their aquatic mobility unfolds within fishing/kin networks that facilitate transit to areas where fishing is most productive at any point in time. All Vezo, from childhood on, participate in fishing, men in boats, women and children on the reef. But today, because of the industrialization of fishing and climate change, the Vezo way of life is "on a knife edge" (Carter, 2023). The local aquatic habitat is being destroyed and fish populations are dropping. The Vezo are losing their ability to feed and support their families, making them among the most vulnerable people in the world.

The UN estimates that currently 75% of fisheries are being harvested to their full capacity, and increasingly overexploited. Today the oceans contain only 10% of the marlin, tuna, sharks, swordfish, grouper, cod, and halibut compared to the 1950s. The poster child of overfishing is the destruction of the bluefin tuna fishery. Since the 1960s the western Atlantic bluefin population has been severely depleted, driven especially by high-end sushi markets. The largest tuna species, bluefins, are shaped like torpedoes, with retractable fins for great speeds up to 43 (70 kilometers) per hour. They are fierce predators who rely on their keen sight to spot prey fish. The greatest catch of bluefins has been in the Mediterranean, which is also the most overexploited fishery for many species (Pinchin, 2023). Only heroic efforts by conservationists saved the Mediterranean population of bluefins from extinction.

Desertification, Drought, and Malnutrition

The term desert is derived from the Latin word for abandoned place. This word expresses the popular Anglo-European conception of areas like the Sahara, Arabian, or Kalahari. In fact, far from being empty and lifeless wastelands, deserts are home to a complex array of plants, animals, and other organisms, including people. The scientific definition of desert is a location on land that receives no more than 10 inches (25 cm) of precipitation per year. In deserts, evaporation often exceeds the annual amount of rain or snowfall. Also, deserts commonly are pictured as hot, dry areas covered by shifting sand dunes. But the polar deserts found in parts of the Arctic and the Antarctic are very cold, while sand dunes are only found in about 10% of the world's deserts. Deserts are widespread around the world and are situated on every continent. They cover about one-fifth of Earth's total land mass. While most deserts are caused by natural forces, desertification is the rapid, human-promoted formation of desert from previously arid or semiarid land. Desertification has been defined by the UN as a "diminution or destruction of the biological potential of the land which can lead ultimately to desert-like conditions" (UN Secretariat, 1977). Since the colonial era, assumptions made about deserts have led to the creation of top-down programs and policies that systematically damage dryland ecosystems while marginalizing Indigenous peoples who have lived in dry areas for centuries and used these lands sustainably.

Contemporary examples of significant dryland degradation are found primarily in places where centralized political economic forces have shaped socioeconomic development. Generally, this has involved a combination of capitalist expansion, highly controlled authoritarian rule, and a developmentalist state bent on the modernization of both cities and the countryside. Across various countries in Africa, for example, modernization efforts were steeped in a Eurocentric economic and conceptual bias that did not allow for sufficient attention to the unique historical, cultural, geographic, and social contexts of different regions of the continent. Often overlooked were the deep impacts of colonialism on social relationships, the dark legacy of slavery, the wide diversity of African peoples (within and across regions), and the significant challenges of and lack of preparation for postcolonial governance. Further, development programs often do not address the unequal distribution of vital resources that were greatly exacerbated under colonial rule, the effects of globalization on local affairs, the rise of resulting conflicts, or the value of Indigenous knowledge about the environment.

The worst failures of top/down development are seen in the Mahaweli Development Program (MDP) in Sri Lanka. Launched in the 1960s, the MDP was supposed to create self-sufficiency among small-scale, village-based rice farmers. Built into the plan, however, was a drive to enhance Sinhalese nationalism and suppress the Tamil minority. Despite this hidden objective, the World Bank funded the ambitious project, the largest in Asia, with a series of loans. Subsequent evaluations showed that the project fostered ethnic conflict, exacerbated existing poverty, and failed to deliver on the creation of an egalitarian society of small-holder farmers (World Bank, 2004).

In many locations, the consequence of development has been environmental deterioration and the jeopardization of the livelihoods of millions of people. The Saharan Desert, for example, has expanded by about 3000 square miles (7600 km^2 a year) for a century and is now 10% larger than it was in 1925.

Who is to blame? Often it is Indigenous people who are faulted, with claims that their sheep and goat herds overgrazed the land while their fuelwood gathering practices eliminated trees and other plants. But as Ganz and Orlovsky (1984) indicate, "The use of [modern] technology in arid, semi-arid and subhumid environments is the result of the policy-makers' desire for economic development... It has been shown that desertification can result from road building, industrial construction, geological surveys, ore mining, settlement construction, irrigation facilities, and motor transport." Some researchers have labeled this process as "policy-induced desertification" (Hogg, 1987). Also implicated is anthropogenic climate change. Increases in weather extremes such as rising temperatures and droughts lead to land degradation. At the same time, desertification may enhance climate change. Land degradation reduces surface moisture and the amount of water available for evaporation drops. As a result, more energy is available for warming the ground and the lower atmosphere. Under drying conditions, wind erosion in dry lands blows dust and other particles into the atmosphere which can contribute to fewer rain showers and even drier land.

Drought, driven by climate change as well as the clearing of trees for raising livestock and the extraction of clay by the large, water and wood-consuming tile industry is impacting parts of Brazil. Large sectors of the well-populated drylands in the northeastern part of the country are now subject to desertification characterized by parched soils that are nearly devoid of nutrients. The region had its longest known drought historically between 2012 and 2017, followed by another drought in 2021. Especially hard hit are poor farmers and field workers who are being pushed off the land. Other places desertification is occurring are the Southwestern USA, remote sites in Russia, and northern China.

The health consequences of desertification are multiple, including increased risk of malnutrition from reduced food and water availability, a rise in water- and food-borne diseases due to poor hygiene and a lack of clean water, added cases of respiratory diseases caused by atmospheric dust from wind erosion, and increased vulnerability to infectious diseases as populations are forced to migrate to new areas. Drought and desertification in the Horn of Africa, for example, have created a humanitarian crisis that is affecting the lives and livelihoods of millions of people. It is estimated that over 22 million people in the region are highly food insecure and at grave risk. In Somalia alone approximately 1400,000 people have been displaced by deteriorating conditions. High levels of acute malnutrition persist in parts of Somalia, putting over 1.5 million children under age five at risk.

Hurricanes and Disasters

Hurricanes are the biggest storms that occur on Earth. Their ferocity is used using the Saffir-Simpson hurricane wind scale, which was developed in 1971 by a civil engineer, Herbert Saffir, and a meteorologist, Robert Simpson. It categorizes hurricanes into five levels based on the intensity of their sustained winds. A Category 5 hurricane has wind speeds greater than 156mph (251 km/h). In the over 50 years that the Saffir-Simpson scales has been in use, there have been 24 recorded Category 5 hurricanes in the Atlantic, eight of them during the last eight years. Hurricane Katrina, one of the five worst hurricanes to hit the USA, was responsible for over 1800 deaths and over $100 billion in damage. It left 80% of New Orleans under flood waters. The historically massive and powerful storm, with wind speeds at times of 140 mph (225 kph), annihilated the Gulf Coast. Katrina left behind a landscape of devastation as it swiftly destroyed over 300,000 homes and 150,000 businesses and caused enormous anguish. The immediate experience for those in the path of the hurricane left an indelible imprint on their lives. Recalls one survivor:

> "We were about an hour inland but that didn't stop the massive winds. Pine trees snapped and crashed down all around us blocking everyone in our neighborhood. I had never seen trees bend like that. It was horrifying. The rain blew sideways for days it seemed. The wind howled like rabid wolves in the night. Then, the lights went out. And they stayed out for two weeks… Days after the storm it seemed apocalyptic. No power, no gas to run generators, no water."

Before Katrina, New Orleans was a city of about 460,000 people. Of these, it is believed that 350,000 were able to evacuate before landfall. Those who were the most likely to evacuate were middle- or upper-class individuals and families with access to cars and other resources. Many who were left behind, especially those from minority and low-income households, wanted to evacuate but lacked the resources to do so (Bullard & Wright, 2009).

Katrina began as a tropical depression that formed over the southeastern Bahamas in the Atlantic Ocean. In tropical regions, as sunlight beats down on the surface of the water, it causes evaporation. The resulting rising air mass, in turn, produces a low-pressure zone that draws in air from the area around it. This air becomes wind that rushes to occupy the vacated space. If atmospheric conditions are right, these winds can develop into what is known as a tropical disturbance. The rotation of Earth causes the wind to spin around the low-pressure zone, creating an "eye" at the center of the gathering storm. During summer months, when sea surface temperatures are highest, the increased rate of evaporation can push the disturbance (with winds speeds below 39 miles per hour) to strengthen into a hurricane (with winds above 74 miles per hour). Hurricanes (or tropical cyclones as they are known) are categorized in magnitude on the Saffir–Simpson scale by their sustained wind speed, ranging from a damaging Category 1 storm (with speeds of 74–95 miles per hour; 119–153 kph) to a catastrophic Category 5 event (with speeds that exceed 157 miles per hour; 253 kph). When it made landfall, Katrina was a Category 3 hurricane. Hurricane Maria, a Category 5 storm, devastated the northeastern Caribbean islands in 2017, especially Puerto Rico, which suffered almost 3000 deaths.

In 2022, there were 40 hurricanes identified worldwide, an increase from 37 hurricanes the prior year. This rate, however, is below the average of 47 hurricanes per year that were registered from 1990 to 2022. In the USA, the most active storm year on record was 2020, when 30 hurricanes formed. Such years are known as "hyperactive" or "explosive" by climate scientists. Since 2018, the USA has seen an average of 18 devastating weather and climate-related events each year that have caused more than a billion dollars in damage. Record years occur when ocean waters are unusually warm because tropical storms and hurricanes gain their power from warm ocean water. Global warming, which is heating the oceans, in short, is fueling hurricanes. In 2023, ocean temperatures around Florida rose above 100 °F (38 °C). This is nearly hot-tub level. Super-heated oceans can rapidly turn minor storms into major ones. Rapid storm intensification in offshore regions is especially threatening to coastal populations and their economies. A study of rapid intensification that occurred within 248 miles (400 km) of a coastline found that the frequency tripled from 1980 to 2020 (Li et al., 2023). The bigger shifts are seen in storm intensity. Since 1975, the number of Category 4 or 5 hurricanes has about doubled. Also increasing is the number of back-to-back storms. Sequential storms, like Hurricanes Katrina and Rita in 2005 or Hurricanes Harvey, Irma, and Maria in 2017, are especially deadly. By 2100, such multipart storm events are likely to become common.

Notably, on September 26, 2024, Hurricane Helene made landfall in the Big Bend region of Florida with maximum sustained winds of 140 mph (220 km/h). This devastating Category 4 tropical storm caused widespread destruction and fatalities across the Southeastern part of the USA. It was the deadliest hurricane to strike the US mainland since Katrina 19 years earlier. Over 200 people were killed by Helene and property damage, including washed out infrastructure, amounted to almost $40 billion. The storm gained strength as it moved through very warm ocean waters of 86 °F (30 °C). Two weeks later, as Florida residents were still cleaning up from Helene, Hurricane Milton made landfall near Siesta Key, Florida, as a Category 3 storm. At least 16 people were killed and Florida suffered as much as $50 billion in property damage. This one-two punch is a likely harbinger of things to come.

The threat to human health and the health of all organisms in the pathway of intense storms continues to climb in an era of rapid climate change. This has led some meteorological researchers to propose that the Saffir–Simpson scale be updated to include a sixth category (Wehner & Kossin, 2023). They argue that Category 5 hurricanes are becoming more prevalent, with wind speeds in excess of 157 mph (253 km/h). The destructive potential of these storms suggests we have entered the era of the mega-hurricane.

Tornadoes represent another type of violent storm but they tend to be much smaller than hurricanes. Tornadoes are rapidly forming *narrow columns of air swirling at as much as 300 miles per that extend from the base of a powerful thunderstorm to the ground. The atmospheric conditions that generate tornadoes*—low-pressure systems, warm moist environments, and high winds—*also tend to produce hail of varying sizes. Tornadoes can devastate a built environment of homes, other buildings, and infrastructure in a very short period of time with a damage path* of more than a mile (1.6 km) long and 50 miles (80 km) wide. Of concern, tornado patterns have been changing in recent years, with more severe storms in rapid succession, possibly because of climate change and its effects. An increase in tornado clustering has been observed by scientists and people caught on the ground since the 1980s. According to Jana Houser, an atmospheric scientist at Ohio State University, "We are seeing a reduction in the total number of days where there are tornadoes, but those that do occur are almost 'supercharged,' producing substantially more tornadoes than what we would otherwise expect" (quoted in Zhou, 2024). At the same time, the location of tornadoes is shifting. In the USA, this has meant a decrease in the number of tornadoes in the lesser populated plains states (from South Dakota to Iowa, Oklahoma, and Texas) and an increase in the Midwest and Southeast sections of the country (Mississippi, Alabama, Arkansas, Missouri, Illinois, Indiana, Tennessee, and Kentucky). This means tornadoes are encroaching on areas with larger population densities with resulting increases in damage and casualties (Gensini & Brooks, 2018).

As assessed by disaster anthropologists Anthony Oliver-Smith, so-called natural disasters are not natural nor are they accidents or acts of God. Rather, "they are deeply rooted in the social, economic, and environmental history of the societies where they occur. Moreover, disasters are far more than catastrophic events; they are *processes* that unfold through time, and their causes are deeply embedded in societal history. As such, disasters have historical roots, unfolding presents, and potential futures according to the forms of reconstruction. In effect, a disaster is made inevitable by the historically produced pattern of vulnerability, evidenced in the location, infrastructure, sociopolitical structure, production patterns, and ideology that characterizes a society."

The Spread of Infectious Diseases

Like all species, humans have a long history dealing with pathogens and the infectious diseases they can cause. For much of human history, our ancestors lived in small, mobile, foraging communities, in which population densities were very low. These communities were too small to support epidemics, but depending on where they lived, our ancient ancestors had to contend with certain parasites and some zoonoses (diseases that spread from warm-blooded animals, primarily mammals but also birds) like sleeping sickness, avian tuberculosis, malaria, and leptospirosis. Beginning about 8–12,000 years ago, an increase in the spread and impact of infectious diseases occurred. It was shaped by various, often linked, factors, including a decline in mobile foraging, plant and animal domestication, settlement into more or less permanent villages, and subsequent urbanization. The latter entailed mass rural-to-urban migration, long-distance trade and mobility, war and colonialism, and significant human-induced changes in the environment, including forest clearance, dam building, and increasingly unsanitary living conditions. *As this brief history suggests, infectious diseases do not occur in the absence of pathogens (e.g., bacteria, viruses, prions), but the mere presence of such agents does not cause significant outbreaks. Rather, it is in interaction with socioenvironmental conditions that epidemics and pandemics occur.*

Today, the outbreak of emerging infectious diseases in humans is occurring with increasing frequency and with greater consequences. These emergent diseases have potentially long-lasting effects on human populations, but on wildlife and domesticated animal populations as well, with direct and indirect impacts on the world's ecosystems. In addition to the emergence of new infectious diseases like Zika, HIV/AIDS, Ebola, and COVID-19, there is a resurgence of older infectious diseases like malaria, cholera, tuberculosis, yellow fever, plague, rabies, and dengue fever. Worldwide, an estimated 56 million people died from all causes in 2001 (i.e., pre-COVID). Almost one-third of these deaths (26%) were due to infectious diseases and the vast majority were in lower income countries (14.2 million of 14.7 million). Mortality from infectious diseases was greatest in sub-Saharan Africa, with 6.8 million deaths, followed by South Asia, with 4.4 million deaths, or about 75% of all infectious disease deaths worldwide. Among non-human animals, there have been significant outbreaks of white-nose-syndrome in bats, epornitic conjunctivitis in birds, and the pandemic chytridiomycosis that is killing amphibians across several continents.

At the heart of the burst of new and renewed infectious diseases are the already noted assemblage of anthropogenic impacts on the environment/climate, including global warming, loss of biodiversity, deforestation and habitat degradation, infrastructure construction, more frequent wildlife–human contact, and the human-driven spread of pathogens and invasive disease vector species like mosquitoes, ticks, and rodents through the movement of trade goods and travel. As more people come into contact with a disease-causing animal pathogen, the greater the probability that it will infect and adapt to humans, resulting in many cases of human-to-human transmission. Observations made over recent decades indicate that we should expect a continued increase in the frequency of epidemics and pandemics caused by newly emergent human pathogens. In this sense, COVID-19 heralds a dystopic future of infectious disease. Emerging as a zoonotic pathogen, the SARS-Cov2 virus spread to people in Wuhan, China, and then, because of our modern hyperconnected, globalized world, rapidly diffused to every corner of the globe. Along the way, it, like other emergent infectious diseases, interacted with other diseases and health conditions to form a varied set of COVID-19 syndemics (Singer et al., 2021). COVID-19 exposes the error in thinking that it is possible for even the wealthiest of nations to escape the threat of contemporary ecocrises.

Infrastructure Maladaptation

Health is shaped not only in interaction with the natural environment but with the human-built environment as well. From cities to rural villages, from infrastructure to everyday commercial products, the human constructed world was built for a world that no longer exists. This maladaptation is evident in the mismatch between the existing climate and our physical infrastructure, including buildings, roads, bridges, dams, and the power grid. For example, in July 2024, very early in the season Hurricane Beryl knocked out power to over two million homes in the Houston, Texas area. Less than two months earlier, a storm with winds up to 100 mph blacked out electricity for more than a million people in the same area. Even a brief power outage is an immanent health risk, especially for medically fragile people and those dependent on electricity-powered medical equipment. Part of the problem is that the electric grid has the same hub-and-spoke basic architecture (which connects a central electric hub to outlying nodes) that it did 100 years ago. It was built for yesterday's climate and that climate is history. Similarly, there are the raging wildfires that hit California around the same time that Hurricane Beryl smashed into Houston. The fires began during a heatwave that broke many all-time temperature records in the West, reaching a scorching 122 °Fahrenheit (50 °C) in Palm Springs, California. The wilting heat was too high for firefighters to confront the fires because of the immediate risk of heatstroke. Had it gotten much hotter, aerial firefighting vehicles like water bombing planes and helicopters would not have been able to fly. In Phoenix during the summer of 2024, the surface temperatures of streets and sidewalks climbed to 160 °Fahrenheit (71 °C), hot enough to cause severe burns upon contact. During heat waves, cities, in effect, are transformed into human frying pans. Across the Atlantic, most of the buildings and homes in European cities like London, Paris, and Madrid lack air conditioning. During an extreme heat wave, as occurred in the summer of 2022, heat-related deaths skyrocket. Also stressed by climate change are reservoir dams around the world, especially from heavy rains and flooding which erode dam structure. The average age of dams in the USA, for example, is 60 years but there are over 8000 dams that are 90 years old, and many of them are at risk of failing resulting in significant loss of life. Equally, encumbered are airport tarmacs, which soften as the temperature rises causing flights cancelations. Sea walls that were built to protect coastal cities from flooding are increasingly ineffective as sea level rises and storm surges gain power in an overheated world. As Jeff Goodell (2024), author of *The Heat Will Kill You First: Life and Death on a Scorched Planet* (Goodell, 2023), maintains "The sooner we stop clinging to the old ways and focus on building a smarter, more sustainable, more equitable future for everyone, the better off we—and every living thing on this planet—will be."

Where Are We Headed?

A burning question—in some senses literally—is this: will anthropogenic environmental/climate disruption result in global societal collapse or even human extinction? Needless to say this question has stirred a range of popular and scientific responses. Some trace the origin of what might be called the ultimate existential question to the World Conference on the Changing Atmosphere: Implications for Global Security, which was held in Toronto, Canada, from June 27 to 30, 1988. Conferees, a mixture of policy makers, scientists, representatives of non-government and government organizations, and the UN, discussed climate change, ozone depletion, air pollution, release of acidifying substances, and threats to water resources. At the close of the conference, participants issued a powerful warning.

> Humanity is conducting an unintended, uncontrolled, globally pervasive experiment whose ultimate consequences could be second only to a global nuclear war.... Other major impacts are occurring from ozone-layer depletion resulting in increased damage from ultra-violet radiation. The best predictions available indicate potentially severe economic and social dislocation for present and future generations, which will worsen international tensions and increase risk of conflicts among and within nations. It is imperative to act now.

Those who deny that the world is entering into a severe environment/climate crisis label such statements as alarmist overreactions to questionable evidence. Even leading politicians and high office holders in various countries have denigrated even modest scientific statements about the seriousness of environmental disruption as a hoax intended to attract research funding or media attention. Javier Milei, president of Argentina, for example, has repeatedly asserted that environmental protections are an unnecessary and burdensome constraint on business freedoms and that climate change is a lie. The fact is, however, "scientists are biased not toward alarmism but rather the reverse: toward cautious estimates" (Bryse et al., 2013). As a result, most scientists have tended historically to shy away from making dramatic assessments or drawing doomsday conclusions. But, more recently, the perspectives of some scientists have begun to change, and there has been an increase in their willingness to at least entertain the possibility of worst-case scenarios. Why is this rethinking occurring?

One factor was the sweeping and sudden nature of the COVID-19 pandemic, which produced a confirmed *death toll of over seven million people* worldwide. The pandemic convinced many researchers that we must at least consider the prospect of very high-impact global risks and the systemic and various cascading threats they can create. A second factor is that research technologies have improved to the point that scientific confidence in worrisome findings has increased. Scientists focus on available data, not on opinions, and the ample amount of evidence from diverse sources as well as the improved quality of evidence has convinced many scientists that things are getting rapidly worse. One stark expression of this emergent understanding is the conclusion drawn by Díaz et al. (2019): "The fabric of life on which we all depend—nature and its contributions to people—is unravelling rapidly." A final factor at play is indication that worse-case scenarios with regard to climate change most closely match current greenhouse gas emission patterns. This does not translate to human extinction any time soon, but it is now recognized that many environment/climate risks are more serious than was previously believed and that this spells catastrophe for many people in many places. As expressed by climate scientist Adam Schlosser, the Deputy Director of the MIT Joint Program on the Science and Policy of Global Change, "there is a massive disruption coming to our way of life, and a potentially existential disruption to the way of life of many people around the world who have very little control over future climate change" (quoted in Krol, 2023). This disruption also means mass extinctions of an array of non-human species that cannot adapt to rapidly and radically changing conditions. On one point scientists agree: we have more than enough evidence to try to minimize worst-case outcomes.

What Does "Us" Mean? The Lesson of Forever Chemicals

Without question, human actions are the motor engine of our ever more impactful contemporary environmental crisis. The implication is that we are all to blame for the severe environment/climate crisis we face. While unavoidably we are all participants in this process—we drive cars, eat food grown by industrial agriculture, and relish consumer goods and the latest powerful technologies—responsibility is not shared equally. First, there are the poor of the world who contribute the least (but suffer the worst consequences) of our growing environmental chaos. Then there are those who are a little better off, people described as working and middle. They consume more than the poor but exercise limited decision-making power. Finally, and most responsible are the elite polluters, people with lifestyles, investments, and positions in major corporations, who are particularly responsible for the decisions and actions that pollute the planet and drive disruptive change. For example, a study by Oxfam (Khalfan et al., 2023) found that the richest people in the world were responsible for more carbon emissions than 5 billion people who were not rich (or about 66% of the overall human population).

Moffett Field, a federally owned airfield located on the banks of San Francisco Bay, is a 30-min drive from one of the homes of Nike CEO John Donahoe located in Portola Valley. Donahoe also owns a condo in Portland, Oregon. These homes are easily affordable given Donahoe's $29 million compensation package in 2023, making him one of America's highest-paid executives. Flight-tracking records show that Nike's G650ER Gulfstream jets landed at Moffett more than 100 times in the first three and a half years of Donahoe's CEO tenureship, after which they landed more frequently at a different airport with a similar drive time to Portola Valley. These repeated flights occurred aboard an eight passenger, four crew plane that its manufacturer describes as having a spacious and comfortable interior that provides "a refined getaway above the clouds." This frequent—air polluting—travel flies in the face of statements by both Donahoe and Nike executive chairperson Mark Parker that climate change is a crisis needing urgent action. In Donahue's words, "We are more committed than ever to help save the planet," while Parker has stated, "It's about leading with actions, not words" (quoted in Davis et al., 2024). Despite the company's commitment to sharply reduce emissions, Nike's jets emitted almost 20% more carbon dioxide in 2023 than they did in 2015, the year Nike uses as the baseline for its climate goals. Nike, the largest athletic apparel company in the world, claims to be a corporate leader on the environment, promising to slash carbon emissions in line with the Paris climate accord. But flying in a private jet is far more polluting than going on a commercial carrier. A private jet releases about 4.5 times as much carbon dioxide per passenger as a Boeing 737. Donahoe has an agreement with Nike that allows him to use the company jets for more than business. He can also use them for personal travel at his own expense.

Also consider the very rich, large shareholders and decision-makers of 3 M, a multinational corporation operating in the fields of industry and healthcare, and the maker of numerous consumer goods like tapes, scouring pads, bandages, facemasks, and glues (Lerner, 2024). Founded, in 1902, 3 M originally was called the Minnesota Mining and Manufacturing Company. Its mining ventures, however, were unproductive and the company shortened its name pivoted to making sandpaper. When an employee noticed that autoworkers were having trouble painting sought-after two-tone cars, he invented masking tape. Another worker created Post-it notes. Yet another successful product adopted by the company was a compound consisting of fluorochemicals which were an outgrowth of the US Manhattan Project effort to build the first atomic bomb. After the war, 3 M hired some Manhattan Project chemists to begin mass-producing chains of carbon atoms bonded to fluorine atoms. The resulting chemicals were found to be very versatile as well as long-lasting. Because they are resistant to degradation in the environment, as well as in human bodies, they have earned the nickname "forever chemicals." In a spray foam, named Scotchgard, fluorochemicals protected fabric, carpets, and leather from staining because they lowered the surface energy of fiber and slowed the penetration of liquids. Used as a coating known as Scotchban, fluorochemicals prevented food packaging from getting soggy. They also were of appeal among firefighters in extinguishing jet-fuel fires. In the early 1950s, 3 M began selling one of its fluorochemicals perfluorooctanoic acid to the DuPont chemical company for use in making of Teflon, widely used as a slippery coating on cookware.

From that point on through 2000, 3 M produced at least a hundred million pounds of fluorochemicals and was rewarded with billions of dollars in profits. But the company had been keeping a dark secret. During the late 1970s, 3 M scientists found that fluorochemicals were toxic in animals and they were accumulating in humans. Company scientists found that a relatively small daily dose, 4.5 mg for every kilogram of body weight—comparable to the dose of aspirin in a standard tablet—could kill a rhesus monkey within a few weeks. This means fluorochemicals should fall into the highest of five toxicity levels established by the UN. A 1979 internal 3 M report stated that fluorochemicals the company was making were more toxic than had been anticipated. In time it was found that forever chemicals made by 3 M (and others) were being spread through groundwater and were showing up in drinking water, the blood of people living all over the world, and human breast milk. Other evidence also began to build up, but 3 M kept silent about it.

3 M's well-kept secret began to unravel in 1999 when a West Virginia rancher named Wilbur Tennant noticed that no matter how much he fed cattle, they kept losing weight. Many of them also developed tumors, foamed at the mouth, and died. Knowing that his farm was located near a DuPont factory, Tennant reasoned that might be the source of his problem. As it turned out, waste from the factory, which produced Teflon, was running into a nearby stream which his cattle used for drinking. The Tennant family sued DuPont and their attorney discovered a document written by DuPont scientists to the Environmental Protection Agency that admitted the presence of toxins in a company landfill and that DuPont had been testing its employees' blood for the presence of dangerous chemicals and found fluorochemicals *had* accumulated in their blood. Further investigation unearthed records exposing the fact that DuPont knew for *decades* that fluorochemicals were toxic. But DuPont hid, like 3 M, this information from the public for years, maintaining that the chemicals were safe.

The Minnesota attorney general's office sued 3 M and released thousands of damning internal 3 M records to the public. Subsequently numerous scientific papers reported that in adults, even at very low levels, fluorochemicals could interfere with hormones, fertility, liver and thyroid function, cholesterol levels, and fetal development. In children, the chemicals interfered with vaccines. During Congressional hearings on the issue, US Rep. Harley Rouda of California called the contamination of the country's drinking water, groundwater, air, and food supplies a national emergency, adding, "These companies got away with poisoning people for more than a half century" (quoted in Winter, 2022).

The fight against forever chemicals and their manufacturers continues. Although some older compounds have now been banned, companies are inventing new ones with different molecular structures they claim degrade more rapidly and are allegedly less harmful to health. The chemical industry, however, does not disclose its formulations. Consequently environmental and public health scientists are skeptical. As Philippe Grandjean of Harvard T.H. Chan School of Public Health has warned, "We're going back to square one" (Lim, 2019).

The 3 M case is not unique. To cite one similar example of the many that exist: the multinational fossil fuel company ExxonMobil hid its research that was conducted in the 1980s that showed the connection between oil extraction and use and global temperature rise but used various forms of deception to keep this information from the public (Supran & Oreskes, 2021).

Elite polluting of the environment as a result of industrial production and the release of unwanted waste from the production process in the air, on land, and into water without regard for cost or consequence, in the view of Rice Marcantonio and Augustin Fuentes (Marcantonio & Fuentes, 2023), constitutes a violent act. They use the term "environmental violence" to label this phenomenon because it is the result of intentional, excessive human consumption of resources and energy that is well beyond what is needed to maximize human flourishing. Elite pollution which is prolific in every corner of the world is a form of environmental violence because it leads to growing environmental hazards that directly and knowingly harm human health.

In sum, as author/activist Dan Voskoboynik (2018) aptly asserts, "we are all to blame" statements suffer from what he calls "the hollowness of we" because only a portion of human beings, not all of humanity, are responsible for our ecological crisis.

Case Study 1: Gaslighting and the Gas Company
The term "gaslighting" is a verb that refers to an insidious form of manipulation. Victims of gaslighting are deliberately and systematically given false information as a way of influencing their behavior. The term first appeared in a 1938 play called *Gas Light* by British playwright Patrick Hamilton, and was later adapted into a feature motion picture called *Gaslight* starring Charles Boyer and Ingrid Bergman. While initially used to describe the psychological manipulation of one person by another, the term eventually acquired a social-level and marketing application. In the book *State of Confusion: Political Manipulation and the Assault on the American Mind,* Bryant Welch (2008) comments that the contemporary popular use of the term "comes directly from blending modern communications, marketing, and advertising techniques with long-standing methods of propaganda." Citing an example, the Sierra Club (2024) observes, "Polluters tend to "greenwash" their destructive impact on our communities by gaslighting the public and decision-makers into believing that a project (natural gas pipelines, gas plants, biogas, etc.) is good for the environment and climate." An egregious case, ironically, involves the gas company.

The American Gas Association (AGA), the leading industry trade group and lobbying effort, which represents over 200 investor-owned gas utility companies, has consistently maintained that natural gas is an environmentally clean product. The AGA, for example, maintains that gas stoves and furnaces are very minor sources of nitrogen dioxide, a known disease-linked pollutant, despite extensive scientific evidence revealing the association of natural gas exposure in the home with asthma, other respiratory diseases, and cancer. Beginning in the 1930s, the gas utility industry began an ad campaign called "cooking with gas" designed to convince American consumers to buy gas stoves. The industry redoubled its efforts beginning in 1969 because the sale of electric stoves began to outpace gas stove purchases. The industry was also focused on getting consumers to buy gas furnaces, water heaters, and clothes dryers, which use a lot more gas than stoves. To try and counter the mounting scientific data on the health risks of burning natural gas, the industry commissioned its own studies by authors and laboratories that failed to disclose their source of funding. Predictably, these paid for studies found no link between health risk and natural gas. Some of these laboratories had previously done the same kind of (thoroughly discredited) work for the tobacco industry. Beginning in 2018, the AGA launched a campaign on Instagram and Facebook that minimizes the risk natural gas poses to human health and the environment. TikTok also has been used by industry linked influences who praise the benefit of gas appliances. The industry also set up front groups like Californians for Balanced Energy to promote the use of natural gas and to oppose local bans on gas hook-ups in new homes and buildings. Gas industry lobbying has convinced legislatures in several dozen states to pass laws that make it illegal for environmentally conscious cities and counties to restrict gas hook-ups. Year after year, gaslighting by the gas company continues.

Discussion Questions

1. How did syndemics theory influence the research of Paula Skye Tallman?
2. What is critical health anthropology?
3. What is the origin of the syndemics approach?
4. Name and discuss five different expressions of climate change.
5. What is a forever chemical and why are such chemicals important in human health?
6. What does the term "gaslight" mean and how was the practice used by the American Gas Association?

Project Ideas

1. Focus on the city/town/area where you live and investigate how it has changed environmentally over the past 25 years.
2. Pick one of the following forever chemicals and investigate its health effects:
   (a) PFOA (Perfluorooactanoic acid)
   (b) PFOS (Perfluorooctanesulfonic acid)
   (c) PFHxS (Perfluorohexane sulfonic acid)
   (d) PFNA (Perfluorononanoic acid)
   (e) PFDoA (Perfluorododecanoic acid)

The Shift to Planetary Health in the Twenty-First Century

Abstract

This chapter examines the emergence, definition, and scope of the planetary health perspective and further explores the role of the environment in health and health equity. The chapter examines the scientific effort to eliminate disease and why it is so difficult to achieve. It also assesses the health of animals, plants, and their shared environments. Contemporary discussions of the safe environmental limits within which humanity can flourish are reviewed. Of special concern in the chapter are Indigenous voices commenting on the planetary health approach and the integration of indigenous perspectives in the shaping of what is here labeled Planetary Health 2.0. Planetary Health, in its revised, collaborative expression, it is argued, represents a critical advance in our collective understanding and participatory response to the issue of health in its full meaning.

Keywords

Planetary health · One Health · Health and social equity · Social determinants of health · Safe environmental limits · Ecocrises interaction · Rethinking plants and animals · Indigenous knowledge · Colonial roots of public health

Eliminating Disease

The term "planetary health" has been formally defined as "the achievement of the highest attainable standard of health, well-being, and equity worldwide through judicious attention to the human systems—political, economic, and social—that shape the future of humanity and the Earth's natural systems that define the safe environmental limits within which humanity can flourish" (Whitmee et al., 2015). Let's break that complex sentence down and along the way explore why disease and health are not simply biological phenomena. This inescapable fact was made abundantly clear by the COVID-19 pandemic. As explained by Devi Sridhar (2020), Chair of Global Public Health at the University of Edinburgh:

> Of all the lessons we've learned from this pandemic, the most significant is how unequal its effects have been. Wealth, it turns out, is the best shield strategy from Covid-19. Two of the largest risk factors for dying from Covid-19 are being from a deprived background and being from a minority-ethnic background, pointing to the underlying role of social inequalities, housing conditions and occupation.

We begin by asking: What is the highest attainable standard of health, well-being, and equity worldwide? We actually don't know, although we are certain based on many comparative studies that we have not achieved it at least in modern times, and certainly not for most people. We do know that it does not mean an elimination of all disease because that is considered not to be achievable. Disease-causing mutations that occur as our genes replicate, the continued human exposure to diseases from the animal world, and unequal structures of social relations that make subordinate groups more vulnerable all hinder disease elimination. Nonetheless, for over a century, the eradication of human disease has been the subject of a long list of conferences, invited speeches, planning sessions, and public health initiatives. That dream continues. In 2023, Mark Zuckerberg and his wife Dr. Priscilla Chan announced their plan to eradicate all human diseases by 2100 using AI to develop digital models that allow a deeper understanding of how the human body responds to diseases and new medications.

To date, however, we have effectively eliminated only one human infectious disease: smallpox (and one infectious disease among animals: rinderpest). Historians have observed that smallpox, a scourge for thousands of years, spread globally due to exploration and colonial expansion. Due to the development of an effective vaccine and a concerted global vaccination campaign, the last known naturally occurring case of this deadly disease was reported almost 50 years ago. There are a number of somewhat unique reasons why it was possible to eliminate smallpox from the wild (i.e., the natural world). The disease is easily detectable because it causes a characteristic skin rash. Smallpox has no animal reservoir, which means it cannot spread from other animals to humans. Once someone has been infected they acquire permanent immunity from subsequent infection. The vaccine for smallpox is heat-stable (and does not need refrigeration), is inexpensive, and provides protection with only one dose.

Beyond smallpox, two of three types of virus that cause polio have been eradicated worldwide. One type remains, primarily in eastern Afghanistan and the Khyber Pakhtunkhwa province in neighboring Pakistan. The polio virus has also been discovered in sewage samples in London, Finland, and Jerusalem. The goal of the Global Polio Eradication Initiative was to eliminate the disease by 2000 through mass vaccination. In parts of Africa, however, vaccine-derived strains of the virus have led to new cases. These strains originally were part of the oral polio vaccine but after they were shed in human stool by individuals who had been inoculated, they mutated in the wild and became every bit as dangerous as the original virus. There are several other infectious diseases we may eliminate in the near future, but as the case of polio suggests, while we adapt to and find ways to prevent and treat infectious diseases, these diseases adapt to our innovations, and many of our actions promote disease, however unintended.

One reason we continue to face disease is genetic mutation. In and of itself mutation is not a bad thing. Indeed, mutation and sexual reproduction expand genetic variation in a population over time and place. Evolution is driven by natural selection acting on mutations. This process tends to favor the survival of individuals within a population that are better adapted genetically and behaviorally to the contingencies of their environment. But evolution does not produce perfection; rather, it is geared to producing sufficient changes to allow for survival and reproduction (and thus the passing on of genetic information) in a given habitat at a particular period of time. But environments change and yesterday's adaptations may become tomorrow's liabilities. Further, mutations can cut both ways, conferring some advantages and some disadvantages. Thus, some of the same mutations that enable humans to fight off deadly infectious diseases also make us more sensitive to inflammatory and autoimmune diseases, like Crohn's disease. Similarly, a parasite that causes malaria has infected various African populations for millions of years. The human genome responded to this deadly threat through evolutionary processes that selected people with genes that favor resistance to infections. This adaptation involves increased inflammation in the body. This change, however, contributed to making contemporary African peoples being somewhat more prone to the development of cardiovascular diseases, such as atherosclerosis, as they grow older. This risk is magnified by oppressive social factors and associated unhealthy living conditions.

Globally, cancer killed an estimated 9.5 million people in 2018, more than the combined lethal impact of malaria, tuberculosis, and HIV. During the twenty-first century, cancer is expected to become the leading cause of death worldwide. Yet for many years people have asked, "If we can put astronauts on the moon, why can't we do away with cancer?" For example, in 1969 the Citizens Committee for the Conquest of Cancer, prompted by the success of the Apollo 11 space mission, ran full-page ads in *The Washington Post* and *The New York Times* calling on President Nixon to "cure cancer." Nixon (1971) responded in his State of the Union address, telling the world: "The time has come in America when the same kind of concentrated effort that split the atom and took man to the moon should be turned toward conquering this dread disease." In 2016, Microsoft Corporation also vowed it would "solve the problem of cancer" and do so within a decade using computer science to reprogram diseased cells back to a healthy state. The plan was to treat cancer like an information processing system that is suffering from a computer virus. According to medicinal chemist Derek Lowe (2016), the problem at the heart of this assertion is that "the cell/computer analogy is too facile to be useful.... On one level, these things do sort of fit, but it's not a level that you can get much use out of. DNA is much, much messier than any usable code ever written, and it's messier on several different levels and in a lot of different ways." Adds Madeline Drexler (2020), editor *Harvard Public Health,* "Cell division is an imperfect process; like a biological keyboard with a letter missing, it makes mistakes." Additionally, it must be stressed, cancer is not one disease; it is dozens of diseases (about 200) with some similarities and many differences. In the USA alone, 600,000 people die from cancer annually. For these reasons, as we approach Microsoft's target date for the elimination of cancer—and despite much progress in cancer treatment—cancer is not close to being solved.

There are some non-infectious "diseases" that have disappeared, but these disappearances only highlight the role of society in disease construction. In 1952, the American Psychiatry Association developed the first version of a volume known as the *Diagnostic and Statistical Manual of Mental Disorders* (DSM). The DSM was the first itemization and description of recognized mental health conditions. The book included homosexuality as a sociopathic personality disturbance. The publication of the revised DSM-II in 1968 included homosexuality again, but the American Psychiatric Association removed homosexuality from the DSM-II in 1973. Psychiatrists no longer see homosexuality as a disease but rather as part of normal human diversity. The official medical depathologizing of homosexuality essentially affirmed that difference is not defect.

Drapetomania was the name given to the "mental illness" that American physician Samuel Cartwright asserted was the cause of slaves running away to freedom. Cartwright, who practiced medicine in Mississippi and Louisiana in the 1800s, reasoned that (in his view) slavery was such a fundamental improvement in the lives of the enslaved that they must be suffering from a mental illness if they wanted to escape bondage. Cartwright, who never visited the societies from which slaves were stolen, also never commented on the sudden disappearance of drapetomania among slaves who succeeded in escaping oppression. With emancipation, this "disease" faded into history.

The term hysteria derives from the Greek word "*hystera*," which means womb. It became a prominent medical concept during the nineteenth century based on the work of the neuropsychiatrist Pierre Janet at Salpêtrière Hospital in Paris, France. He described hysteria as "a nervous disease" that causes women to behave in extreme ways or to feel very intense emotions. Sigmund Freud also promoted this diagnosis based on the culturally dominant view that by nature women are given to over-dramatizing symptoms, have heightened sensitivity, and are more easily influenced than men. Hysteria patients were said to exhibit extreme states of nervousness or anxiety as well as eroticism. Doctors were slow in coming to recognize the sexism inherent in the diagnosis of hysteria and its use to control women's behavior. Although the term did not appear in the original DSM, it was included in the revised DSM-II in 1968. It was finally dropped as a psychiatric diagnosis in 1980. In retrospect, hysteria was a fallacious disorder that reflected gendered social inequalities.

How Epidemics End

Another example of the social nature of disease as well as its impact is seen in research designed to determine when epidemics (or pandemics) end. How do people know when the threat of an epidemic is over and it is possible to resume their normal lives and activities? It is tempting to assume that epidemics end through the successful eradication of a disease or through the discovery of a preventive vaccine. Yet, as noted above, we have not eliminated or fully prevented the vast majority of the diseases that imperil human life. Some epidemics, such as recent local outbreaks of cholera, have ended through a combination medical, social, hygienic, and political interventions. But stopping a local outbreak in one area does not mean there are not subsequent outbreaks elsewhere. This is the case with cholera which has seen outbreaks during the 2020s in various African countries, Haiti, Afghanistan, and Syria. Similarly, the end of plague caused by the bacterium *Yersinia pestis* in Western Europe in the early 1700s tends to hide the fact that plague did not disappear from the rest of the world. Other epidemics like influenza and HIV/AIDS never ended. Rather, they persist as cyclical epidemics or endemic diseases.

Historians Erika Charters and Kristin Heitman (2021) have suggested that most often an epidemic ends when health authorities declared it to have ended because the frequency of new cases falls to a level that the disease has been accepted as an unwelcome but manageable part of normal life. Further, they point out that epidemics end at different times for different groups, both across regions and within individual societies. Analyzing the process of ending "reveals the nature of epidemics as social and political events, and not simply biological phenomena" (Charters and Heiman 2021).

Worldwide Equity

The second theme expressed in the definition of planetary health is equity across political, economic, and other social systems, including health care. The Centers for Disease Control and Prevention defines health equity as the state in which everyone in society has a fair and just opportunity to attain their highest level of health. Achieving this goal requires redressing historical and contemporary injustices, economical and social barriers to health and health care, and the elimination of preventable class, racial, ethnic, and gender health disparities. Again, knowing exactly what someone's highest attainable level of health is somewhat elusive but this language is only meant to focus attention on identifiable factors that diminish health and are preventable. Collectively, many of these factors have been called the social determinants of health. As Amartya Sen (2005) observes, "unnecessary suffering, debilitation, and death from preventable or controllable illness characterize every country and society, to varying extents." The study of the social determinants of health has proliferated during the twenty-first century. Researchers have asked questions like does structural racism—i.e., the totality of pathways used within societies to promote racial discrimination and racial inequality—harm health? A related question for the social determinants approach is precisely "how do social relations and society become literally 'embodied,' 'incorporated,' and result in pathology?" (Hahn, 2021). In other words, how do unjust social relations "get under the skin" and cause disease in human bodies?

Answering these questions begins by examining how people are categorized in society (e.g., by sex, gender, race, ethnicity, classes) and how groups that hold power both make and administer rules and allocate or withhold societal resources, including social rights and statuses, based on these categories. The notion of the totality of pathways refers to interconnected and mutually reinforcing components of social systems like housing, living conditions, education, employment, income, the media, health care, and the criminal justice system. A growing body of research indicates that built-in discriminatory features of social systems cause higher rates of various diseases and other health conditions in affected populations. For example, prolonged exposure to racism across the various components of a social system constitutes a form of chronic stress, a process that leads to pathophysiology. Some of the most common stress-related diseases are cardiovascular diseases like heart disease, metabolic diseases like diabetes, neurodegenerative disorders like depression, and cancer. Cortisol released from the body during periods of stress can cause physiological and psychological damage, which can be transmitted across generations. Emerging research suggests that the effects of trauma may even be genetically passed down from one generation to another. Epigenetics, which is the study of how genes are turned on and off, shapes gene expression, boosting the activity of some genes and quieting the expression of others. This may be the mechanism through which a parent's experience of trauma is imprinted in the genes of their children.

Stress can damage the body through processes like inflammation. Inflammation is part of the body's normal defense apparatus. When, for example, pathogens like a species of virus gains access to the body, the immune system responds by triggering the release of inflammatory cells. These cells trap the virus, while attracting a kind of white blood cell that kills the virus, and starts healing any tissue injured by the virus. Inflammation may cause some pain, swelling, or even discoloration, but these short-term changes are signs that your body is healing itself. Inflammation can be either acute or chronic. When stress is chronic and continues over a prolonged period (even years), the body keeps producing inflammatory cells, which, in itself, is harmful to body tissues. Chronic inflammation, in short, is a misguided or over-healing process that damages rather than benefits the body. Thus, a study by Thames et al. (2019) of 71 individuals, 37 of whom were HIV-seropositive (HIV+) and of whom were 34 HIV-seronegative (HIV−) who self-identified either as African American/Black ($n=48$) or European American/White ($n=23$), provided an opportunity to examine the independent effects of race and HIV on inflammation. Relative to European Americans, Blacks showed increased activity of two key pro-inflammatory transcription control pathways and two stress-responsive signaling systems. These patterns did not differ significantly as a function of HIV infection. These results suggested that differences in experiences of racial discrimination can potentially account for more than 50% of the total race-related difference in chronic pro-inflammatory activity. In effect, racism and the chronic stress it causes wear down or age body systems including the immune system. The result is more sickness.

Lisa Molix (2014) proposes that sexism, a structural factor experienced by women involving stressful prejudice, stereotyping, and discrimination, should also be examined as a risk factor for stress-related cardiovascular disease. This proposal stems in part from findings showing that while the incidence of death due to cardiovascular disease has decreased in recent years among men, it remains the leading cause of mortality and disability among women. It is theorized that this contrast may be due to underdiagnosed, misdiagnosed, and undertreated heart conditions among women because of sexual bias among researchers and providers. Moreover, Berg's (2006) study of the correlations between everyday (nonviolent) sexism and the development of trauma symptoms in women found a moderately strong relationship between the experience of everyday sexism and posttraumatic stress disorder (PTSD). In the study, 382 women completed a subjective measurement of their experience of sexism, a checklist of gender-based stressors, and a measurement of PTSD. A stepwise multiple regression revealed that when all variables were analyzed the most predictive variable for trauma was recent experience of sexist degradation, which accounted for 20% of the variance in PTSD scores.

As this research suggests, inequality is bad for human health. Inequalities often have intersectional interactions. The term intersectionality is used to describe how systems of power and oppression (like racism, sexism, heterosexism) entwine to shape people's everyday lived experiences as well as their health. Thus, while Black women in the USA have experienced notable improvements in health, disparities persist. These health disparities reflect the combined race and gender inequalities experienced by Black women across various social and economic measures.

An important set of social determinants of health stems from the effects of human activity. Neighborhoods that are home to lower-income, racially minoritized, and immigrant residents often are subject to human-made environmental risks such the placement of toxin-producing facilities or the building of low-income housing on or near known toxic sites. Also, it is not uncommon for shopping malls, schools, or other commercial entities to be built on brownfields or otherwise polluted land and airscapes. Research in the UK, for example, shows that most new schools with enrollments of thousands of students are being erected in areas with unsafe levels of air pollution. Children are especially sensitive and vulnerable to the harmful effects of polluted air because their bodies and immune systems are still developing. Polluting facilities and toxic dumps, which include power plants, congested highways, and industrial facilities, rob people of the power to shape their own neighborhoods while damaging their health. The term "environmental justice" was coined to label the ability to be part of decisions, like government or corporate policy making, regarding community environment issues.

Safe Environmental Limits Within Which Humanity Can Flourish

The final part of the defining statement on planetary health focuses on the existence of environmental thresholds or conditions beyond which humanity cannot flourish. The concept of flourishing, which has garnered considerable attention in the broader health field in recent years, especially positive psychology, has various definitions.

These definitions utilize terms like living the good life, attaining well-being, and functioning well both psychologically and socially. What factors allow human flourishing? As Sarah Willen and her colleagues (2022) emphasize, the ability to flourish is shaped by the circumstances in which people live, including the political, economic, legal, housing, and educational systems that structure their world. In other words, "for individuals to flourish, they must be situated in societies that promote their flourishing" (Roberts, 2019). Those that do not, like impoverished neighborhoods or marginalized communities, thwart flourishing. Thus far, the discussion of flourishing has tended to focus on privileged groups within society and less so on those subject to discrimination and other forms of injustice. In their own study, Willen et al. (2022) asked a socioeconomically diverse sample of over 150 residents of Greater Cleveland, Ohio, to share their personal perspectives on and experiences with flourishing using a set of open-ended, semi-structured interviews. They found that even when they controlled for income, Black study participants reported lower levels of flourishing. Even achieving a higher standard of living did not protect Black interviewees from the insults and injuries of racism. These findings affirm the fundamental role of structure, power, and historical racial injustice in people's ability to flourish.

A broader lens on human flourishing locates it within the field of exposome science, which is the multidisciplinary study of impacts and exposures to the total environment (Logan et al., 2023). Of central importance to this way of thinking about flourishing is recognition that human life on Earth, indeed all life on the planet, is sustained by a delicate balance of a number of vital biogeochemical systems that sustain a livable environment. Scientific focus on what makes up the key biogeochemical subsystems of an inhabitable world was significantly advanced during the mid-2000s by Johan Rockström, director of the Stockholm Resilience Center, along with an interdisciplinary team of scientists (2009). Their goal was to define the boundaries of a safe operating space for humanity on Earth. In other words, across the various biological, geological, chemical, and other natural subsystems of our planet, their aim was to identify the key boundaries that make Earth a place where life as we know it can flourish. This also entails finding the thresholds we should never cross to avoid environmental peril. If these subsystems are pushed too far through human actions, Rockström and co-workers indicated, they will lose their resilience and transition, rapidly and possibly irreversibly, into a new self-reinforcing state for the planet, a state that might not support humanity. The nine crucial subsystems they identified, all of which interact and need to be treated as one networked system, are:

- Climate change: As we have seen, ever greater health and other consequences emerge as Earth grows warmer. The accepted guard rail on global warming—a 3.6 degree Fahrenheit (2 degrees Celsius) rise in temperature above pre-industrial levels—has already been crossed for short periods of time. This has begun to unleash a cascade of concerning changes. Because of the myriad of adverse impacts stemming from climate change, climate stability is perhaps the core boundary in maintaining a livable Earth.

- Introduction of novel environmental substances: The harmful substances introduced by human activities include chemicals, plastics, heavy metals, and radioactive materials. They constitute a vital boundary because they negatively impact the air, the water, and the land on which all life depends.
- Biosphere integrity: This term refers to the innate value of biodiversity. Scientists estimate that there may be over 8 million species of plants and animals currently, although only a little over one million have been formally identified and described. The rapid rate at which species, including mammals, birds, reptiles, amphibians, fish, and insects, are now going extinct has led scientists to declare that we are in a biodiversity crisis. Over the last half billion years, due to natural events (e.g., volcanoes, asteroids), there have been five mass extinction events involving a dramatic contraction in Earth species. Some scientists believe we are currently experiencing a sixth extinction, and this time it is human actions that are picking apart the intertwined web of life. But, argues Justin McBrien (2019), while still a doctoral candidate in global environmental history at the University of Virginia, "Let's start calling it what it [really] is: the first great extermination." He explains that what we are experiencing is not a passive natural event but an "active, organized eradication" in the name of corporate profit-making (McBrien, 2019).
- Atmospheric aerosols: Small particles suspended in the atmosphere. Aerosols include blown desert dust, air pollution, and soot from wildfires. Aerosols have multiple physical, biogeochemical, and biological effects on the Earth system. For example, observational studies suggest that there has been a global doubling of mineral dust deposition since 1750 as a consequence of drying and desertification. The Sahara Desert is the largest source of dust in the world. Now very dry, it previously had many lakes and wetlands. Mineral dust enters the atmosphere when wind blows over deserts and lifts up and carries away particles. As aerosols fall back to Earth, some land on snow or ice, decreasing their reflectivity and causing the surface to absorb more light, which has a significant warming effect. Aerosols also can cause damage to plants, nonhuman animals, and humans.
- Ocean acidification: A process stemming from the ocean uptake of CO_2 from the atmosphere appears to be happening faster now than at any time in the past. Beyond the adverse effects on corals and shellfish, acidification confuses fish (hindering their ability to smell food, mates, predators, and suitable habitats) and contributes to harmful algal blooms. Toxins produced by algae cause a variety of human food poisoning syndromes through the consumption of contaminated seafood. Collectively, these changes pose a severe risk to marine biodiversity.
- Biogeochemical flows: Human activities, especially industrial agriculture, have critically changed Earth's natural nitrogen and phosphorus cycles. Enormous quantities of synthetic pesticides and chemical fertilizers applied to crop lands over the last 60 years have seeped into various ecosystems. Nitrogen and phosphorus pollution contribute to global warming. Nitrous oxide is a powerful greenhouse gas as well as an ozone-depleting substance. Another component, ammonia, causes air pollution, with severe health impacts. Nitrates seep into estuaries and cause oxygen-depleted dead zones.

- Freshwater use: Agriculture, industry, and the growing size of the global population are straining Earth's freshwater cycle, at a time when climate change is causing droughts in some regions and flooding in others. A threat to freshwater is a threat to many species and all human populations.
- Land-system change: Changes in land-use patterns, especially the cutting of tropical forests and their conversion into farmland, have a major impact on climate, biodiversity, freshwater availability, and the solar reflectivity of Earth's surface. Land cover is an environmental boundary of vital importance to a land-dwelling species like our own.
- Stratospheric ozone depletion: The depletion of ozone in the stratosphere by chemical pollutants was first discovered in the 1980s. Actions taken beginning in 1987 appear to have been effective and the ozone layer is showing signs of recovery. However, an area of severe ozone depletion opens up annually over Antarctica. In recent years, the hole has remained until December, well into the Antarctic summer, when plants and animals are most vulnerable. What is causing this dangerous shift: climate change. All of these changes impact aquatic life (Fig. 2.1).

When Rockström and his colleagues around the world first explained how they identified planetary boundaries, they reported that three of the boundaries—biochemical flows, biospheric integrity, and climate change—had already been transgressed. In a follow-up study with new data in 2015, land-system change was

Fig. 2.1 Marine biodiversity

added to the list of boundaries that had been crossed. Most recently, in 2023, these researchers reported that the introduction of novel entities and freshwater change have also been added to the list. This means we have already crossed two of the above listed boundaries, and the only three we have not crossed thus far are ocean acidification, aerosol loading, and atmospheric ozone depletion. Fortuitously, drastic changes are not expected to occur immediately as we blindly push past boundaries, but already we see the warning signs that severe risks to human and nonhuman health, indeed planetary health, are accumulating as we enter a new era characterized by a confluence of crises. We are speedily undermining essential features of the Earth's vibrant system that have kept conditions stable for the last 10,000 years and at some point we will cross tipping points, or points of no return, and Earth as we know it (and need it to be) will be gone.

Ecocrises Interaction

The multiple anthropogenic environmental and climate disruptions that are putting life as we know it on Earth at risk are not only occurring at the same time but, more gravely, interacting with one another in complex and often hard to predict and unexpected ways. There are, for example, potentially critical interactions between the transgression of the safe planetary boundaries for climate change and the loss of biosphere integrity (including the decline or disappearance of biological diversity, from genes to ecosystems). The natural world that is under, over, and around us forms one interdependent system made up of various component subsystems, and "[d]amage to one subsystem can create feedback that damages another" (Abbasi et al., 2023). Further, human and natural systems are increasingly interconnected such that the impacts of human actions in one part of the globe can be felt at distances far from their source. In December 2020, under the auspices of the Intergovernmental Panel on Climate Change and the Intergovernmental Science-Policy Platform on Biodiversity and Ecosystem Services, 50 of the world's leading biodiversity and climate experts participated in a four-day virtual workshop to examine the synergies and trade-offs between biodiversity protection and climate change mitigation and adaptation. Among their conclusions was the following: "Only by considering climate and biodiversity as parts of the same complex problem…can solutions be developed that avoid maladaptation and maximize the beneficial outcomes." Additionally, they pointed out a number of pathways of interactions, including climate-related decline of snowfield and glacier sizes leading to a reduction in late-summer streamflow that negatively impact biodiversity, ocean warming and acidification acting together to reduce the fitness of tropical corals and the consequent degradation of coral reef ecosystems, and the synergistic interactions between deforestation and droughts that promote wildfires that lead to the replacement of forests by savanna-type vegetation or fire-prone secondary forests (see Fig. 2.2). The term "ecocrisis interaction" refers to the synergistic interface of two or more adverse environmental events or pollutants. These interfaces can multiply impacts and produce harmful health effects that are greater than their additive outcome (Singer, 2021a, b). Simply put, in terms of environment consequences, one plus one equals more than two because of the additional effects caused by ecocrises interaction. Indeed, going beyond the issue of subsystem interaction, in 2023 over 200 health journals from across the world published an editorial calling on world leaders and health professionals to recognize that "climate change and biodiversity loss are one indivisible crisis and must be tackled together to preserve health and avoid catastrophe" (Abbasi et al., 2023).

Alaina Pfenning-Butterworth et al. (2024) illustrate the nature and threat of ecocrises interaction through an examination of each of the six causal pathways that link climate change, biodiversity loss, and infectious disease, as discussed below.

Climate Change → Biodiversity

Climate change restructures biological communities through various mechanisms. Both rapid changes in local climate and extreme climatic events can cause local species extirpations (including local keystone species), or even global extinctions, reducing the diversity of local ecosystems. If a keystone predator is removed from an ecosystem by climate change, for example, prey species may explode in number, a change that can lead to the displacing of other species. This kind of shift, called a "top-down trophic cascade," can have major long-term damaging impacts on an ecosystem. Climate change also pushes range shifts that can lead to novel community compositions that reshape species interactions. Changes in temperature and precipitation can shape the flow of energy through ecological networks. Climate-induced changes can modify the resilience of food webs, or mismatches between food availability and need (e.g., the availability of food for newly hatched birds, fish, or reptiles) which then cascade into the termination of a species in a geographic area.

Biodiversity → Climate Change

Increases in biodiversity are associated with reduced effects of climate change. More diverse and species-rich natural forests, for example, have higher potential for carbon sequestering (and hence not released to the atmosphere). Conversely, the loss of biodiversity reduces carbon sequestration while simultaneously increasing greenhouse emissions by increasing the quantity of plant biomass undergoing decomposition and carbon release (Fig. 2.2).

Biodiversity → Infectious Disease

A considerable body of research shows that high biodiversity frequently is associated with reduced rates of pathogen transmission, decreasing infectious disease risk for humans, wildlife, and plants. The inhibitory effect of high biodiversity on

Fig. 2.2 Deforestation in Brazil

pathogen transmission is based on several mechanisms: (1) most pathogens appear to be host generalists; they encounter and potentially infect more than one host species; (2) these host species differ substantially in their susceptibility to infection, and in their capacity to transmit infection to other hosts; and (3) the hosts most likely to acquire and transmit infection (called the reservoir hosts) tend to be species that are abundant, widespread, and resilient. Consequently, reservoir species tend to persist when biodiversity is diminished, increasing in abundance relative to those species that are more sensitive to disturbance. Because of these factors, species living in ecological communities with high biodiversity tend to dilute the effect of the reservoir species and reduce disease risk. This "dilution effect" has been seen in plant, wildlife, and human pathogens (Ostfeld, 2017). Changes in the abundance of vectors due to "ecological release" (which occurs when the population of a species increases or even explodes because it is freed from limiting factors in its environment like predators), species introductions and invasions, or climate-induced range shifts can also alter disease transmission, with either positive or negative effects on disease prevalence.

Infectious Disease → Biodiversity

Infectious disease is a direct driver of biodiversity loss through species declines, local extirpations, and global extinctions. Infectious diseases can cause population declines in species by reducing maturation and development, ecological fitness (including ability to cope with change), and survival of their hosts. Infectious agents constitute a particular risk to already threatened and endangered species. Diseases also can manipulate the behavior of hosts. For example, parasites can modify host feeding behavior leading to increases or decreases in the consumption of nutrients. Beyond a few publicized examples, such as the fungal disease chytridiomycosis in frogs around the world and white-nose syndrome among bats in North America, infectious disease is probably underestimated as a cause of both local and global extinction. This is because infection often co-occurs with other more visible drivers of extinction, and its signs can be easily missed.

Climate Change → Infectious Disease

The various effects of climate change on infectious diseases transmitted by biological vectors like ticks and mosquitos were explored above. Other such vectors include aquatic snails, fleas, lice, sandflies, and triatome bugs (called "kissing bugs," although they are actually insects). Kissing bugs transmit Chagas disease, the most important vector-borne disease in Latin America. Several studies suggest that rising temperatures associated with climate change may lead to a reduction in the frequency of Chagas disease. This, however, is not the case with other vector-borne diseases.

During the spring of 1993, an initially puzzling respiratory disease appeared in the Four Corners region of the southwestern USA. The initial identified patient was a 19-year-old man from the small reservation village of Crownpoint who became ill while driving with family members through New Mexico in the area where the state comes together with Arizona, Colorado, and Utah. Prior to his illness, he was a very fit, competitive marathon runner with some local celebrity. The family was on its way, however, to the funeral of the young man's fiancée and the mother of his infant child. She too had been an active runner but had died suddenly several days earlier. As they drove toward the city of Gallup, the young man became severely short of breath. Alarmed, his family members pulled into a nearby service station to call for assistance. By the time an ambulance crew arrived, he had collapsed because of respiratory failure. He was taken to the emergency department at a hospital in Gallup where he was diagnosed with florid pulmonary edema. Despite aggressive resuscitative efforts, he died in the hospital. Over the next few days, it became clear to a local medical investigator that several other young, previously healthy tribal members recently had died from a mysterious, fast-moving respiratory illness. People who became ill were generally young and previously healthy before suddenly developing influenza-like symptoms and succumbing to an acute febrile illness that led to death by pulmonary edema and cardiovascular collapse. Epidemiologists from the CDC were called in to identify the cause of the outbreak. Ultimately, they determined that it was a previously unknown hantavirus. In Asia, infection with hantaviruses is associated with hemorrhagic fever and renal disease. This family of viruses had not previously been known as a cause of human disease in North America (Van Hook, 2018).

The primary vector of the outbreak was identified as the deer mouse. Researchers found that the deer mouse population in 1993 was ten times greater than it had been during the preceding spring. The cause of the population explosion was increased moisture brought on by an El Niño winter. This led to an abundance of springtime vegetation that provided food and shelter for the mice and increased human exposure to the mouse vector.

The outbreak reflected a broader pattern linking climate change to infectious diseases. A review of the literature by Camilo Mora et al. (2022) found that 58% of infectious diseases that afflict human populations worldwide have at some point been aggravated by climate change while 16% were at times diminished. These researchers identified 1006 unique pathways through which climatic hazards led to the spread of pathogenic diseases.

Infectious Disease → Climate Change

Strong evidence for direct links through which infectious disease alters climate is generally lacking. One identifiable indirect link involves hospital treatment of infectious disease. Hospital waste from patient diagnostics, immunization, surgery, and therapy increases the healthcare sector's carbon footprint, making it a major contributor to anthropogenic climate change. Left untreated, disposed hospital waste can cause illness and environmental contamination. The most common methods of hospital waste treatment, such as incineration and autoclaving, are high-energy demand procedures. To be effective, their operation requires high temperatures, and the use of large amounts of energy. Moreover, incinerators produce various pollutants like fly ash, bottom ash, and fugitive gases, including both vapors and particulate matter. As a result, the hospital treatment of infectious disease has unexpected effects, including the degradation of the environment and the contribution to climate change (Zikhathile et al., 2022).

These pairwise links among infectious disease, biodiversity, and climate change often are intricately interconnected, resulting in feedback loops and consequential chains of interactions. Together, they constitute part of the multiple factors in Earth's contemporary ecocrises dilemma.

The Social Context of Planetary Health

The precise origin of the term "planetary health" in its current understanding is uncertain. However, the philosophical and social context of its emergence is generally understood. It involved the appearance of social concern during the Victorian era in Britain about the environment among middle-class individuals living in the suburbs, with the support of a few wealthy and politically influential backers. This varied collection of lovers of nature (especially birds), Darwin-influenced intellectuals, amateur naturalists, influential authors, and monied philanthropists recognized that the world around them was changing, an experience that triggered a sense of loss and a sense of the actual finiteness of native plants and animals, and the habitats they required for survival. A somewhat parallel development occurred in the USA involving the rescue of rapidly disappearing native species like bison and the desire to save iconic and awe-inspiring landscapes like Yellowstone and Yosemite. Along with this budding environmentalist/conservationist movement, there was a growing dissatisfaction about the narrow disease focus that had come to dominate biomedicine. As influentially articulated by physician George Engel (1977), the traditional biomedical approach, which was heavily influenced by the discovery of pathogens and infection, "assumes disease to be fully accounted for by deviations from the norm of measurable biological (somatic) variables," which leaves no room for understanding the social, psychological, and behavioral contexts of illness. The merging of these two expressions of social disquiet provided the social milieu for the birth of planetary health.

While concern about the environment has deep historical roots (including social concern about dismal factory pollution introduced by the Industrial Revolution), environmentalism as a distinct and conscious social movement traces back to 1835, the year Ralph Waldo Emerson wrote *Nature*, a text dedicated to encouraging an appreciation of the natural world and proposing a limit on euromerican expansion into the North American wilderness. Subsequently, Henry David Thoreau wrote his seminal and very personal ecological volume, *Walden*, which has inspired the work of many awakening environmentalists. In 1892, John Muir founded the Sierra Club in the USA to protect the country's scenic wilderness. Rachel Carson, a marine biologist, brought the environmental movement into sharper focus with the 1962 publication of *Silent Spring*, which sold over two million copies. The book offered a vivid description of the impact of chemical pesticides like DDT on biodiversity. As she wrote, "For the first time in the history of the world every human being is now subjected to contact with dangerous chemicals" (Carson, 1962). Her central message was the need to appreciate the complex and fragile nature of the ecosystem and the environmental threats facing humanity. Her work helped launch a global environmental movement of conservation activists.

One result was the celebration of the first Earth Day on April 22, 1970, an annual event first sparked by the impact of an oil spill off the coast of Santa Barbara, California. Soon after, new, often more radical, environmentalist groups like Greenpeace and Earth First! followed. In more recent years, especially with the recognition of climate change, we have seen the formation of large groups like Extinction Rebellion and the Sunrise Movement, as well as smaller environment/climate action collectives around the globe. Just Stop Oil, for example, uses nonviolent direct action in their protests, such as members gluing themselves to the frames or pedestals of famous works of art in museums. Typical of such actions, on July 1st, 2022, two Just Stop Oil activists glued themselves to the ornate frame of J. M. W. Turner's Tomson's Aeolian Harp (painted in 1809) while it was on display at the Manchester Art Gallery in Manchester, UK. Just Stop Oil released a press statement saying: "According to flood risk mapping carried out by Climate Central, the areas of London [the River Thames seen from Richmond Hill] depicted in Turner's painting could be underwater as early as 2030" (Escalante-de Mattei,

2022). The activists who joined the Sunrise Movement have been described as being "furious at what they see as [government] inaction on climate and [being] ready to take matters into their own hands. In this they're joined by young, angry activists around the world" (Malle, 2019). As Naomi Klein (2014) explained at the start of the youth climate movement, there has "been a huge shift ... with Sunrise's organizing and the global student climate strikes that were inspired by Greta Thunberg in Sweden.... I think young people have a particular moral voice that is just getting stronger and clearer, a combination of optimism and existential terror. There's also a rage and rightful disappointment with the people who were supposed to protect their future." Observes Tyler Harper (2024) of the Environmental Studies Department of Bates College, the most radical elements of the climate change movement "pin the blame for climate change on all of humanity. This is misguided: We should be pursuing an environmental humanism, one that wants to defend both the planet *and* the human estate from the predations of dirty-energy billionaires and the oil addiction they supply."

Environmental protest has not been limited to privileged sectors of the Western world. During the early 1970s, for example, Gaura Devi, a woman living in the farming village of Reni, India, tightly hugged a tree and used her body to shield it from being cut down by industrial loggers. This individual act of courage, which followed in the footsteps of other women engaged in such open defiance, inspired the Chipko environmental movement (*Chipko* means "to stick" or "to cling" in Hindi). Ultimately, this village initiative garnered international attention and gave rise to India's Forest Conservation Act of 1980.

As noted, the other cultural stirring that influenced the creation of the planetary health approach was both popular and physician disaffection with aspects of the dominant medical system. By isolating disease from its social/environmental framework and limiting the medical lens to the domain of biology, doctors were trained to not consider social conditions (which were seen as the domain of social workers) in disease causation. In this narrowing of focus, biomedicine supported the global consolidation of the capitalist economic system and its view of the environment as a source of endless resources and a depository of industrial waste and people as faceless sources of labor (Berliner & Salmon, 1980-81). As a result, heart disease, cancer, and auto accidents were accepted as inescapable diseases of needed economic growth and industrialism.

The crack in this way of thinking began in part as people watched the effects of public health initiatives. The greatest decline in the death rate, for example, did not come from biomedicine but from a sharp drop in infant mortality, attributable primarily to public health programs that supported improved nutrition, enhanced sanitation (e.g., cleaning the market milk supply), and advances in knowledge about essential infant care. However, it was not until the 1960s that the growing disaffection with biomedicine became especially vivid. Several factors were involved. Doubts emerged regarding the value of a medicine to effectively prolong life to old age, but often resulting in people living their final years in a hospital or nursing home in a way that often robbed them of human dignity. Moreover, ethical questions developed about inequitable access to extremely scarce medical resources, from artificial organs to dialysis machines. Another influence was the explosion in costs in a treatment-centered (prevention-weak) healthcare system. Finally, there was a growing scientific awareness that much disease occurred because of degradation of the physical environment as well as the conditions under which people were forced to work. The holistic health movement arose in part from these concerns but, at the same time, also helped to generate them.

Holistic comes from the Greek word "holos" which means whole, which in the context of healing means a focus on the wellness of the whole person and not just their identified disease. Those who embrace holistic health often cite Hippocrates, known as the father of medicine, because he encouraged self-healing of the body, or Plato, who is credited with saying that "the part can never be well unless the whole is well." From the perspective of holistic health, healing is most effective when you consider the whole person, their feelings, experiences, and social environment, rather than concentrating only on specific illnesses, body parts, or symptoms. Thus, health is conceived as a state of balance, not simply as an absence of disease.

The modern Western holistic health movement began in the late 1960s, primarily as an out-growth of the counterculture and human potential movements that evolved in this era, as well as influence from contemporary Chinese medical practices, Eastern philosophies, and a re-examination of nineteenth-century Western health practices. By the late twentieth century, a full-blown holistic medicine came into its own. What came to be known as the International Association of Holistic Health Practitioners was founded in 1970. The first National Conference on Holistic Health was held at the University of California, San Diego School of Medicine, in 1975. The Holistic Medical Association was founded 1978 and the American Holistic Nurses Association in 1981. These developments caused many biomedical practitioners to reconsider their approach to medicine and helped in the development of planetary medicine.

Birth of Planetary Health

Today, the planetary health paradigm is widely discussed in the health and medical literature, at conferences and policy discussions, and through numerous health initiatives, including those of the World Health Organization. As Susan Prescott and Alan Logan (2019) point out, while many issues about the precise history of planetary medicine remain unresolved, what is known is that in the early 1970s, Frederick Sargent (1972), a practicing physician and ecologist at Western Washington State College, laid the groundwork when he authored an article in the *American Journal of Public Health*. This paper was about the interrelations between the natural ecosystems (before the evolution of humans), the human intentional and inadvertent role in reshaping the environment (i.e., the rapid transformation of natural ecosystems to the human ecosystem), and the (largely human-caused) environmental health problems faced by our species. Although he did not use the term planetary health, in this paper, Sargent argued that humans and environment constitute a system, while health is a process of human–environment interaction within a particular ecological context.

Two years later, Russian philosopher Gennady Tsaregorodtsev (1974) introduced the concept of "planetary public health" as part of an argument for the creation of a new integrative center of contemporary science. His perspective was similar to that of Sargent on the need for improving our understanding of the biopsychosocial needs of humans in the context of local and global ecosystems, and in light of the human health consequences of past, current, and future environmental degradations. His goal was to be able to forecast the health consequences of human-induced changes to the natural environment.

Before long, this more holistic, ecological perspective on health was picked up by environmental groups concerned about pollution, deforestation, and other disruptions. In 1980, a global environmental network of organizations, known as Friends of the Earth, in an effort to broaden their appeal, retooled the World Health Organization's comprehensive definition of health—a state of complete physical, mental, and social well-being—to include ecological factors, maintaining that "personal health involves planetary health" (Prescott & Logan, 2019). James Lovelock, a renowned British scientist who had cautioned the world about industrial chlorofluorocarbons being released in our environment, developed the Gaia Hypothesis which, somewhat controversially, posited the idea that Earth is a living, self-regulating organism of physical and biological processes. He subsequently published the book *Gaia: The Practical Science of Planetary Medicine* (Lovelock, 1991) to address the profound relationship between the health of the planet and the health of its most disruptive species: us.

At the beginning of the 1980s, Theodore Roszak (2001), an American academic and novelist, was a founder of the ecopsychology movement. As a scholar, among other topics he examined the 1960s counterculture (a term he coined) in the USA and Europe and a philosophical orientation referred to as "deep ecology." The latter is an environmental philosophy and social movement that embraces the idea that humans must radically shift their relationship to nature from one that values it primarily because of its instrumental usefulness to humans to one that sees nature as having intrinsic value independent of humans. He argued that "the needs of the person are the needs of the planet. The rights of the person are the rights of the planet" (Roszak, 2001). This perspective provided the conceptual foundation for the rights of nature movement, a total rethinking of humanity's relationship with nature in which nature is placed at the center and humans are seen as interdependently connected to it rather than the dominate player in the relationship. Advocates argue that not just humans but ecosystems have the right to exist and flourish without human-caused disruptions. This movement to go beyond viewing nature as property gained a foothold in a number of countries, culminating in formal recognition of the rights of nature in Ecuador's 2008 Constitution under President Rafael Correa. This groundbreaking law was promoted by the National Confederation of Indigenous Nationalities of Ecuador, which embraced the concepts of *sumak kawsay* (meaning "ecologically balanced good living") and respect for *Pachamama* ("Mother Nature"). Today, over 35 countries recognize such rights, as do numerous US municipalities. In 2010, the Global Alliance for the Rights of Nature, a global network of organizations and individuals, drafted the Universal Declaration of the Rights of Mother Earth patterned on the 1948 Universal Declaration of Human Rights. The Alliance forms tribunals to investigate and publicize cases that show national and international legal systems that do protect the natural world (e.g., the disastrous Deepwater Horizon oil spill off of the coast of the USA in the Gulf of Mexico by BP fossil fuel company).

The holistic health movement also came to see the value of planetary health. Included in this transition were early promoters of plant-based diets, especially those supporting a macrobiotic regime beginning in the 1980s. Proponents maintained that reducing meat consumption contributes to both individual and planetary health. Influenced by new ways of thinking about the human/nature relationship, spirituality, and nursing, Christina Stohl, wrote a short editorial in *Beginnings,* the journal of the American Holistic Nurses Association, which she entitled "Planetary Health: Are You Part of the Solution or Part of the Problem?" In this statement, she espoused the view that "the health of each of us is intricately and inextricably connected to the health of our planet" (Stohl, 1991). Stohl recognized that as the largest contingent of healthcare workers worldwide, nurses provide care for patients from diverse backgrounds and in varied settings from hospitals, to local clinics, to far less formal locations. Even earlier, Rosa Williams (2017) edited a book entitled *A New Era in Global Health: Nursing and the United Nations 2030 Agenda for Sustainable Development.* The chapters in this text examined the relationship between global nursing and global health. The book advocated for the role of nurses in advancing the "United Nations Agenda on Sustainable Development Goals," which was intended to achieve both health and healthy environments worldwide. The initial embrace of emergent ideas about planetary health among registered nurses reflected an historic consideration within nursing of environmental factors that may affect the health of individuals and communities. Designation of environmental factors as being within the concern of nursing practice was incorporated into the American Nurses Association's *Nursing: Scope and Standards of Practice* (1994). In this vein, Judith Parker (1993) developed a nursing ethic for planetary health. By this, she meant an understanding of health "as a reintegration of our human relationships with nature [along with an] openness to nature's healing power."

Some researchers and practitioners trace physician concern about the environment and health back to Hippocrates, a renowned fifth century BC Greek physician and philosopher. His text, *On Airs, Waters, Places,* advised physicians to pay attention to all aspects of the environment, including the seasons, the direction of blowing winds, and the quality of both soil and waters. While this orientation did not have much influence on the day-to-day practice of biomedicine as it consolidated into its modern form, changes began to be visible in the late twentieth century. In the early 1970s, immunologist turned-human-ecologist Stephen Boyden (1972) began to fear that "trends in the relationship between human society and the total environment constitute a serious threat to the survival of civilization and mankind." Like his mentor René Dubos, a medical scientist, Boyden explored the link between health and the global environment. Both Boyden and Dubos adopted the nascent "planetary thinking" that emerged after World War II, which was stimulated, in part, by the work of Rachel Carson, as well as by the advent of nuclear weapons. As one expression of this turn, a group of physicians in Boston formed an organization called Physicians for Social Responsibility (PSR) in 1961.

In Canada, Trevor Hancock was an early leader of an environmental approach to public health. Trained in family medicine, in 1985 Hancock published a scholarly article in the journal *Family & Community Health* in which he argued that "a major transformation in the understanding of health and disease has taken place. The emphasis has shifted from a simplistic, reductionist cause-and-effect view of the medical model to a complex, holistic, interactive, hierarchic systems view known as an ecologic model" (Hancock, 1985). On this foundation, he maintained that we should "talk about planetary health as the ultimate determinant" of human health and development (Hancock, 1997). Over the course of his career, Hancock focused much of his work on the relationship between health and the natural and human-built environment. During the 1980s, he helped co-found both the Canadian Association of Physicians for the Environment and the Canadian Coalition for Green Health Care. Also, he became the first leader of the Green Party in Canada.

Subsequently, Anthony McMichael, a medical school graduate and internationally influential epidemiologist, became a pioneer in research on the health risks of global climate change and other major environmental alterations. Born and raised in Adelaide, Australia, as a student, McMichael spent a summer volunteering in a community of Hansen's disease (leprosy) sufferers in New Delhi, India. There he witnessed how patients were stigmatized as social outcasts, suffering even though they were no longer contagious. McMichael was convinced by the experience that he did not have to become "a stethoscope-carrying doctor" to contribute to people's health. His shift toward epidemiology was influenced by Paul and Anne Ehrlich's book *Population, Resources, Environment*, which addressed the question of how long Earth can sustain the growing human population and consumption patterns. McMichael wrote a review of the book that he titled *Spaceship Earth* as a way of accentuating the point that our planet is a closed system with limited resources and not an open trash pit. As McMichael was finishing his doctorate in 1972, he was attracted to the ideas of René Dubos. In his own book, *Planetary Overload: Global Environmental Change and the Health of the Human Species*, McMichael (1993) argued that global environmental change is a critical public health issue, especially for vulnerable populations. He urged researchers to escape "the prison of the proximate" (McMichael, 1999), meaning that in the study of population health, we must look beyond individual-level risk factors (e.g., drinking, smoking, eating) to the upstream roles of social and ecologic systems. Thus, he urged adoption of a social-ecologic systems perspective in the study of population health. In his view:

> For the past two centuries, epidemiologists have lived and worked in a world in which large-scale, natural life-support systems have not been perceptibly perturbed and weakened. We no longer live in such a world. We must therefore now think beyond the traditional striving for incremental health gains within populations; we must also address the issue of

the sustainability of population health against the prospect of a deteriorating natural environment (McMichael, 1999).

One Health

A conceptual model called One Health emerged in response to the growing recognition that the health of people is closely enmeshed with the health of animals as well as with our shared physical environment. The One Health (of human and animal) approach stresses the fact that most people live in close proximity and contact with wild and domestic animals, including as food, a source of products and livelihoods, travel, recreation and entertainment, sports, education, profit, and as pets. Close contact with animals and their environments provides opportunities for diseases to spread between animals and people (moving in both directions). Anthropogenic changes to the climate/environment help to drive interspecies disease movement. Further, the movement of people, animals, and animal products has increased through international travel, trade, and contact. As a result, diseases can move quickly across national borders and around the globe. One Health stresses that disease in animals can sometimes serve as an early warning sign of potential human illness. For example, bird die-offs usually occur before people in the same area are infected and become sick with the mosquito-borne West Nile disease. From a One Health perspective, key issues of concern include the human–animal–environment interface, vector-borne diseases, food-borne diseases, antimicrobial-resistant microbes, and water contamination.

One Health is traced to an article by a physician named Laura H. Kahn (2006) entitled "*Confronting Zoonoses, Linking Human and Veterinary Medicine.*" Kahn argued that closer collaboration is needed among veterinarians, physicians, and public health professionals in addressing individual health, population health, and comparative medicine research. Reading this paper prompted Bruce Kaplan, a veterinarian, to contact her and together they formed the One Health Initiative team which is dedicated to uniting human and veterinary medicine.

While similar in many ways, there are differences that developed between One Health and the effort to develop planetary health, including focus and emphasis. Planetary health tends to stress the importance of climate change and other anthropogenic planetary changes, non-communicable diseases, issues related to food systems and diet, and physical activity (Ruiz de Castañeda et al., 2023). Practitioners have tended to play down any sense of rivalry between these two somewhat different but often parallel approaches.

Formal Organization of Planetary Health

Against this backdrop, in 2015 a scholarly body known as the Rockefeller-Lancet Commission on Planetary Health issued an eye-catching and influential report. The commission that issued the report was a joint initiative of the Rockefeller Foundation and *The Lancet*. The Rockefeller Foundation, based in New York, has long had a significant international influence on health policies and practices. The foundation served as a model for the development of the World Health Organization, the US National Science Foundation, and the US National Institutes of Health. It also influenced the health work of the United Nations. According to Vieira-da-Silva (2018), in the early years of the twentieth century, wealthy capitalists like John D. Rockefeller foresaw the need for social reform as a way to quell social unrest that might threaten the survival of the prevailing economic order, one that allowed them to gain great riches and enormous power. Among other outgrowths of this understanding was the formation of the Rockefeller Foundation, which originally was established with the goal of assisting in the industrialization of the agrarian US South in the service of the capitalist interests of the North. Also of concern were the diseases that were hindering the work of the Western colonial enterprise, beginning in the Philippines. Tropical diseases decimated the ranks of the personnel of colonial governments and limited the productivity of the Indigenous populations drafted into service in colonial labor forces on plantations, in mines, and at factories (Brown, 1976). Consequently, early in the twentieth century, the foundation, under the banner of humanitarian philanthropy, launched a series of single disease/vector campaigns to eradicate hookworm disease, malaria, and yellow fever. These public health initiatives were replicated by the World Health Organization when it set out to eradicate smallpox. The Foundation also established both the Johns Hopkins School of Public Health and the Harvard School of Public Health, as well as the London School of Hygiene and Tropical Medicine. In more recent years, the Foundation has attempted to distance itself from its roots in the fossil fuel industry, the original Standard Oil Co. (now ExxonMobil), the primary source of Rockefeller wealth, and to emphasize issues like climate change and pollution as global threats to health.

Founded in London in 1823, *The Lancet* is a peer-reviewed general medical journal (which today has multiple affiliated specialty journals). Among the world's oldest and most prestigious medical periodicals, *The Lancet* has one of the highest-impact rankings in the field (first among the 167 general and internal medicine journals internationally in 2022). It is widely considered one of the leading sources of knowledge on clinical, public health, and global health and is highly influential in discussion of global health issues. In the last several decades, under the leadership of Richard Horton, the journal has addressed many urgent health issues, initiated debate on social and environmental factors in health, and sought to influence health decision-makers around the world. Over the years, *The Lancet* has set up a series of commissions on issues of science, medicine, and global health. These commissions are based on the idea that organized science provides an enlightened and effective platform for advocacy and policy recommendation. Over a period of two or three years, commissions assemble multidisciplinary, international teams of recognized health experts to review and analyze existing and emerging data. The commissions then issue detailed, evidence-based reports intended to spark transformational change with a special focus on urgent and often medically or socially neglected or understudied health problems. Commission reports often attract considerable discussion and widespread media reports, and may lead to identifiable changes in health policy and practice.

With funding from the Rockefeller Foundation, in July 2014 members of the Commission on Planetary Health convened at the elegant Rockefeller Foundation Bellagio Center, a former villa on the shore of Lake Como in Bellagio, Italy, and subsequently in New York City. Commissioners included 15 experts in environmental health, medicine, biodiversity, and ecology. At Richard Horton's request, Andrew Haines, a physician and renowned professor of Environmental Change and Public Health at the London School of Hygiene and Tropical Medicine, chaired the Rockefeller/Lancet Commission on Planetary Health. Haines (2019) describes planetary health as "a new field of study rooted in understanding the interdependencies of human and natural systems." This assessment was echoed by Howie Frumkin (2017), now the Director of the National Center for Environmental Health/Agency for Toxic Substances and Disease Registry at the CDC, who described planetary health as "a breakthrough" and "new way of thinking." The commission defined its audience as health professionals, public health practitioners, politicians and policy makers, academics, international civil servants working across the UN and in development agencies, and, above all, every person who has an interest in their own health, that of other human beings, and in the flourishing of future generations (Horton et al., 2014). The time has come to reject an unjust global neoliberal economic system that favors the success of a small, wealthy elite over everyone else.

Planetary health was thus envisioned as an attitude toward life as well as a philosophy for living that focuses comprehensively on the human condition, and not just on diseases. The goal is to build a social movement that seeks health and social equity and rejects the further perpetuation of unjust societies. This requires a sustainable environment that supports the diversity of life with which humans coexist and on which we depend. It also demands paying close attention to the planetary boundaries framework advanced by Johan Rockström and his colleagues. The Commission report emphasized that human modifications of Earth have become so far-reaching and transformative that it is appropriate to adopt a new name for the current human-shaped geophysical epoch. The commission joined with other scientists who had begun to label this new era the Anthropocene. As a result, we cannot engage in siloed thinking about human health, animal/plant health, and environmental health; rather, we need an interconnected multi-species and animate/inanimate lens on these critical issues. This new approach was called "the principle of planetism" (Horton et al., 2014). In this light, planetary health was defined as

> the achievement of the highest attainable standard of health, wellbeing, and equity worldwide through judicious attention to the human systems—political, economic, and social—that shape the future of humanity and the Earth's natural systems that define the safe environmental limits within which humanity can flourish. Put simply, planetary health is the health of human civilisation and the state of the natural systems on which it depends (Whitmee et al., 2015).

Johan Rockström (2015) soon commended the report and its call for the global community to focus on synergies between human and planetary health.

The impressive 55-page report produced by the Commission had four key messages (Whitmee et al., 2015):

1. The concept of planetary health is based on the understanding that human health and human society depend on flourishing natural systems. However, these systems are being degraded to a degree that is unprecedented in human history.
2. Mounting environmental threat is characterized by surprise and uncertainty. Actions are needed now to protect present and future generations.
3. The existing systems of governance and assemblage of human knowledge are inadequate to address the threats to planetary health.
4. Solutions lie within reach and should be based on the redefinition of prosperity to focus on the enhancement of quality of life and delivery of improved health for all, together with respect for the integrity of natural systems. This means supporting sustainable and equitable patterns of consumption, reducing population growth, and harnessing and enhancing the power of technology for change.

Publication of the commission's report drew keen interest among researchers, physicians and other healthcare workers, educators, and the worldwide media and inspired a subsequent flood of new publications, meetings, lecture series, keynote addresses, and institutional pronouncements. It also led *The Lancet* to create a new specialized journal to advance scientific and medical knowledge on planetary health. Soon, research centers on planetary health were established at various universities, including the University of California Center for Planetary Health and the Institute for Planetary Health at Johns Hopkins University, as well as at independent think tanks like the Centre for Planetary Health Policy in Berlin, Germany, and the Planetary Health Alliance in Tokyo, Japan. The Open University of Catalonia in Spain added a master's degree program in Planetary Health while the City University of New York's Graduate School of Public Health and Health Policy created a PhD degree in Environmental and Planetary Health Sciences. As Cristina O'Callaghan-Gordo and her colleagues (2022) argue, "Universities and higher education institutions [are] called to embed the concept of planetary stewardship in all curricula and train the next generation of researchers and change makers as a matter of urgency." The Global Inventory of Planetary Health Courses was developed as a list of Planetary Health programs and/or courses that have been implemented at educational institutions worldwide and includes both virtual and in-person teaching, undergraduate and graduate programs, open-access courses, and summer schools (see https://www.planetaryhealthalliance.org/for-learners).

Although the planetary health initiative has been generally well received, issues have been raised. As Prescott and Logan (2019) observe, in presenting planetary health as a new concept, the Commission ignores decades-old holistic discussions of planetary health in and beyond biomedicine, as reviewed earlier in this section. The general ahistorical nature of the Commission's report is further indicated in the author contribution section, which states, "The original idea for the concept of planetary health was devised by RH" (Richard Horton) (Whitmee et al., 2015: 2019). While in the grand scheme of things, this oversight does not distract from the laudable nature of the report, and at least some prior work is acknowledged (e.g., that of Anthony McMichael), it serves to remind us that in science we all build on the ideas of those who came before us.

Also, concern has been expressed with the way the human/environment relationship is presented in the Commission's report. As contrasted with the report's emphasis on Earth as a place that holds human benefits like food, fuel, timber, and medicinal compounds, Indigenous peoples commonly describe a mutualistic interdependence with their ancestral land or a deep-seated entwinement of people and the planet. This means that far more than a place to acquire needed material resources, Earth is also a source of identity, ancestry, spirituality, and cultural meaning. In short, absent from the report "are discussions concerning the ways in which emotional bonds are developed between person and place, and the psychological asset of nature-relatedness" (Prescott & Logan, 2019). The theoretical concept of "the ecosocial self," as described by Neely Myers, is relevant here. Based on ethnographic fieldwork with the pastoral Maasai women living on the Kenya-Tanzania border in East Africa, Myers underlines the intimate relationship these women have with their ecological setting and the positive and (as a result of climate change) negative impacts that relationship can have on their health. Notes Myers (2022), "While the Maasai do not use the term "ecosocial self," they did emphasize the importance of their sense of self as being in an intimate relationship with the land and livestock which had consequences for their well-being and so inspired [my adoption of] the term."

Other critics have pointed out that in the Commission's report nonhuman animal and plant residents of planet Earth tend to only be of concern to the degree that they have instrumental value because of their role in human health. This attitude toward nonhuman life is rooted in the view that animals are mechanistic bundles of instinct and not salient beings, while plants lack brains, and do not have subjective experience or feelings. The influential Greek philosopher, Aristotle (who lived from 384 BCE to 322 BCE; BCE stands for before the common era), asserted that nonhuman animals had no interests of their own and were not capable of rational thought. Embracing human exceptionalism, he did not believe that animals have agency (the ability to act with intent), which he considered to be a distinctly human capacity. While noting some similarities between humans and other species, he denied that animals had moral equality. In Aristotle's view, plants have life, animals have both life and perception, and human beings have both of these characteristics as well as rationality. Further, he believed that plants exist for the sake of animals and animals for the sake of humans (Gary, 1995). Reflecting this centuries-old and culturally embedded attitude, science has long warned against anthropomorphizing, which is our tendency to attribute human emotions, desires, or behavior to animals or even to plants.

Missing from the Commission's report is any recognition of the movement to recognize that animals, and in the view of some, even plants, have intrinsic moral and legal rights independent of their utility. Further, there is no acknowledgment in the report that scientific thinking about plants and animals has undergone a seismic shift. Expressing this change, on July 7, 2012, a group of eminent cognitive neuroscientists, neuropharmacologists, neurophysiologists, neuroanatomists, and computational neuroscientists from around the globe signed the Cambridge Declaration on Consciousness. This document highlighted the evidence that shows that many types of nonhuman animals have the capacity for consciousness. As the Declaration states:

> Convergent evidence indicates that non-human animals have the neuroanatomical, neurochemical, and neurophysiological substrates of conscious states along with the capacity to exhibit intentional behaviors. Consequently, the weight of evidence indicates that humans are not unique in possessing the neurological substrates [or nervous systems] that generate consciousness. Non-human animals, including all mammals and birds, and many other creatures, including octopuses, also possess these neurological substrates (Low et al., 2012).

In other words, a human-like brain is not necessary for consciousness. Research on this issue has expanded greatly since 2012, affirming many intellectual and emotional capacities in nonhuman species. In the case of plants—life forms seemingly far less like us than animals—newer research reveals the ability to recognize their genetic relatives alters their behavioral response to their environmental neighbors. For example, the beach and dune dwelling succulent known as the American searocket (*Cakile edentula*) has been found to limit root growth, perhaps to allow their nearby relatives to share soil resources. Plants may also avoid growing vertically to provide shade for their neighbors if they are recognized as genetic kin (Dudley & File, 2007). Discovering kinship recognition in plants began to suggest that the divide between plants and animals (including us) was narrower than previously believed. Exhibiting another capacity, a vine (*Boquila trifoliolata*) found in the Chilean rainforest mimics nearby plants, including their leaf shapes, textures, and vein patterns, yet it remains unclear how, without eyes, the vine can "see" its host plant neighbors. In the laboratory, this vine will even replicate the features of an artificial plant with plastic leaves. Moreover, the common lima bean plant (*Phaseolus lunatus*) can protect itself by making and releasing biochemicals that attract the predators of insects that devour the seemingly defenseless lima bean. The beach-dwelling evening primrose (*Oenothera biennis*) produces sweeter nectar when it "hears" a recording of a honeybee, a key plant pollinator. In laboratories, pea shoots have been found to be able to navigate mazes and respond to the sound of running water.

To summarize a growing body of research, while plants do not have a central nervous system or eyes and ears, they are still able to process information from external sources and respond effectively to them. This conclusion is affirmed by the work of Anthony Trewavas, emeritus professor in the School of Biological Sciences of the University of Edinburgh. In his book, *Plant Behaviour and Intelligence,* Trewavas (2014) marshalled extensive research evidence on how plants deal with threats and opportunities in their environment to support his conclusion that plants living under competitive, wild conditions exhibit purposeful behavior that can be accurately described as intelligent. Moreover, they react to negative or unpleasant sensations and have ways (e.g., stored proteins) of retaining memories of these events. Plants also communicate, including across species. Of note in this regard is the mycorrhizal interaction between fungi and plant roots, a pattern found in about 90% of plant species. Through these underground networks, plants communicate with fungi and other plants, transfer nutrients like nitrogen, carbon, and phosphorus, and send stress signals.

Reflecting this sea change in thinking, some plant scientists have begun to argue that the field had been engaging in self-censorship by failing to ask questions about the possible parallels between the neurobiology of animals and the phytobiology of plants. The many "choices" that plants appear to make and their use of signaling (communication), these researchers argued, suggest that it is time to stop worrying about anthropomorphizing plants and study them as behavioral organisms with the capacity to receive, store, share, process, and use information.

In light of the growing realization of plant capacities and their place in the world, in his book *The Life of Plants*, the Italian philosopher Emanuele Coccia (2018) reverses dominant thinking about the living world by placing plants at the top of the hierarchy and humans at the bottom. Coccia argues that our biological classification system is not firmly grounded in science. Rather, it is heavily influenced by theological ideas about the supremacy of the human race and the planet as something humans are supposed to manipulate to meet their needs. Coccia highlights the fact that plants have been evolving their abilities on land for 700 million years and humans for only about 300,000 years. In Coccia's view, humans are a by-product of a world shaped by plants, from the oxygenated air we need to breathe to the food we depend on for survival. Unlike most of us in our human-build worlds, plant life is "in absolute continuity and total communion with the environment" (Coccia, 2018).

In the case of animals, where intelligence has long been accepted (and widely documented experimentally), some rights advocates assert that, "The question is not, Can they *reason*?, nor Can they *talk*? but, Can they *suffer*?" (Bentham, 1789). Older still is the ninth century BCE Indian religious principle of *ahiṃsā* which preaches nonviolence toward all living beings. In recent times, the work of Peter Singer, Emeritus Professor of Bioethics at Princeton University, helped to promote the animal rights movement with his argument that all animals, human and nonhuman alike, are equal. In his book *Animal Liberation* (1975), he proclaims, "there can be no reason—except the selfish desire to preserve the privileges of the exploiting group—for refusing to extend the basic principle of equality of consideration to members of other species."

As succinctly summarized by University of Cambridge wildlife scientist Alex Schnell (2024), "Traits of intelligence once thought to be uniquely human are now being discovered in distantly related species. We know [for example that] octopuses show curiosity, can problem solve, use tools, and are rapid learners. The more we learn about them, the more it removes a barrier of otherness" (quoted Fobar, 2024). She adds,

> "It's like when Nicolaus Copernicus dethroned Earth as the center of the cosmos and realigned the way we think about our planet, the way it works in the solar system, and our place in it… We're not the pinnacle of intelligence anymore. We share the planet with a lot of different sophisticated minds, we're not better, we're just different" (quoted in Hutchison, 2024).

Today, it is widely recognized that animals are sentient beings capable of experiencing pain, suffering, and even joy. Indeed, Schnell and other marine researchers helped convince the British government in 2021 to legally recognize octopuses and their cephalopod relatives (i.e., cuttlefish) as sentient beings. This means that for the first time these invertebrates are protected under UK animal welfare law. This change was especially influenced by the work of Jonathan Birch at the London School of Economics. He is the principal investigator of the Foundations of Animal Sentience project, which is examining whether animals can feel. This examination even extends to the presence of feelings in insects and their ethical treatment as we begin commercially farming them for mass consumption by cattle, chickens, and humans.

In the view of animal rights activists, if assuming men are superior to women is sexism, and that whites are superior to Blacks is racism, treating humans of greater value than other animals is speciesism. Ideas like these, which remain controversial for some but compelling for others, found no voice in the Commission's report, nor what such a realization means for a truly planetary health approach, one that is committed to protecting the health of all species and the natural environment.

Finally, the Commission's report has faced criticism because of its "overreliance on western eurocentric understandings of health and natural systems" (Jones et al., 2022). For example, the report calls for the "training of indigenous and other local community members" in order to "help protect health and biodiversity." Indigenous leaders like Nicole Redvers, an assistant professor in the Department of Epidemiology and Biostatistics at Western University and a member of the Deninu K'ue First Nation, responded to this call by raising the inverse of the Commission's equation. She and others asked: what about the training of technologically oriented biomedical healthcare providers by Indigenous peoples so that they can better understand how to protect both health and biodiversity? In other words, as voiced by Indigenous commentators, sprinkled throughout in the Commission's report is a biomedical bias that is rooted in a Western conception of the world. They noted the incongruity of trying to solve the global environmental crises we all face using the same conceptual framework that produced the problem in the first place (Redvers, 2021). As Audre Lorde (1984) comments, "the master's tools will never dismantle the master's house. They may allow us temporarily to beat him at his own game, but they will never enable us to bring about genuine change." The planetary health movement launched by the Commission's report emerged from Western biomedical and environmental sciences with support from Western social sciences. These academic disciplines have their conceptual foundations in an understanding of the world that separates humans both from each other and from the rest of nature. Taking the field of anthropology as an example, the Statement on Anthropology, Colonialism, and Racism of the Department of Anthropology at the University of Pennsylvania (2021) acknowledges that:

> No form of scholarly enquiry is neutral, and anthropology is no exception. Anthropology began as a colonial science, the product of a settler colonialism uniquely focused on the study of the languages, history, culture, and biology of non-European peoples seen as

'primitive,' or 'ancient' all around the world. Anthropology was, until recently, primarily the study of the exotic 'other' in space or time, an orientation that presumes an unmarked normative 'self'—white, Euro-American, and often male—positioned as the distanced and 'objective' observer. While this conceit has been thoroughly discredited, it helped obscure the field's historical implication in projects of domination, rule, and control.

Coming to terms with the discipline's distant and recent history is an ongoing, painful process of self-critique and rethinking, an endeavor that has not been without controversy or debate. A core task of this process is recognizing and directly confronting anthropology's colonial legacy and the ways it may have assisted in the marginalization, exploitation, and erasure of Indigenous peoples, woman, ethnic minorities, sexual minorities, and the poor and working classes as well as their knowledge and understandings of the world (Allen & Ryan, 2016).

Fay Harrison, a pioneer in the effort to decolonize anthropology, raises the issue of epistemological imperialism, which she uses to label the fact that anthropologists from or located at universities in the Global North (especially in the USA, the UK, and France) are positioned to define the key issues and directions in the discipline with little consideration of the ideas of anthropologists living in the Global South. She further argues that anthropologists must take "the subaltern, the indigenous, the indigen*ized* and the minorit*ized* seriously. To the extent that we truly recognize people's full humanity, that of course means we recognize their wisdom, their intelligence, their capacity to produce forms of knowledge that include potentially powerful interpretations and explanatory accounts of the world, which give us the clues to then create strategies to change the world" (quoted in McGranahan et al., 2016).

In a similar vein, the theoretical approach known as political ecology, which emerged from anthropology and has been adopted by other social sciences, has "long worked to expose the uneven power dynamics involved in knowing and managing nature, including the knowledge politics that privilege Western science while marginalizing local knowledge (Goldman et al., 2018). Political ecological analyses draw attention to the persistently uneven power dynamics that shape what is accepted as valid knowledge. Political ecologists call for the recognition of other ways of knowing about and experiencing "nature," including local and Indigenous understandings and knowledge.

The Colonial Roots of Public Health

While healthcare providers like doctors and nurses, who primarily treat or care for individuals after they become sick or are injured, public health professionals (who may be doctors or nurses, but also includes nutritionists, community educators, vaccinators, and many others) are concerned with preventing illness and injury in targeted populations. The American Public Health Association (APHA), the largest professional organization of public health workers in the USA, defines public health as a broad-based effort to promote and protect the health of all people and their communities. In other words, it is the science and practice of health promotion at the population level. Founded in 1872, the APHA has participated in every major public health campaign, debate, and policy initiative for more than 150 years. Today the organization defines its mission as improving the health of the public and achieving equity in health status across communities. Public health is active on multiple levels. At the local level, this would include media campaigns to reduce smoking and encourage the use of seatbelts, or it might involve running a community's childhood immunization program. At the far more complex global level, this includes efforts by the World Health Organization in preventing malaria, promoting safe pregnancies, and trying to eradicate polio, or it might involve the work of non-government organizations like PATH, a global team of scientists, clinicians, designers, engineers, advocates, and other experts working among other issues on the prevention and effective management of postpartum hemorrhaging.

This sanguine description of public health, however, does not fully reflect the history of this field, especially as it has engaged with Indigenous communities. Instead, research reveals that public health practitioners historically were complicit in colonization by contributing to the persistent negative physical and mental health outcomes among Indigenous peoples. This colonial legacy, from the Indigenous perspective, means that anyone "seen as an actor, or appendage, of the government which dispossessed Indigenous peoples of land, enacted policies of Indigenous erasure, and failed to formally apologize for the aftermath," such as government employed public health officials and other public health professionals, has played a role in causing historic and ongoing trauma (Gartner & Wilbur, 2022). Gartner and Wilbur (2022) itemize five ways public health is entrenched in systems of oppression. The combined effect of these five factors is the reinforcement of unequal power relations between public health and Indigenous and other marginalized communities. The consequence is mistrust of public health research and interventions.

First, early public health efforts focused on controlling disease in colonial nations helping to ensure that colonizers could survive and acquire and settle new lands at grave cost for Indigenous peoples. In other words, the ability of colonial nations to support the subjugation of Indigenous people was enabled in part by public health programs in colonizing nations. In the UK, for example, Edwin Chadwick, a lawyer, and social reform advocate, wrote a report in 1842 titled the "Sanitary Condition of the Labouring Population of Great Britain," which helped launch efforts to control widespread and recurring cholera epidemics. This improvement supported the workforce that built the ships, produced the food, and manufactured the weapons of the imperial enterprise.

Second, public health emerged from the same socio-intellectual milieu as the development of racialized hierarchies that asserted Indigenous people were less human than people of Western European ancestry. In these schemas, Western Europeans societies and their offshoots in the USA and elsewhere (and especially the richest people in these nations) were held up as the most advanced while other peoples were seen, to varying degrees, less evolved and less capable. Many Indigenous societies were labeled as primitive or barbarian. This pseudoscientific distortion rationalized colonial expansion, exploitation of Indigenous peoples around the world, and genocide as acts that improve the human species. For example, early British sociologist Herbert Spencer mobilized the concept of "survival of the fittest" in defense of *laissez-faire* or unrestrained capitalism during the Industrial Revolution. Spencer opposed any laws that would help workers, the poor, and those he saw as genetically weak. Protective laws for "the weak," he maintained, were pernicious and only delayed the extinction of the "unfit." These ideas later were picked up and applied by Hitler and his Nazi followers in his campaign to exterminate Jews, Roma, homosexuals, and others maliciously deemed to be subhuman or unfit.

Third, public health research contributed to the stigmatization of Indigenous people. As Linda Smith (2012) illustrates in her book *Decolonizing Methodologies: Research and Indigenous Peoples*, there are telling intersections between research and imperialism. Imperialism, she argues, is deeply embedded in academic disciplines of knowledge and tradition, which are presented as "regimes of truth." She borrows this concept from French historian Michel Foucault who used it to refer to socially embedded mechanisms used to distinguish true statements from false ones, the acceptable methodologies for identifying each of these, and the status of those with the power to say what counts as true. Within the realm of public health research, this historically involved focusing on Indigenous communities as riddled with deficits and despair (e.g., disease, family break up, alcohol and other drug abuse, suicide, child abuse). This disparity labeling and social construction provided justification for public health intervention in Indigenous communities. As O'Neil et al. (1998) indicate, "epidemiological portraits of Aboriginal sickness and misery act as powerful social instruments for the construction of Aboriginal identity. Epidemiological knowledge constructs an understanding of Aboriginal society that reinforces unequal power relationships; in other words, an image of sick, disorganized communities can be used to justify paternalism and dependency." Public health interventions tended to overlook the multiple structural causes of the disparities they encountered (e.g., racism, classism, sexism) and instead targeted Indigenous beliefs and behaviors in need of reform. As Askew et al. (2020) indicate, Australia public health discourse "has manifested as an oft-used convention of beginning reports about Indigenous health with a recent epidemiological portrait, thus creating a visual metaphor of Aboriginal and Torres Strait Islander peoples as a problem to be solved."

Lost in this venture were the underlying strengths that had enabled Indigenous peoples to survive all forms of abuse from outsiders. Among these underappreciated features were community solidarity and support, meaning systems anchored in spiritual beliefs, and deep attachment to place (the local natural environment).

Fourth, the legacy of public health research about Indigenous peoples largely consists of data extraction and exploitation for the benefit of Western science and the academic careers of researchers rather than contributing to Indigenous interests. Historically, health and other research failed to meaningfully engage Indigenous communities in the identification of research topics, culturally sensitive research methodologies, appropriate study designs, selection of data analysis strategies, dissemination of findings, or the utilization of research findings in teaching, policy recommendations, or intervention development. A noted example of this pattern occurred in Bolivia after the Movimiento Nacionalista Revolucionario (MNR) gained power in 1952. The MNR used its newly gained authority to expand rural public health programs, ostensibly to improve public health but guided by a desire to address what early twentieth-century Bolivian elites called the "Indian problem" as part of a wider nation-building program. This vexing "problem" was the continued existence of Indigenous peoples (who accounted for well over half of the country's population) and their cultures, which were seen as an obstacle to the modernization of Bolivia. The MNR mobilized public health as a project for cultural assimilation, and state-sponsored deIndigenization of rural populations through a so-called "civilizing process." This required that Indigenous peoples change their cultural patterns and everyday behaviors with a special focus on their "loathsome" hygienic practices. As part of this campaign, public health officials used off-road vehicles equipped with movie projectors and loudspeakers to show hygiene-related films on topics like the value of hand-washing, teeth-brushing, and basic understanding of diseases like smallpox, yellow fever, and tuberculosis. In supporting this approach, the Health Ministry referred to rural poverty (which was in fact widespread), by conjuring "images of poor Indians in torn clothing living in dilapidated shacks that needed to be rescued from their misery by government benevolence and patriotic health workers" (Pacino, 2017). Framing condescending attitudes in medical language allowed MNR public health officials to practice what Marisol de la Cadena (1998) called "silent racism." Such coding embedded the distain of wealthy Bolivians toward Indigenous people as backward, diseased, and ignorant, an impediment to modernity.

Finally, public health science values the use of biostatistics and quantitative approaches like the use of surveys over qualitative forms of research like ethnography or oral history collection. Most public health researchers engage data collection by counting people, behaviors, health problems, and information on discrete risk events/conditions (e.g., toxic exposures) to assemble sets of measurable data for comparison. Missing from this approach usually are the "lived experiences" of patients, practitioners, and affected communities. For example, in 2016, the *British Medical Journal* published an open letter from 76 senior scholars in 11 countries asking the editors of the journal to "... *reconsider their policy of rejecting qualitative research on the grounds of low priority"* (Greenhalgh et al. 2016). While acknowledging the value of qualitative methods, the journal did not change its practices. Additionally, when sharing its research findings, public health practitioners prefer to communicate through the use of statistical tables, charts, graphs, and other modalities of scholarly messaging that are inaccessible to nonpractitioners.

Current efforts in public health, such as community-based participatory research (CBPR) orientations, are designed to address some of the concerns raised above. While traditional research approaches tend to be investigator-driven (addressing questions of interest to the researcher), research within a CBPR model begins with issues raised within communities and involves members of the community in every phase of the research process, including data analysis, interpretation, and the use of findings in actions for change. Further, it seeks to go beyond mere tokenistic approaches to participation to total participation. CBPR places value on community expertise in the pursuit of shared research objectives and emphasizes mutual respect, a balance of power, free-flowing communication, mutual learning, and community capacity building. In this collaborative approach, people previously seen only as the objects of research become participants and co-owners of the research process. This shift demands that researchers be honest about their relative power and privilege while accepting a degree of humility about how their social and cultural backgrounds influence their way of interpreting the world. Researchers also are required to not claim the role of experts but be open to community expertise and criticism. This may be uncomfortable for some researchers but is a critical element of CBPR. The ultimate goal of CBPR is advancing social and health equity through collective action (Wallerstein et al., 2017). As Crosse et al. (2021) maintain, "the role of a truly engaged and empowered community in the research process (i.e., as equal partners in the process of knowledge production, problem definition, decision-making, implementation, evaluation, and dissemination) is integral to success" in this kind of research.

Even in CBPR framed studies, academic researchers must reflexively assess their positionality, including the class, racial, gender, ability, and related components of their social identity and worldview. Part of this process entails critical reflection on how issues like class, race, gender, culture, and education shape their view of Indigenous people. Another component is the consideration of how these factors might limit or distort their capacity to interact in mutually agreeable ways with Indigenous counterparts in the research process. This involves critical preparatory work to allow the framing of research within the participating Indigenous group's historical context, cultural approaches to ethical issues, and decision making.

Applying Indigenous Knowledge

The term Indigenous knowledge is used here to refer to insights and know-how rooted in the worldviews, lifeways, and experiences of specific communities and peoples. In such systems, knowledge is not differentiated from practice (as in the Western dichotomy of science vs. technology), and the rational is not divorced from the spiritual (as in the Western divide between science and religion). As a result, Indigenous knowledge encompasses empirical and deductive approaches borne of observation and experience as well as ideas and behaviors (e.g., rites and ceremonies) embedded in a spiritual understanding of an integrated world of animated components (from people to rocks and from the sky to bodies of water). The structure and order attributed to the wider cosmos is seen as giving direction for relations among people and between people and everything around them.

As contrasted with Indigenous understandings, the dominant Western worldview was strongly influenced by the Enlightenment, an eighteenth-century intellectual and cultural movement that emphasized reason over faith and gave birth to both science and public health. Included in this perspective were ideas about the primacy of personal autonomy, agency, individual rights, and materiality. By extracting our identity and sense of self from a rootedness in community and shared purpose, some have suggested that the Enlightenment gave rise to our current dilemmas of loneliness, depression, and alienation. Among them is Canadian writer, thinker, and activist, Charles Taylor, who at age ninety-two, authored a new book that he titled *Cosmic Connections: Poetry in the Age of Disenchantment* (Taylor 2024a, b). In this book, Taylor says that we have become estranged from a historic sense of belonging and meaning. By way of rejecting participation in this estrangement, he praises communities that still are pulled together by what he calls "the interspace of enchantment." Before the consolidation of modern societies, he believes, people occupied an enlivened and enchanted world of shared meaning. Now common agreement on meaning is no longer possible. According to Taylor (2024a), in a disenchanted world meaning is "in our own mind." We give meanings to things (e.g., having the newest iPhone is valued, only the god of my religion is the true God, deriving joy when the sports team you root for wins a championship), but there is no meaning intrinsic to anything; it's all in our heads. By contrast, in an enchanted world, not only is there meaning inherent in the world, including in objects and invisible agents (e.g., spirits), but they can communicate meaning to us. In an enchanted world, we are in direct communication with the visible and invisible realms around us, while in a disenchanted world, we only communicate with other humans and other objects created by humans (e.g., computers).

These are the kinds of issues raised in the Indigenous assessment of the planetary health paradigm discussed earlier in this chapter. A key document in this assessment was developed by a collaborative team composed of Indigenous scholars, healthcare practitioners, land and water defenders, respected Elders, and knowledge-holders from around the planet who met together as a consensus panel to define the determinants of planetary health from an Indigenous perspective (Redvers et al., 2022). As Durie (2004) indicates, "[a]lthough there is no simple definition of Indigenous peoples, two important characteristics are a relationship with some geographical place and an ethnic distinctiveness from others now living alongside them."

Participants in the Indigenous assessment began with the premise that Indigenous peoples—who number over 475 million around the world—have a sacred mandate and right to speak on behalf of Mother Nature. Taken together, Indigenous peoples comprise about 6% of the world's total population and live in at least 90 countries. Indigenous peoples are known to play important roles in the management, conservation, and sustainable use of natural biodiversity. Many Indigenous communities are located in places with historically high biodiversity. These communities have strong emotional and spiritual ties to their local territories and use their traditional knowledge, garnered over thousands of years, to protect, oversee, and sustainably use natural resources. Although often perceived as wild places, it has been shown that the ecosystems and species in areas that are in fact carefully managed by Indigenous peoples are often less threatened than in other areas, as Sze and co-workers (2022) found in tropical forested areas in the Americas and Asia. Prior to the arrival of Europeans, Indigenous peoples living on the West Coast of what would become the USA built rock walls at the low tide line, which caused sand to pile up behind. One effect was that the slope of the beach became gentler. Another was that it expanded the area of the intertidal zone where edible clams and other shoreline species dwell. Indigenous clam gardens increased shellfish numbers and food security for local peoples.

Members of the Indigenous assessment were also fully aware that Indigenous people are three times as likely to live in extreme poverty than non-Indigenous peoples (Cajete, 2020). Additionally, they have the lowest life expectancy of social groups globally, living as much as twenty fewer years than their non-Indigenous counterparts. While acknowledging their historic and ongoing mistreatment, Indigenous peoples firmly reject the deficit lens through which they have been portrayed in the Western scholarly literature. Commonly, this literature has focused narrowly on their lifestyles and health problems, sometimes framed as self-caused shortcomings, thereby creating an image of Indigenous peoples that hides their resilience and the strengths they bring to the global community on a warming, disrupted planet.

Although they recognized that their claim to special rights with regard to nature and that their knowledge generally is not respected by prevailing legal systems, Indigenous peoples have always asserted their responsibility to protect their human and nonhuman relatives on the planet. Eurocentric political and economic narratives, participants maintained, deprive the land, water, and air of being equal rightsholders in the world. They then pointed out that this "denial of the right of being is a direct product of ongoing capitalist and colonial mandates, which will continue to exacerbate the environmental crisis" (Redvers et al., 2022). In this time of crisis, they argue, we need a new set of mandates and point to the traditional knowledge of Indigenous peoples: "Traditional knowledges are not meant to be an assortment of information that can be simply merged with western scientific knowledge systems. Instead, traditional knowledges are collective, holistic, community-based, land-informed ways of knowing that are inherently interconnected with people and the environment" (Redvers et al., 2022). Their perspective includes the following three key points:

First, they call attention to gender issues noting that Indigenous worldviews commonly recognize Mother Earth's creative power as the primordial First Mother. On this foundation, it is women who "foster community, strengthen resilience, and enhance collective vitality and wellbeing." Further, they emphasized that "violence against Mother Earth is violence against women, and vice versa" (Redvers et al., 2022). By contrast, planetary health was created within a patriarchal and intensely competitive world of colonization, militarism, racism, social exclusion, and poverty-inducing economic and questionable development policies. Indeed, during European colonization, violence against Indigenous women became a core part of the colonial strategy for conquest, resource extraction, servitude, and genocide.

Second, since the beginning of colonialism, people have lost their identity as beings within a larger natural system and with it they have forgotten how to live sustainably with Mother Earth. The rapidly advancing ecological destruction exposes the impaired human relationship with our inner self (i.e., that we are Nature and not separate from it). The dominant Western "ideology of independence has resulted in a sense of entitled ownership, a kind of utilitarian perception of the natural world that relates to it through transactional relationships that do not have a sense of responsibility, care, or love. This worldview will only continue to perpetuate planetary harm" (Redvers et al., 2022). At the center of Indigenous understanding is the belief that we are not parasites who are driven to consume the world but rather we need the world and the world needs us. As Lyla June (2023) of the Dine' people explains, "The Earth may be better off without certain systems we have created but we are not those systems… The Earth needs us.… We belong here."

June (2012) illuminates this point by sharing an interview she conducted with an Indigenous Winnemem Wintu man, a member a band of the Wintu people who lived traditionally along the lower McCloud River near Redding, California. She reports:

> "His words were sure and penetrating and offered me a shocking introduction into the Winnemem Wintu world. I learned how deeply a person could love a stone, a pool of water or a mountain when he said: We're hanging on by a thread by keeping these sacred sites together and visiting these areas. These are places that were given to us by Creator to go to. We doctor there. It doctors us. Without this then we're just another displaced tribe. We're just another people who have no spiritual connection to the earth. Without that, without these sites to be taking care of, then we are not Winnemem anymore. If we can't do that anymore then who are we? Why are we? …. With tears in his eyes and a certainty in his voice, this man told me that without this collection of special places he would have no reason to live. While I could not understand why at the time, I would eventually learn that these areas provide the basis for the spiritual, social and medicinal practices of his people."

Third, although they have been abused and disrupted, Indigenous communities historically tended to be collective in nature. Individuals raised in collective-based societies learn as they grow up that interdependence with others and with place (i.e., with the total landscape where they live) helps to maintain their sense of wellness and balance. For example, the traditional healers of the Dine' (Navajo) people of the US southwest assemble medicine bundles during their lives which are essential to performing healing ceremonies in order to restore their patients' balance, harmony, and spiritual grounding. Consequently, Indigenous peoples like the Dine' "are more likely to consider the present and future impact their thoughts and actions have on others and place rather than focus on immediate self-gratification or reward (i.e., life about service vs life about gain)" (Redvers et al., 2022). This collective orientation toward life sharply contrasts with individualist societies like the eurocentric world that developed the planetary health paradigm.

Like the Dine', in an ethnographic study of Indigenous Oneida people in Southwestern Ontario, Canada, Paul Beaudin (2012) found that study participants held a cultural belief in the connectedness among all things. This attitude of connectedness was seen as essential for health and well-being across the physical, spiritual, mental, and emotional parts of human experience. Participants, moreover, described themselves to Beaudin as being stewards of the land. Across the Atlantic in Southern Zambia, Kennedy Kanene (2016) carried out an ethnographic study among the Indigenous Tonga people that examined the steps they have taken to sustain their local biophysical environment. Kanene observed that some native fruit trees and other plants of the types that people generally relied on for food, fuel, shade, medicines, and as windbreakers were protected and left untouched; not even fallen branches from protected trees were collected for firewood. When gathering medicinal plants, the Tonga were careful to only gather the required parts of the plant they needed because killing the plant was believed to be the equivalent of killing a human. Similar cultural rules applied to the treatment of water sources, where crops could be grown, wild animals, and soil. These culturally based actions and beliefs helped sustain local biodiversity. In Kanene's (2016) view: "Governments and policymakers should also integrate indigenous knowledge into environmental policies and take advantage of this knowledge to minimise environmental degradation… Finally, I would appeal for genuine partnership regarding scientific and indigenous knowledge towards environmental sustainability."

Western science uses the scientific method to theorize, hypothesize, select variables, measure properties, and describe relationships, an approach that usually is framed in mathematical, economic, or even political terms. But because it is linear, reductionistic, and mechanistic, this approach struggles to explain complex, multidimensional relationships that unfold over time. There is, additionally, a core interest in Western science in finding ways to influence and even control the natural systems of the world, including humans and their behavior. American marine biologist Sylvia Earle, a researcher who has led over 100 ocean expeditions and spent more than 7500 hours underwater, expresses deep frustration about this aspect of Western society. Having witnessed deep-sea ocean environments and their unique life forms, she is critical of the tendency to destroy nature and extract something profitable to someone, "as if it isn't useful keeping us alive… I dream, sometimes, of what the world would be like if whales made the rules, or tuna, or even trees" (quoted in Hobson, 2024).

In the early 1990s, Per Fugelli, an internationally celebrated Norwegian general medical practitioner and professor of social medicine at the University of Bergen, expressed the biomedico-centric mindset from which the planetary health approach emerged, saying: "The patient Earth is sick. Global environmental disruptions can have serious consequences for human health. It's time for doctors to give a world diagnosis and advice on treatment" (Casassus, 2017). From an Indigenous perspective, it is Western techno-profit culture and its medical system that are sick and in need of healing.

With the rise of what has been called "Indigenous science," since the early years of the twenty-first century the pendulum has begun to swing toward a more community-centered, ecological-based networking approach to knowing and being. Meade Krosby (quoted in Jones, 2020), a conservation biologist with the University of Washington, affirms, "One of the things that comes across really clearly is the fact that indigenous peoples are by far the most effective stewards of biodiversity… They do the best job."

Thus, consensus panel participants concluded their assessment by stating:

> As equitable and inclusive societies, institutions, and fields are built, embracing diverse knowledges will get us closer to a well and just planet for all. Indigenous voices are a powerful and beneficial solutions-oriented force for Mother Earth's wellbeing and for all living beings that inhabit her. We therefore call for an inclusion of wisdom that is not mere knowledge or information but is an insight that comes from the heart—from the heart of Mother Earth (Redvers et al., 2022).

In a parallel effort, a collaborative group of Indigenous and non-Indigenous health promoters (Tu'itahi et al., 2021) also has sought to elevate and center Indigenous voices and worldviews in the struggle to achieve a healthy planet. As health promoters, they define their job as improving public health and well-being in communities through education, community action, and the development of healthy public policy. These activists have called on mainstream non-Indigenous public health workers to engage in a process of critical self-reflection. In light of the challenge of the UN Declaration on the Rights of Indigenous Peoples, they expressed support for the reclamation, restoration, and celebration of Indigenous culture, identity, and belonging. In promoting public health, they encourage providers to learn from Indigenous cultures and help cultivate a sense of place in their target audiences, and by including discussion of the spiritual dimensions of ecosystems in their approach to the environment. Similarly, there has appeared an interest in embedding Indigenous perspectives and knowledge systems in medical education. Advocates urge a collaboration that combines Indigenous and Western knowledge in developing planetary health medical education. This would entail forging a respectful reconciliation between people and place in medical schools. A first step in this process is land acknowledgment. This is a statement issued by an institution or individual that honors the Indigenous peoples who first inhabited the land on which universities or other educational hubs are built. Land acknowledgments recognize the forced removal of Indigenous peoples from their ancestral homes and express a keen awareness of the rights of their descendants. The administration of the University of Massachusetts Chan Medical School, for example, has publicly acknowledged that their academy was built on the ancestral lands of the Nipmuc people and that there is evidence that parts of it were constructed on Nipmuc burial grounds.

The University of Minnesota Medical School, in Duluth, a region with a considerable Indigenous population, has gone beyond acknowledgment to the inclusion of a seven-hour group of Indigenous lectures for first-year undergraduate medical students. At the university, Indigenous students have comprised about 9% of the student body. These lectures are taught primarily by Indigenous faculty from several departments at the University of Minnesota. These talks examine the history of Indigenous peoples, issues of sovereignty and politics, Indigenous identity, local Indigenous cultures (namely Anishinaabe and Dakota) with a focus on seasonal ceremonial rounds and spirituality, the well-documented (and far from over) history of medical racism, introduction to the federal Indian Health Service, respectful approaches for working with Indigenous populations generally and as patients, and the need for physician cultural humility (Lewis & Prunuske, 2017). Other universities, like the University of Washington, have implemented the faculty position of elder-in-residence as a way of increasing the presence of Indigenous people and their knowledge in medical education. The program is intended to create a welcoming environment for Indigenous students, foster intergenerational learning, and showcase the experience and insights that elders from Indigenous communities have to offer. The Indigenizing of the medical school curriculum and medical school experience, while still in its emergent phase, is attempting to help reduce Western biomedical bias toward Indigenous views of health and the environment, as well as to change the systemic racial biases present in medical schools and decrease Indigenous health inequalities. Because health providers enter the workforce unprepared and unconfident to respond to health-related climate and environmental impacts, these curricular changes will help prepare current and future healthcare workers for acquiring a planetary consciousness and related healthcare practices.

Archaeogenetics and the Indigenous Struggle for Recognition in Argentina

A common idea perpetuated in anthropology, museology, and beyond is that most areas in Argentina were sparsely populated by Indigenous people at the time of the arrival of European colonialists and that in the nineteenth century Indigenous people were nearly or completely destroyed by wars with the colonial government. Many Argentinians still believe there are no Indigenous people in their country, either because they died out or were assimilated long ago into the dominant mestiza society. According to Argentine anthropologist José Grosso (2008), Indigenous people are powerfully absent from the popular narrative about the asserted homogeneous Argentinian identity, a worldview perpetuated by the elite large landowners and corporate businessmen of Buenos Aires. Yet, Indigenous identities continue to survive in Argentina, and in recent years the peoples who cling to their ancestries have organized and are fighting to be seen, heard, and protected from land grabs by the agricultural and lithium industries.

In 2022 alone, native forests covering an area almost four times the size of Manhattan were cut down in the tree-covered Santiago del Estero region of northern Argentina. Blanket deforestation destroys rural and Indigenous people's lives and livelihoods forcing displacement (Castro & Singer, 2004). In response, thousands of Indigenous activists and their supporters have taken to the streets in the capital in protest. Activists have blocked traffic and disrupted commerce and tourism. This Indigenous movement unites land rights, environmental, and anti-racist activism.

This is where archaeogenetics and ancient DNA research has become part of the story. María Pía Tavella, a biological anthropologist at the National University of Córdoba in Argentina, studies ancient DNA found in the excavated bones and teeth of long dead individuals. Her specialty is archaeogenetics, a research field that involves the analysis of genetic material preserved in archaeological remains using approaches like genome-wide DNA sequencing. Archaeogeneticists attempt to answer questions about the genetic relationships, geographical origins, natural selective processes, and the genetic structures of past and present-day human and nonhuman populations. From an ethical standpoint, Tavella (2024) is concerned about the impact of her field on Indigenous narratives about continuity in their local territories. She points to an intense controversy that erupted in 2021 when researchers sequenced partial genomes of roughly 1500-year-old individuals excavated from the Calingasta Caves in San Juan, an Argentine province to the southwest of Santiago del Estero.

To recover the DNA, scientists crushed and chemically dissolved one tooth, one inner ear bone, and lice nits from the hair of mummified bodies. They then compared the ancient genomes to a genomic dataset of present-day Indigenous populations. Based on this comparison, they concluded that the original peoples of San Juan migrated to the area from Amazonia about 2000 years ago. Based on a very narrow database, they also concluded that San Juan's present-day Indigenous population was genetically unrelated to the original people of the area. Moreover, they repeated the assertion that claimed the Indigenous peoples of Argentina were completely eradicated by the twentieth century. The contemporary Huarpe people maintained that this research was false and disrespectful of their ancestors' bodies, little more than a continuation of the colonial legacy that disconnected them from their homeland. Further, it offered fuel to the efforts to dispossess them of their land to make way for elite resource extraction. Tavella (2024) notes, "Archaeogeneticists should consider the potential harm that comes from publishing conclusive-sounding results based on limited—and exclusively genetic—data."

At the same time, Travella recognizes that genetic data can also support the land claims and recognition demands of Indigenous communities. In her own research, Travella analyzed mitochondrial DNA—a small piece of maternally inherited genetic code—from 45 individuals who lived 500 years ago in the area that after Spanish colonization became the provincial city of Santiago (Rodrigo et al., 2022). When she and her colleagues compared the ancient people's maternal lineages to those of present-day inhabitants of the province, she found that many individuals shared nearly identical genetic sequences. This suggested that the modern people are descendants of those living in the same place at least five centuries earlier. Other researchers pushed this genetic continuity back even further to at least 8000 years ago. Travella emphasizes the importance of developing collaborative and trusting partnerships between Indigenous or rural communities and archaeogeneticists. Such science/community alliances, she believes, are necessary, not only to proceed in a more ethical way as part of the effort to decolonize science, but also to produce better science.

Planetary Health 2.0

The foregoing discussion of Indigenous critiques of planetary health and science more broadly should not be read as an additional contribution to the contemporary resurgence of politically or economically motivated anti-science diatribes or pseudoscientific false narratives about natural reality. As but one example of this trend, since the middle of the twentieth century there has been a renewal of efforts to claim that Earth is flat and not the oblate or imperfect sphere established by multiple strains of scientific research. Advocates of flat-Earth ideologies, or comparable notions like the claim that astronauts never landed on the moon, COVID-19 is not a deadly disease, or that global warming is not occurring, are often motivated by religious beliefs or conspiracy theories. Today such ideas are widely spread by social media but they are false, nonetheless. Of course, if you reject science, you can simply ignore the enormous evidence base that affirms the true shape of Earth, that 12 humans have walked on the moon (thus far), that COVID-19 has killed millions of people around the world, or that the overall temperature of the planet is rising with significant consequence. A lot can be learned about current struggles with the self-interested promotion of misinformation by examining the concerted and well-financed effort by the tobacco industry during the latter half of the twentieth century to sow doubt about the known causal role of smoking in cancer or the more recent fossil fuel industry's campaign to knowingly confuse the public about climate change. Rather than endorsing anti-science attitudes, the foregoing discussion attempts to highlight the fact that science is subject to a range of social, cultural, political, and economic influences, but it has time and again demonstrated the capacity to ferret out these influences and overcome them. This key feature of the scientific method expresses the foundational assertion that all findings in science are subject to refutation through open discussion and further research. The knowledge built by science always is open to question and revision. Further, science is always seeking new evidence, some of which may reveal shortcomings in our current understanding. This valuable trait is notably lacking in the worldviews of conspiracy theorists, anti-science contrarians, religious authoritarians, and other detractors of our capacity to collectively produce ever more accurate natural explanations of the world.

A good example of the way scientists engage in the difficult task of revising older conclusions based on new evidence comes from the field of archaeology. Western scholars have long pointed to the fate of the Indigenous population on Easter Island (known Indigenously as Rapa Nui) as a case study of the disastrous costs of environmentally unsustainable living. This explanation asserts that the Polynesian people on the island cut down all of the trees found there when they arrived to build massive stone statues, ultimately triggering a population collapse. Easter Island, now a colony of Chile, has become famous for its giant monumental statues, called *moai*, built around 800 years ago, typically mounted on platforms called *ahu,* and sometimes topped with red stone headwear. Scholars have puzzled over the *moai* on the small island for decades, curious about their cultural significance as well as by how an Indigenous society with only wood and stone tools managed to carve, transport from quarries, and put into place statues weighing as much as 92 tons. In his bestselling 2005 book *Collapse*, anthropologist Jared Diamond offered an ecocide theory. Namely, he posited that the societal collapse on Easter Island was caused by the destruction of the island's historic ecological environment. This began a downward spiral of internal warfare and significant population decline, culminating in a breakdown of the Indigenous social and political structure around the year 1600. When the first European explorers arrived in the seventeenth century, they found only a few thousand inhabitants on the island, which is just 14 by 7 miles across, and positioned thousands of miles away from any other land. In order to explain the presence of so many *moai*, Diamond assumed that the island was once home to tens of thousands of people. This number would be needed to carve out the statues, haul them several miles to their selected destination, and set them up.

New research, however, questions the collapse explanation. This research reveals three things. First, it did not take hundreds of people to carve, transport, and erect the *moai* statues in line on an *ahu*. For smaller *moai*, this task could be accomplished by just a few dozen people and three strong ropes using a back-and-forth rocking motion (the way we often move refrigerators into place). The impressive red hats, which can weigh up to 13 tons, could be moved atop the statues using ropes to pull them up ramps and set them on top of the *moai*. Secondly, researchers now question the capacity of the island to have ever supported tens of thousands of people. People living on the island, prior to the arrival of Europeans, survived on a combination of fish and other marine resources and growing crops, primarily sweet potato, taro, and yams. Some researchers now estimate that the island could at most support about 3000 people, which is about the number European explorers found when they arrived. Finally, archaeological excavation found no fortifications, and the wear patterns on the obsidian tools that have been found show they were used for agriculture not warfare. Also, there is not much evidence of violence on skeletal remains. There is evidence, however, that the Indigenous Rapa Nui people—who still comprise about 45% of the island's population—were still flourishing after the alleged "collapse" of 1600.

In short, new research is pushing toward a rethinking of earlier conclusions. Instead of being a case of the failure of an Indigenous society, Easter Island suggests how Indigenous populations have sustainably adapted to limited resources even in remote locations. Cast away in this new understanding are older conclusions about the fragility and backwardness of Indigenous peoples. In this light, the goal here is to underline the ways an urgently needed planetary health initiative can be advanced without repeating older racist and colonial patterns of science in the service of oppression. This involves sincere efforts to build an open and participatory process that incorporates Indigenous input, leadership, and criticisms. In this effort, Indigenous scientists are helping lead the way.

Indeed, in response to Indigenous efforts, there has developed a movement to decolonize planetary health and to bring it into greater harmony with Indigenous voices, understandings, and direction. At the heart of this movement is the task of changing the privileging of the knowledge of those with power to those who are subject to the effects of colonization. An important influence on this shift to what might be called Planetary Health 2.0 is an alteration that occurred in social and physical scientific attitudes about the key driver of our environmental and health crisis. This involved realization of the need for the incorporation of Indigenous knowledge, know-how, and direction into research on climate impact and vulnerability assessment, mitigation, and adaptation. An example of this change is found in the extensive ethnographic study conducted by Sebastien Boillat and Fikret Berkes (2013) among Indigenous Quechua farmers living in the Tunari Mountains of Central Bolivia. Traditional ecological knowledge in Quechua communities in this area is a product of a centuries-old accumulation of insights gained through daily and seasonal life or death interactions with a never static environment. This knowledge/practice belief system is transmitted across generations but also is open to the incorporation of new information and behavioral adjustments. It is rooted in paying close attention to observable associations between phenomena in the world, finding analogies between natural events and living beings, seeing changes as constituting parts of natural cycles, and learning lessons from past as well as new experiences. Based on their research, Boillat and Berkes (2013) concluded that traditional knowledge offers a critical resource for improving adaptive capacity in a time of global warming. However, they argue "knowledge must be acknowledged as process, emphasizing ways of observing, discussing, and interpreting new information. Problem-oriented coproduction of knowledge can take place if both indigenous people and scientists recognize that their knowledge is partial, and apparent contradictions are solved if knowledge is not taken out of its cultural context."

The same conclusions were reached by Whitney et al. (2020) based on their interviewing with Indigenous members of the Heiltsuk and other Indigenous Nations residing in the central coastal region of British Columbia, Canada. Among the Heilksuk, primarily dwelling on Bella Bella Island, their view of stewardship is guided by a recognition of change and adaptation, and this idea constitutes one of their core values. Others include valuing the Heilksuk language, community, innovativeness, and resilience. Traditional Heiltsuk knowledge is shared across generations through storytelling (called ornúyṃ́). This traditional oral history practice encourages connection with community and land. Many stories provide a framework for appropriate interaction with and understanding of one's place in the world. One such narrative, called the Story of the Salmon People, provides a lens with which to view Heilksuk connection with the natural environment while emphasizing recognition of nature's vulnerability. The story describes a boy's journey involving negligent action (mistreating salmon in the river), repercussion (resulting in salmon avoidance of swimming in the river causing the death of the boy's twin sister), recognition (involving sorrowful prayer by the boy at the river, who was then sucked underwater, and learned about the salmon's anger because of his disrespectful behavior), and renewal (the boy then taught his people the respectful way to treat salmon and ensure food security) (as told by 'Qátuẃas Jessica Brown, 2018). More broadly, the edited volume *Indigenous Knowledge for Climate Change Assessment and Adaptation* (Nakashima et al., 2018) brings together an array of local studies from around the world that similarly argue for the benefits of including Indigenous knowledge to understand and cope with climate change.

Layla June (2023), based on the Indigenous understanding of her own Dine' people and those of other Indigenous communities she studied during her doctoral research, outlines four techniques, or approaches to living a healthy life on a sustainable, healthy planet.

1. Tap into and align with the forces of nature. Rather than trying to control her, "work with her." For example, Indigenous use of alluvial farming techniques using rainwater in natural floodplains is productive without outside irrigation or the use of fertilizers. This farming system has been used for millennia in arid and semiarid areas. Research on the traditional alluvial farming practices of the Zuni people of New Mexico, for example, evaluated nutrient (especially nitrogen and phosphorus) and hydrologic processes, farm management, maize productivity,

and soil quality. This ancient agricultural approach has been used on the same plots of land by the Zuni for centuries without conventional irrigation or fertilization. Carefully placed fields intercept rain runoff as well as water-borne sediments and organic debris transported from forested uplands hills. Findings of the study indicate that the "condition of Zuni agricultural soils suggests that their knowledge and management of soils contributed to effective conservation" (Sandor et al., 2007). Elsewhere, farming in this way has been productive on the same plots of land for centuries without soil depletion in places like Myanmar in Southeast Asia.

Another example of the practice of working with nature is seen in what is known as "three sisters agriculture," a traditional practice among the Indigenous peoples of the Americas. It involves the companion planting in a shared space of corn, beans, and squash. Grown together, these plants form a symbiotic relationship. Indigenous farmers saved the best seeds of each of these plant species for planting in the following season, resulting in a wide variety of cultivars well-suited for the local environments in which they were grown. These farmers placed corn in small hills planting beans around them and interspersing squash throughout the field. The corn's fibrous roots occupied shallower parts of soil and gave stability to the soil which supported the other two sisters. Beans have taproots that go deep into the soil and do not interfere with the corn or squash. The bean roots, in turn, carry a bacteria called rhizobia which collects nitrogen from the air and converts it into ammonia. This conversion fixes nitrogen into the soil helping the next year's corn and squash crops. In return, as the beans grow, they are supported by wrapping around the corn stalks. As their contribution to the sisterhood, squash leaves provide ground cover between the corn and beans, preventing weeds from overtaking the field. Squash provides many vitamins that corn and beans need but do not produce. These three plants thrive together better when planted together than when they are planted alone.

Other plants may be grown alongside the "three sisters" and sometimes get referred to as a "fourth sister." In eastern North America, the "fourth sister" could be amaranth (a grain with a high vitamin C content) or sunflower. In the US Southwest, Mexico, and Central America, other plants like chili pepper and tomato were used as companion plants. For Indigenous people, the Three Sisters were not just physical sustainers of life, but also spiritual sustainers of well-being. The crops were understood as human-like spirits and were venerated with ceremonies and other spiritual practices. Calling these plants "sisters" was a reminder that they are not just resources to exploit, but that they are part of the web of relationships linked by responsibility, care, and love (Hill, 2016).

2. Identify opportunities for intentional habitat expansion, such as traditional Native American augmentation of grasslands to support bison herds. On the plains, Indigenous people used controlled, soft burning of seasonally dead grass to produce nutrient-dense ash and refreshed topsoil while triggering the growth of new pyro-adapted grass species. This approach also eliminated seedling trees from taking over the grasslands, sustaining the diet of the bison on which people depended for food, fuel, clothing, shelter, and cultural identity. In this way, the

fertile soil of Mother Earth, bison herds, and people all benefited. In her dissertation, June (2022) concluded that "the extent and sophistication of Indigenous food systems were minimized in the historical record precisely because they are living contradictions to the narratives used to legitimize land seizure and attempted genocide."
3. The time has come for a return to a world in which we de-center humans by supporting nonhuman-centric systems. For example, coastal people like the Salish of British Columbia enhance fish habitat by planting kelp to expand the underwater forests where herring lay their eggs. The increase in herring eggs and eatable herring cascades up the food chain nourishing many other species, including salmon, orca, eagles, wolves, and humans. Strategies like these affirm that humans need not be a bane to Earth, but rather something integral to planet flourishing, a vital piece of the ecological puzzle.
4. Initiate the process of returning traditional lands to their Indigenous caretakers. Beyond healing the soil, the water, and the air, it is necessary to heal the damage wrought by the traumatic histories of colonized Nations. This dark legacy will not be healed by simply appropriating Indigenous knowledge in a new wave of neo-colonial extraction. Effort must be made to restore at least some of the stolen lands to their former Indigenous stewards and to support self-determination for the world's Indigenous communities.

In the Dine' language, the word *Hózhó* refers to a set of principles that should guide one's thoughts, actions, and speech. Doing so produces a sense of well-being as part of all creation, of being in harmony with the world, of living a good and moral life. June (2023) draws on this traditional concept as a way to talk about the personal and planetary benefits of Indigenous values. Indeed, her own life is a microcosm of the wider transition and cultural reclaiming she supports. Born in Taos, New Mexico, to a family with Dine', Tsétsêhéstâhese (Cheyenne), and white ancestry, she grew up uncertain of her identity and confused about her life direction. Like many of the Indigenous youth around her, she was introduced to using alcohol and drugs when she was 11 years old. The use of psychotropic chemicals was the norm in her social world; she literally assumed that was just how everyone lived. Later she realized that because of the drugs she never learned how to fully feel and process emotions or deal with trauma, including experiencing childhood sexual abuse. Drugs were an escape from the pain of having feelings. This period in her life was also shaped by sexual exploitation and rape, which occurred when she was 16. As she explains, "When you are alcohol or drug induced you can't really choose. There is no one there to choose… Rape is like a trick. It tricks people into thinking that they lost their worth and they lost their sacredness" (June, 2020). Because she did not resist, or even know how to resist, she felt complicit, that she had directly participated in destroying her worth as a person. Despite her struggles, and sense of personal and racial inferiority, she managed to finish high school and was accepted at Stanford University, where her drug use and sexual exploitation continued during endless rounds of campus parties. Even at Stanford, she could not escape her shame and self-blame, which weighed heavily on her shoulders all of the time. She recalls:

"I started to feel ugly, I started to feel tainted. I started to feel gross. I started to feel like a bad person. My entire self-image began to become completely unraveled" (June, 2020). Like many people who are drug dependent, June used more drugs to try and cope with her internal crisis and so her cycle of misery, self-blame, and self-destruction continued. During this time, she even began praying for death. This downward spiral came to a head when she was a sophomore and on a study abroad semester in Peru. There, she was severely injured in an earthquake. In the aftermath of this physically and emotionally painful experience, through a complicated and at times convoluted trail, she eventually turned her life around with the help of several Indigenous elders. In time, she was able to reclaim her cultural identity as Dine', her self-worth, and her spiritual relationship with Mother Earth. Moreover, she was able to complete her Ph.D. based on a doctoral study of the ways in which pre-colonial Indigenous Nations physically shaped large regions of "Turtle Island" (aka, the Americas), and become a musician, scholar, public speaker, community organizer, and advocate for the use of traditional land stewardship practices as well as approaches for mending historical traumas. To advance this work, she co-founded the Taos Peace and Reconciliation Council, which works to heal intergenerational trauma and ethnic division in northern New Mexico. In other advocacy efforts, she has participated in the Nihigaal Bee Iiná Movement, which is a 1000-mile prayer walk through the Diné homeland, organized to expose the exploitation of Diné land and its people by uranium, coal, oil, and gas industries.

One of the enduring traumas experienced by the Indigenous peoples of the USA and Canada were church-run boarding schools. The US government, for example, using the Civilization Fund Act as legal authorization, forced or otherwise coerced Indigenous families to send their children to these strictly run residential schools as part of a focused assimilation plan. While parents often tried to hide their children from this legalized kidnapping, police were empowered to seize them, violently if necessary, and drag them against their will to places like the Sherman Institute in Southern California or the Chemawa Indian School in Oregon. This "educational" system, consisting of 408 schools in 37 states and territories, including seven in Hawaii, was designed to destroy Indigenous cultural traditions, languages, and identities and grab land from Indigenous people. While most children returned from the schools deeply traumatized, many never made it home. According to an ongoing investigation and phase 1 report ordered by Interior Secretary Deb Haaland, a member of the Laguna Pueblo Nation, hundreds of children died in the boarding schools. As the investigation continues, it is expected that the number will climb into the thousands or tens of thousands. The report also concluded that these schools used "systematic militarized and identity-alteration methodologies" (Newland, 2022) that included changing children's names from Indigenous to English ones, cutting their hair short, mandating the wearing of uniforms, preventing Indigenous religious and cultural practices, and assigning children to perform military drills. These institutions also forced children to perform manual labor, such as sewing clothes and agricultural work. Moreover, children were subject to "[r]ampant physical, sexual and emotional abuse; disease; malnourishment; overcrowding; and lack of health care" (Newland, 2022). Survivors suffered deep emotional wounds that continue to haunt Indigenous communities today.

The strategies itemized by Layla June provide a few starting points for a renewed planetary health framework that is sensitive to, reflects, and empowers Indigenous knowledge and its creators. In the view of Rhys Jones, a Māori academic, Papaarangi Reis, also a Māori academic, and Alexandra Macmillan, a scholar-activist living in Aotearoa/New Zealand, in a reoriented decolonial conception of planetary health, benefits that accrue to some because of the exploitation of others cannot be considered health-promoting. In fact, it is antithetical to any moral conception of good health. This team of Indigenous and non-Indigenous researchers believe that planetary health has an important role to play in shepherding humanity away from injustice and a dismal future: "Planetary health action cannot simply be about replacing one form of extractive capitalism with another, protecting elite lifestyles and nationalising notions of ecological sustainability while accepting racist violence against some populations as a regrettable, but unavoidable, externality" (Jones et al., 2022). Transportation and other infrastructure, for example, they argue, should be guided by the local landscape, local relationships, and histories of the land, not by a dominative subjugating the environment to meet the needs of governments, corporations, and car owners and their demands for efficiency and saving time. Similarly, they contend, public health campaigns designed to reduce the consumption of meat among all populations hinge on a colonial disregard of customary and culturally meaningful wild food sources among Indigenous peoples. Denied access to wild foods forces Indigenous communities to rely primarily on commercial food systems that perpetuate exploitative dynamics and carbon-intensive supply chains. Further, initiatives undertaken to improve planetary health must avoid acts of injustice against Indigenous peoples. Such breaches of Indigenous rights already are occurring, including the forced removal of Indigenous communities to make way for forestry projects (e.g., forcibly moving the Maasai in the name of conservation) and efforts to expand biofuel production, which also significantly increases the price of food and exacerbates food insecurity for Indigenous communities. In response to threats to traditional food sources, a food sovereignty movement has emerged that challenges the dominance of the capital-intensive, corporate model of food production. Framed within a larger rights narrative, the food sovereignty movement calls for the right of all peoples to healthy and culturally appropriate food and the right to define their own diets (Coté, 2016).

This understanding of meaningful change involves dismantling established systems of power and the fundamental reorientation of governance at all levels. A change of this magnitude requires a transformational shift in dominant values and ideologies. Such a world-reshaping process, they conclude, should begin with a commitment to "epistemic disobedience" (Mignolo, 2009), which involves the interrogation of the "naturalness" and "superiority" of the Western, individualistic approach to knowing and being in the world. This project also must include a disinvestment from corporation-driven, business-as-usual activities but does not preclude various actions to mitigate the numerous adverse impacts of existing systems. While planetary health scholars (and activist-scholars) may need to continue working in Western academic institutions, they must refocus their work on creating alternative systems that are based on principles of relational well-being and engagement in community environmental and social justice actions. Planetary Health 2.0, in short, envisions a paradigm shaped by relationality, kinship with the natural world, and a commitment to Indigenous rights and their claims to self-determination.

Emergence of planetary health is seen by some as a fifth stage in the historic evolution of the modern population health paradigm (Singer, 2014). As noted earlier, thinking about health as more than an individual condition—the prevailing approach of biomedicine—is rooted in public health efforts, especially in Europe, during the nineteenth century. The second stage of this history also began during the nineteenth century with the creation of tropical medicine in response to the colonial encounter with the infectious diseases of tropical environments. The third stage began during the post-World War II period with the transition from tropical medicine to international health. This involved the expansion of multinational health initiatives like the World Health Organization. During the 1990s, the fourth stage, global health, was launched with the consolidation of a global neoliberal economy and global communication systems, in combination with recognition that risks to health transcend national borders and require multilateral responses. The shift to a planetary health understanding represents a further advance in population health thinking driven by recognition that the health of human communities is multiply linked to the environment and to other species. The planetary health perspective, in short, reveals the fundamental ways in which human beings are not just agents of environmental change but are also vulnerable objects of that change.

A difficult challenge of planetary health is fully comprehending the dynamic and systemic relationships among global environmental changes, the precise and locally varied effects of these changes on natural Earth systems, and how these changes affect the health of humans and other species on multiple levels (i.e., locally, regionally, and globally). To help overcome these challenges, planetary health draws on expertise from various sources, including the physical and social sciences, healthcare providers, and diverse communities including Indigenous ones, to assemble and mobilize effective holistic responses to our current permacrises dilemma. Needed efforts have been initiated in recent years to include Indigenous ideas and people in conceptualizing and operationalizing planetary health, although there is still far to go. Critical to this initiative is the Indigenous understanding that our sights cannot be limited to protecting human health but must be broadened to make planetary health improvement as the true goal. As climate change and environmental disturbances and stressors advance, planetary health offers an ever more popular framework for grassroots/professional/Indigenous collaboration in building a just and sustainable world. To be meaningful, this framework must translate from a set of laudable "ideas" into a practical roadmap that shapes health, environment, and social decision making and action.

Reflections on the Challenges of Collaboration

While she was training to be an Arctic ecologist at the University of Durham in the UK, Ilona Kater (2022) remembers that questions of research ethics were primarily focused on how to appropriately process plant, animal, or human tissue being analyzed in the laboratory. Ethical issues with regard to studying or working with living people were rarely addressed and even then only in informational conversations with peers. Despite her lack of formal training in the ethical challenges of working with human populations, Keter observed a growing push in the field for more interdisciplinary work that includes the knowledge and perspectives of local and Indigenous peoples. Driving this change, in part, was the desire among researchers to replace certain problematic mainstream research practices including ignoring the knowledge of Indigenous peoples and other subjugated groups that are less familiar to Western scientific ways of thinking. For example, a natural scientist's knowledge of a field site often is based only on the experience of a brief visit, a few days or weeks in length, as well as on the published work of other scholars who also may have only spent a limited amount of time in the area. During these visits, researchers collect data which is processed and analyzed back home and then written up and published using scholarly jargon in an academic journal. Local people living in the field site area often never see the results of the study nor do they experience any direct benefits from the work that was done. Their longer-term detailed knowledge of the area commonly is ignored while the expertise of scientists is prioritized. This kind of "helicopter research" scientists began to realize perpetuates a disconnected and detached theorizing that can lead to information being misrepresented, the use of unethical research practices, and communities being harmed. Inclusion of local and Indigenous people in natural sciences research began to be promoted as a way to counteract these problematic patterns. However, the challenges of collaborative work Kater realized were significant and were not getting adequate attention.

Kater learned this lesson while trying to do collaborative work in northern Sweden with Indigenous Sámi reindeer herders. In initiating this project, she was determined that her research would not simply consist of answering an interesting academic question but would also be of some practical use to the Sámi. Specifically, she hoped to answer questions the Sámi had about their environment, or, alternatively, quantify some of the knowledge, called *árbediehtu*; they already held about their environment that might be useful in their conflicted court dealings over land claims with more powerful non-Sámi neighbors and local industries. By doing this work with the Sámi, she hoped it would make a contribution toward improving unbalanced power relations by addressing the legal demand that the Sámi prove land use either since "time immemorial," or at least continually over the span of 90 years.

To begin her work, Kater had to make contact with the Sámi and get their buy-in for the project. This proved to be difficult as her overtures were usually ignored, or even if answered, did not lead to any agreements to participate. As this pattern continued she began to sense that her would-be collaborators were suffering from "research fatigue," a weariness and disinclination toward further participation in research because of offensive power and benefit imbalances with visiting university researchers. As a new researcher, Kater struggled with imposter syndrome, feeling like she was singularly naïve, unaware, and unprepared for the task she had selected. But, in fact, she was not alone; her early field experience is shared by other researchers who have been rebuffed by Indigenous communities that were unwilling to be studied.

Helga West (2020), a Sámi theologian in Finland, explains: "I'm tired of strangers who constantly approach my people for the sake of science." She adds:

> The Sámi have been told to strip naked in order to be photographed and measured. They have been taken blood samples for gene and other tests. Notes have been made about their family background, body length, eye and hair color, joints, bones, and many other physical and non-physical characteristics. Their Indigenous spirituality was demolished, and their spiritual equipment was either destroyed or sent to museums in Europe for astonishment and examination.

Among the research projects to which West refers was one conducted by the Swedish State Institute for Racial Biology carried out from 1922 to 1969. Framed within a eugenics perspective, it focused on Sámi and other ethnic minorities, without their consent. Study "participants" were pressured to undress, be photographed, and have their physical features studied in the context of being viewed as members of inferior races. Other studies have appropriated Sámi knowledge for the career or monetary gains of researchers, further damaging the Sámi ability to ever trust researchers. Reading the literature on these issues, including the writings of many Indigenous scholars, Kater (2022) concluded that as researchers "we need to honestly consider how committed we are to decolonial work. Are we willing to relinquish some of our power and control to tackle some inherent inequalities in research?" Helpful in this effort was gaining acquaintance with using Indigenous methods and values to ensure research is ethically and culturally appropriate (Porsanger, 2004). As Porsanger explains Indigenous approaches to research on Indigenous issues "are not meant to compete with, or replace, the Western research paradigm; rather, to challenge it and contribute to the body of knowledge of Indigenous peoples about themselves and for themselves, and for their own needs as peoples, rather than as objects of investigation." From this perspective, researchers must ask themselves who is the research for, who will most benefit, how will compensation and credit be shared, does this project give back to all those involved, and is the research commitment respectful of participants' time and life priorities?

As a result of such rethinking, it is possible to identify successful collaborative ecological initiatives. A notable example is the co-management arrangement developed for the far northern river known as Näätämo in Finnish (Njauddâm in Sámi), which includes the Skolt Sámi as active partners and knowledge producers (Brattland & Mustonen, 2018). This collaborative effort was developed to carry out research and sustainably manage the wild Atlantic salmon population in Norway and Finland. Since the 1960s, through government policy decisions the coastal and river fisheries in the area have been cut back by shortening the allowable fishing period and limiting the range of permittable fishing gear. This policy was met by fierce opposition from the Sámi who depend on salmon as a vital food source. This activism included yearly occupation of an island in the Tana (or Deatnu) River (south of the Näätämo/Njauddâm) by a group of Sámi activists who called themselves Ellos Deatnu (Long Live Deatnu!). Ellos Deatnu declared a "moratorium" on government salmon regulations on the border of Norway and Finland. Additionally, they asserted autonomy on the island and the waters surrounding it, maintaining that instead of the governments of Norway and Finland the area was now governed by customary Sámi law. They also announced a moratorium on recreational fishing by non-Sámi around the island, which implied that fishing licenses purchased from the state were no longer valid. This conflict reflects the re-assertion of Sámi identity after a long history of government assimilation efforts.

In this context, the co-management project began with shared recognition of the need for ecological restoration of habitats to decrease disruptive drivers like erosion, algae-causing nutrient and organic loading, the loss of salmon spawning areas, and climate change. Skolt Sámi teams produced traditional knowledge observations, including weather and star lore events. This information was compared with those of a science team. Equipped with digital cameras, the Skolt Sámi were the first to report the arrival of a threatening southern beetle species (*Potosia cuprea*) in the area. Similar observations have included sites of algae growth, invasive plant species intrusion, and sites of ecological damage. Results of the Näätämö project were published as work reports, posters, online postings, and in peer-reviewed science journals. Nothing was published without being approved by the Skolt Sámi. The Sámi also agreed upon and initiated self-imposed Atlantic salmon harvest limitations to increase the number of mother fish reaching spawning areas. The mechanisms for including traditional Indigenous knowledge and science in a rigorous, community-led study of the basin proved to be a meaningful tool for the Sámi to include their voices, knowledge, and observations in a process that directly links to observable outcomes. Both the mapping of past damages and weather- or climate-related observations of salmon and rivers provided useful mechanisms for the Sámi to improve their self-esteem. A system and a process were put in place whereby the Sámi, as co-researchers and co-managers, work to improve the health of the fish and the river. A comparable project in Sweden focused on developing and using an electronic tracking tool (affixed to a reindeer collar) to map reindeer movements over time has improved the planning process among Sámi reindeer herders (Sandström et al., 2012).

In a parallel way to the examples discussed above, Planetary Health, in its revised, collaborative expression, represents a critical advance in our collective understanding and participatory response to the issue of health in its full meaning. One further step in this journey is the incorporation of a biosocial syndemics understanding of disease and other negative health conditions, addressed in the next chapter.

Case Study: Is Climate Change Coming for Your Lunch?
In the summer of 2024, the CDC reported a high-profile food poisoning outbreak. Several dozen people diagnosed as being infected with *Listeria monocytogenes*

bacterium were hospitalized and several died. Named after the British pioneer of sterile surgery Joseph Lister, listeria acts as an intracellular parasite in mammals including humans. The outbreak of the resulting disease, listeriosis, was linked to consuming sliced deli meat. Listeria easily spread among deli equipment, surfaces, hands, and food. It is the nation's third-leading cause of death from food-borne illness. It is so deadly because it acts syndemically as a catalyst for other lethal bacterial infections, like meningitis.

Healthy people with mild food poisoning symptoms from listeria infection, including fever and diarrhea, often do not need medical care and recover within a few days. But, of course, not everyone is healthy and children, pregnant women, and seniors are particularly vulnerable. Pregnant women may suffer only mild symptoms but their baby can die in the womb or have a life-threatening infection within a few days of being born. While listeria is not contagious from person to person, it can still be hard to get rid of because it spreads easily from contaminated food to nearby surfaces.

The 2024 outbreak was reminiscent of a far worse event in 2017–2018 in South Africa. This was the largest listeriosis outbreak recorded globally. The source of the outbreak was located in early March 2018 when traces of the bacterium were found in a food production facility that prepares ready-to-eat processed meat products. By the time the source was identified, about 950 cases of disease had been confirmed and 180 deaths were reported, figures which are believed to be underestimates of the actual extent of the outbreak.

The wide-ranging environmental effects associated with global climate change are known to significantly alter the epidemiology of food-borne diseases like listeriosis. Even though listeria microorganisms are ubiquitous in the natural environment, several characteristics of the bacterium make it especially climate sensitive. Jumps in outdoor temperature and high summer temperature peaks have been linked to the occurrence of listeriosis, as with most infectious diarrheal diseases. Hot weather extremes that become more common with climate change enhance the replication cycles of the microbe and could cause breakdowns in food cooling chains, with rapid rises in numbers of the bacteria on food products. Aside from temperature increases, altered rainfall patterns and lengthened dry seasons may influence listeria transmission. Climate change increases the likelihood listeria will spread in food-processing plants, retail outlets, and domestic settings. As temperatures continue to rise due to climate change, so does the risk of suffering food poisoning from various other food-borne pathogens as well.

Discussion Questions

1. What are some of the reasons so few human diseases have been eliminated.
2. How do drapetomania and hysteria inform the planetary health understanding of disease?
3. How does the social determinants of health framework influence planetary health?
4. Discuss what is meant by the "safe environmental limits within which humanity can flourish."

5. What is ecocrises interaction and why is it relevant to planetary health?
6. Discuss some of the key moments and influencers in the development of planetary health.
7. Discuss some of the criticisms of planetary health and changes in response to these criticisms.
8. How have understandings of plant and animal "consciousness" changed in recent decades?

Class Projects

1. Pick a disease, research it, and come up with a realistic plan for how to eliminate it.
2. Form a group to discuss all the ways climate change impacted health in the world this year.

The Making of Ecosyndemics

3

Abstract

This chapter focuses on ecosyndemics in light of the planetary health perspective. Further, it explores known and potential ecosyndemics, pathways of environmental and other disease interaction, and health impacts of ecosyndemics across disparate populations. The chapter reviews the development of the syndemic concept and its engagement with environmental drivers of health, leading to the development of the ecosyndemic framework. The features of several ecosyndemics are examined in some detail revealing the complex nature of these biosocial health phenomena.

Keywords

Ecosyndemics · SAVA · Elder health · Lung disease · Cardiovascular disease · COVID-19 · Pathogen-pathogen interaction · HIV/HCV · Tick-borne diseases · Paleopathology

Lichens, which can be found growing on the surfaces of tree bark and branches, rocks, gravestones, and even roofs, are a symbiotic assemblage of algae or cyanobacteria and fungi. In a thought-provoking essay, nature writer Douglas Chadwick comments that because they are not a single organism but rather an interactive community of species, lichens should be seen as a kind of a doorway between organisms or individual species and ecosystems. "Look out one direction," he writes, "and you see individual things; look the other way, you see processes, relationships, things together. This is the new level in understanding biology" (Chadwick, 2003). This new way of seeing biological interconnectedness is part of the foundation of syndemic theory. In the field of biology, the term "interdependence" refers to the relationships shared by organisms of different species. In syndemic research, interdependence refers, in part, to adverse synergistic relations among diseases or other health conditions in a population. In these interactions, one, two, or more diseases is enhanced in some way to the detriment of the health of the affected population.

Another part of the foundation of syndemic theory focuses on the relationship between macroscopic patterns (i.e., the social or environmental contexts of populations) and microscopic dynamics (i.e., disease processes in the bodies of population members). Not only do diseases interact, but this interaction is initiated and advanced through contextual factors that create vulnerability in populations. Vulnerability refers to physical and emotional susceptibility to harm. Harsh social and environmental conditions weaken body systems, increasing the likelihood of both disease formation and comorbid disease interaction. Attending to this range of issues demands "systems thinking." This means relating different types of structures that shape our lives, including the biological systems of our bodies, the social systems in which live our lives, economic systems that determine quality of life and access to resources, and the political systems that govern public affairs. Systems thinking requires focus on the connections among different components and their interactions, as well as transdisciplinary cooperation. It is a strategy for seeing the bigger picture without losing focus on all of the smaller pictures that comprise the whole.

Syndemics, in short, consist of a specific menu of features. First, they involve two or more diseases or other disease-like health conditions. Diseases can be implicated in multiple different syndemics based on other factors. Similarly, body organs can be the internal site of various syndemics. For example, diabetes is a chronic disease that develops when the pancreas does not produce an adequate amount of insulin or when the body cannot effectively use the insulin it produces to move glucose (a source of energy) into cells. Diabetes and underlying pancreatic problems have been found to be involved in multiple different syndemics. Second, in syndemic diseases interact across various pathways, such as through breakdowns in the body's intercellular signaling systems. All of the cells in our bodies are continually transmitting electronic or chemical signals and receiving signals from other cells. But cell communication can go wrong, resulting in disease. Sometimes cells fail to execute a signal at the proper time or the signal does not reach its target. Also, sometimes cells do not respond to a signal they receive, or they respond even when they have not received a signal. Actually, most diseases involve at least one disruption of cell communication. Multiple sclerosis, for example, is a disease in which the protective myelin covering around nerve cells in the brain and spinal cord is scarred and destroyed. Affected nerve cells stop sending signals from one area of the brain to another. This leads to multiple problems, including muscle weakness, high blood pressure, blurred vision, difficulty with balance, uncontrolled movements, and depression. Disruption of body signal by one disease may help promote the progression of another disease. Thus, the many comorbidities of multiple sclerosis cause the destruction of nerve coverings to progress faster, advancing the original disease. Unhampered cell signaling is vital to the coordination of all body processes. Without proper signaling, for example, all of the many components of the immune system (e.g., white blood cells, antibodies, bone marrow, the thymus) cannot work together to identify and eliminate pathogens that threaten the body. Third, syndemics are local or at most regional. The disease components of syndemics, such as the concentration of HIV disease, hepatitis C, and sexually transmitted infections among Indigenous communities near Albuquerque, New Mexico (Yu, 2023), often are closely linked and geographically clustered. As Mendenhall and Singer (2019) state, "We know from research on diabetes that the disease becomes syndemic differently from one location to another, because variations exist in how diabetes materializes in relation to political and epidemiological histories." Fourth, syndemics impact specific populations based on their demographics, health condition, and existing threats and challenges (e.g., stress levels). Finally, syndemics occur under specific sets of social and environmental conditions, from the nature and forms of expression of social inequality to anthropogenic disruptions of the local environment. All of these characteristics indicate why, for example COVID-19 is not a global syndemic, but rather is a disease ensnared in multiple different local/regional syndemics around the world.

Development of syndemics as a concept dates to the rise of the AIDS pandemic in the Western hemisphere. It is now believed that HIV, the virus that is the immediate cause of AIDS, probably entered this region from its origin in Africa in the early 1970s. For years, spread was slow and limited to a few populations. First to come to light were cases with unusual symptoms (e.g., a rare type of cancer called Kaposi's sarcoma) among men who have sex with men. Thus, an early name of this new disease was GRID (gay-related immune deficiency). Health experts soon began to fear that GRID was an immunological time bomb, a worry that was well-founded. Before long, but with less initial attention, some healthcare workers began seeing a new mysterious disease that was ravaging people who inject drugs. The latter called this condition "junkie flu" or "the dwindles." Ultimately, the viral cause of the disease afflicting both groups, as well as other populations, was discovered by medical researchers. Tellingly, its origin has been traced back to the colonial era in sub-Saharan West Africa and to the stressful and oppressive working conditions, forced labor, and community displacement that supported colonial plantations, construction projects, and other imperial enterprises. Also implicated are various unsafe injection practices by colonial healthcare providers (e.g., reusing unsterilized syringes) and vaccination campaigns intended to control tropical diseases. These factors facilitated exposure to SIV, an infectious disease of nonhuman primates, and the adaptation of this pathological agent to the human body as HIV. Naturally occurring SIV infection of African nonhuman primates is asymptomatic and usually does not induce significant white blood cell loss despite high levels of virus in a primate's blood system. SIVcpz (from chimpanzees) and SIVsm (from sooty mangabeys, a frequent ground visiting Old World monkey) have crossed species barriers leading to the evolution of the generation of both HIV-1 and HIV-2 (the more virulent subspecies), respectively. The exact pathways of this exposure remain uncertain but may have involved increased reliance on the hunting of forest animals (including primates) by the underfed colonial workforce. While eating game meat is not implicated, bites and scratches inflicted by wild animals on hunters, as well as exposure to animal body fluids and feces during handling and butchering, may have been the source(s) of exposure. Whatever the exact pathway of the spillover, the emergence of HIV as a deadly human disease affirms the underlying interconnectedness of the planet's species.

A computer-generated model suggests that the first transfer of SIV to humans leading to the evolution of HIV-2 may have occurred in Guinea-Bissau during the 1940s. Research with primates living on other continents has not found evidence of SIV. This suggests that HIV originated in Africa (Lemey et al., 2003). Study of stored blood samples from a malaria research project carried out in 1959 in what is today the Democratic Republic of the Congo found early HIV infection. It was in Kinshasa, the capital, that the first epidemic of HIV/AIDS is believed to have occurred in the 1970s. It has been hypothesized that HIV was brought to the city by an infected individual who traveled from Cameroon. Soon the virus entered a wide urban sexual network and spread quickly around parts of the city. Accelerated spread in the region was due to a combination of widespread labor migration, a high ratio of men to women in urban populations, the subordinated status of women, and prevalence of other sexually transmitted diseases. Uganda was hard hit by the AIDS epidemic in the 1980s. At the beginning of the decade, Ugandan doctors encountered a surge in cases of a severe wasting disease, as well as a large number of fatal opportunistic infections such as Kaposi's sarcoma. By this point, some doctors in the USA were becoming aware of cases with similar symptoms among their patients.

As AIDS began to spread in the USA during the late 1980s and early 1990s, community-based organizations that addressed the needs of underserved populations began to mount prevention efforts. One of these was the Hispanic Health Council (HHC) in Hartford, Connecticut, which provided research-guided disease prevention and health promotion services to residents of a poor city with a majority Black and Latino population. After several years of underfunded efforts, the HHC was able to secure funding from the National Institute on Drug Abuse to study the epidemic among people who inject drugs and use finding to develop targeted prevention programs. This research focused on identifying the social relations, health risk behaviors, risk environments, and life experiences of people who inject illicit drugs that could contribute to disease transmission. As part of this research, outreach-recruited study participants, people who were actively involved in the illegal injection of drugs, were asked to identify all the diseases they had been diagnosed with by a medical provider. Members of the research team were startled to discover the number of serious diseases reported by participants, triggering concern about the significance of disease interactions on their overall health burden (Singer et al., 2021).

This research led to recognition of the morbid interaction of substance abuse, violence, and AIDS in the health profiles of people who inject drugs. The term SAVA, an acronym formed from the first letters of these three threats to health, was used to label the first syndemic to be described in the academic literature (Singer, 1996). Participants in this study regularly experienced police harassment (e.g., stopping suspected drug users, confiscating and breaking their syringes), routinely suffered street violence (muggings, beatings), lacked easy access to health care, faced major hurdles in trying to enter drug treatment programs, endured daily discrimination and stigmatization, were denigrated in the news and entertainment media and in the speeches of politicians, and suffered high rates of poverty and homelessness. This amalgamation of stressful life experiences was promoted and sustained by a set of political-economic and social structural factors, including the use of class, ethnic identity, and gender in scapegoating and blame-the-victim practices. As Lasco (2019) comments, in the USA and elsewhere in the world, "political leaders have reportedly leveraged illicit drug use as a populist trope to cast suspicion on groups they oppose and to boost support for themselves and their policies."

Based on the findings of this study, the HHC research team published several papers on the SAVA syndemic which caught the attention of other researchers concerned about the health of marginalized populations in the era of AIDS. While some of these researchers were drawn from public health, others were trained in psychology or related fields. Use of the SAVA model was extended from the study of the health of people who use drugs to other populations, including men who have sex with men, sexual partners of people who inject drugs, commercial sex workers, and others in light of the adverse social conditions they experienced. In 2002, researchers at the Centers for Disease Control and Prevention (CDC) began to consider the usefulness of the syndemic approach to public health. Their work helped slowly spread awareness of the concept nationally and even internationally and facilitated its diffusion across multiple health disciplines. Within the medical community, familiarity with syndemics was boosted by Richard Horton's (2020) publication of a commentary in *The Lancet* in which he asserted "COVID-19 is not a pandemic. It is a syndemic." This followed the publication of a set of articles in *The Lancet* in 2017. In 2022, health experts across the US Department of Health and Human Services formed the Syndemic Steering Committee to promote work on syndemics, further disseminating the application of syndemics in health service delivery.

A considerable literature on syndemics, including academic articles, commentaries, book chapters, books, conference reports, and published talks, now exists. The growth in the recognized utility of the syndemic approach is evident in its diffusion across health-related disciplines and the ever-increasing pace of syndemics-related publications. The widening appeal of the syndemic approach stems from recognition that healthcare providers must increasingly address the needs of individuals with multiple coexisting diseases and health deficits. Because individual diseases do not exist in a vacuum, the same can be said of sufferer experience and the management of disease and the burden of diseases on community well-being.

There is growing awareness that many of the most damaging human disease events across time and place—from the deadly influenza epidemic of 1918/19 to the contemporary global COVID-19 pandemic, and from the bubonic plague epidemic that swept fourteenth-century Europe to the European diseases that devastated the Indigenous populations of the Americas—are the possible or probable consequence not of a single disease acting on its own but of two or more diseases acting in tandem under stressful social conditions. Researchers have now described multiple syndemics, including the VIDDA syndemic (violence, immigration/isolation, depression, diabetes, abuse), the CRC syndemic (Chagas disease, rheumatic heart disease, congestive heart disease), diabulimia syndemic (insulin-dependent diabetes and bulimia nervosa), and the WIT syndemic (whooping cough, influenza, and tuberculosis). Still, despite the 30-year history of syndemic work and its broad proliferation and abundant literature, everyday people working in various health fields are still encountering the concept for the first time.

The Changing Environment and Ecosyndemics

The initial definition of syndemics focused on the social factors underlying adverse disease interactions. As the multiple impacts of a changing climate as well as other disruptive environmental alterations began to be reported more widely, it became increasingly clear that many social factors are mediated by the environment. For example, climate change is a consequence of social behaviors like the actions of fossil fuel companies, but these social behaviors are not experienced directly by those suffering the effects of climate change. Only examination of the social drivers of climate change reveals the behind-the-scenes social processes and relations that are involved in destabilizing the environment. In other words, while climate change is an immediate threat to health, social power and inequality are the ultimate determinants. As Kirsch (2000) argues, "pollution is a social relationship not simply an environmental issue." That lower-income, ethnic minorities are more likely to be exposed to pollution in the USA, for example, reflects public policies rooted in structural racism that have led to polluting industries being intentionally located in communities of color (Patel et al., 2021).

The concept of ecosyndemics was developed in the first book on syndemics to advance the framework by acknowledging and incorporating the significant role of the physical environment on syndemic interactions (Singer, 2009a, b). Ecosyndemics recognizes that climate change and altered physical environments foster both disease interactions and biosocial interactions in diverse ways.

The Lungs: A Key Interface with the Environment

The nature of ecosyndemics received one of its earliest examinations in a study of respiratory health (Singer, 2013), which is appropriate in light of the lessons to be learned from the "simple" act of breathing. We tend to take breathing for granted. If we are healthy, we do not usually think about it too much unless we have exerted ourselves. But it is actually a complex process of inside/outside gas exchange. During external respiration, our lungs pull oxygenated air from the environment into our bodies (inhalation) through our nose and mouth and discharge carbon dioxide back out (exhalation). When we breathe, air flows through a series of progressively smaller airways, called bronchioles, and then into microscopic sacs called alveoli. It is here that gas exchange takes placed.

This outside/inside pathway means that breathing is a critical point where our bodies engage the environment around us, an event that occurs thousands of times a day during our lives. In fact, the lungs are the body's largest interface with the outside environment, 30 times that of the skin. Unraveled, the lungs have the surface area of a full racquetball court. This enormous surface area is also far more exposed to the outside environment than areas like the gut.

Indeed, there are no physical barriers (other than the larynx during swallowing) that separate the most distant parts of the lungs from the outside environment. In the average healthy adult, the lungs pull in about 1850 gallons (7000 liters) of air, including all it contains, each day. If air comes in through the nostrils it is warmed and humidified. Tiny hair-like filaments called *cilia* protect the nasal passageways and other parts of the respiratory tract by filtering out dust and other particles that enter the nose along with air. This is seen as one of the ways living organisms have adapted to the challenges of allowing the outside in. For most organisms on Earth, having access to a constant supply of oxygen is fundamental to living. Because it is not stored in the body, every single cell needs a constant fresh supply of oxygen to work properly. Permanent brain damage (loss of brain cells) begins to set in after only four minutes without oxygen, and death can occur between four to six minutes later in most cases.

Our need for oxygen is actually an expression of our dependence on other species. Earth did not always have much oxygen. In what is somewhat problematically called the "Great Oxidation Event" (problematic because it actually was a drawn-out process), about 2.45 billion years ago oxygen began to appear in the planet's atmosphere. The source: photosynthesis by oceanic cyanobacteria (formerly called blue-green algae, although they are not actually algae). Researchers believe that the amount of oxygen released into the seawater by cyanobacteria gradually increased over time. As oxygen accumulated in the ocean, it began escaping into the atmosphere. In addition to providing breathable air outside of the oceans, which allowed for the evolution of multicellularity, this process triggered the formation of the ozone layer that protects us from harmful UV radiation from the sun. Moreover, plants can make food for themselves (and oxygen for animals, including humans) because of cyanobacteria living in plant's cells.

It is not an exaggeration to say that humans and other species owe our very existence to tiny cyanobacteria. Oxygen in the atmosphere that has accumulated over hundreds of millions of years from this source accounts for most of the oxygen humans breathe. Today, however, cyanobacteria are not the primary source of new oxygen. About 50–70% of the oxygen in Earth's atmosphere now comes from marine plants and plant-like organisms, especially plankton, while land-dwelling plants add additional oxygen.

Despite abundant oxygen, respiratory diseases can make it hard for people to breathe. The global burden of respiratory diseases is an increasing threat worldwide. In 2017, there were almost 550 million cases of chronic respiratory diseases recorded around the world. This is almost a 40% increase since 1990. In 2017, respiratory diseases were the third leading cause of global mortality, an 18.0% increase from the rate in 1990 (GBD Chronic Respiratory Disease Collaborators, 2020). One of the most common of these diseases is asthma which is caused by inflammation and muscle tightening around the airways. It is named after the ancient

Greek word for panting. This disease, involving a combination of both genetic factors and environmental exposures, has varied expression across patients. Over time, repeated inflammatory episodes can cause permanent structural and functional changes in the air pathways, including a persistent narrowing of the airways. Resulting symptoms include wheezing, labored breathing, cough, and chest tightness. The World Health Organization estimates that almost 300 million people suffer from asthma, and more than a quarter of a million, mostly in low and lower-middle income countries, die from this disease each year (1000 a day). In 2019, there were over 21 million years of life lost due to premature death and ten million years of life lived with disability attributed to asthma across all age groups globally (Global Asthma Network, 2022). Even in a wealthy country like the USA, asthma inflicts about eight percent of the population. Further, it is one of the most common causes of hospital admission for acute conditions among children. While asthma rates have been increasing worldwide, especially vulnerable are the urban poor.

A wide range of both outdoor (ambient) and indoor environmental factors have been found to be triggers of asthmatic flare-ups. Outdoor factors include vehicular emissions, ozone, and plant pollens. Research with middle school children has shown that traffic-related air pollutants, especially smaller particle particulate matter, nitrogen dioxide, and carbon monoxide, are linked to the prevalence of asthma. Overall, the association of asthma morbidity and air pollutants has been found to be stronger in children than in either adolescents or adults. This conclusion is supported by several longitudinal studies that evaluated the relationship between early childhood exposure to outdoor air pollution and subsequent development of asthma. In a prospective study, the interaction between air pollution exposure in early life and asthma development also has been demonstrated. Both early and recent exposures to air pollution are associated with a higher incidence of asthma until the age of 20. Other research has found a positive association between perinatal exposure to air pollution and asthma incidence during a child's preschool years (Tiotiu et al., 2020).

Studies of nitrogen oxide (NO_2), a traffic-related pollutant emitted from vehicle engines, for example, indicate this gas can penetrate deep into the lungs. In addition to damaging the lungs, it may play a prominent role in creating allergen sensitivity. While greater exposure to a high concentration of NO_2 in early life is more likely to be associated with asthma onset than less exposure, even low levels are associated with symptoms of asthma, reduced lung function, and asthma. Similar findings have been reported for other outdoor air pollutants.

Moreover, there is now considerable evidence, as Murray et al. (2006) indicate, that "a synergistic interaction [occurs] between allergens and viruses" in the development of asthma attacks. To assess this ecosyndemic interaction, these researchers enrolled 84 children between ages 3 and 17 with an acute asthma exacerbation (i.e., an asthma flare-up or attack) that were admitted to a hospital in Manchester, UK, over a one-year period (labeled: the case group). These index cases were matched by age and gender with two control groups: patients with stable asthma seen in the outpatient department and patients admitted to the hospital with nonrespiratory conditions. These researchers found no significant differences between the three groups by ethnicity or in terms of the presence of indoor triggers like parental smoking, pet ownership, or deprivation. All participants were tested for various nasal pathogens, such as rhinovirus, enterovirus, coronaviruses, RSV, influenza A and B, and *Mycoplasma pneumoniae*. Findings showed that participants in the case group were at a significantly higher risk of having been both exposed and sensitive to allergens and of having a higher respiratory pathogen load than participants in either of the control groups. Murray et al. (2006) concluded that their results "indicate that there appears to be a combined rather than an individual effect of natural virus infection and real-life allergen exposure in allergic asthmatic children in inducing asthma exacerbations." This conclusion about the ecosyndemic interaction of viruses and allergens is supported by other studies.

While respiratory infections from viruses are thought to be the most common infectious trigger of acute asthma, some research indicates that bacteria may also contribute to asthma flare-ups. Because viruses and bacteria can interact with adverse health consequences and are capable of exchanging genetic material (Singer, 2009a, b), and viruses and bacteria have been found together in studies using nasal swabs of asthma patients, biological synergy between different kinds of pathogens may be an additional factor in asthma exacerbation.

What are the biological pathways of syndemic interaction between allergy and infection? Several studies suggest that the key element in this interaction is the increase in air pathway inflammation in sensitized individuals exposed to allergens while already infected with one or more respiratory pathogens. Indeed, multiple pathways may contribute to the interaction of allergy and infection in the development and exacerbation of asthma. Note Wark and Gibson (2006): "People with asthma may frequently be exposed to more than one trigger, and these appear to interact in the development of asthma exacerbations."

Anthropogenic climate change also contributes to asthma in several ways. Increases in cold air and humidity are potential triggers for asthma attacks. Climate change also exacerbates or causes allergic respiratory diseases by increasing growth rates of pollen producing plants that release allergic proteins. More intense and prolonged periods of pollen release have caused changes in allergen patterns, increased the severity of respiratory tract infections, and altered the seasonality of allergies.

Another serious respiratory disease of concern from an ecosyndemic perspective is chronic obstructive pulmonary disease (COPD). COPD is actually a linked group of lung diseases, especially emphysema (which damages the alveoli of the lungs) and chronic bronchitis (which causes enflamed bronchial tubes). Vos et al. (2015) estimate that the global prevalence of COPD is approximately 174 million. COPD is the third leading cause of death globally and the fifth leading cause of economic disease burden.

Like asthma, COPD is an inflammatory lung disease that obstructs airflow in the lungs. Its symptoms include difficulty breathing, regular coughing, mucus production, and wheezing. COPD is a progressive disease. Unlike asthma, it is not characterized by episodic attacks stimulated by exposure to a trigger. Rather, symptoms are constant and worsen over time, even with treatment (although it is possible to suffer from both asthma and COPD). COPD typically is caused by long-term exposure to irritating gases (like tobacco smoke) or particulate matter in the ambient air. People with COPD are at heightened risk of developing other diseases, including heart disease and lung cancer. On average, people with COPD suffer from five comorbidities, suggesting that comorbidity is an essential characteristic of people who develop COPD. The most frequent chronic diseases associated with COPD include cardiovascular and respiratory disorders, osteoporosis, muscle wasting, metabolic and neuropsychiatric disorders, chronic kidney disease, gastroesophageal reflux, anemia, and cancer. These comorbidities appear earlier in life in people with COPD, although they often remain undiagnosed and untreated.

The clustering of diseases in COPD is not random; it has a history. As Fabbi (2023) notes, "[s]yndemics … refers to the occurrence of disease clusters with shared risk factors and biological interactions that exacerbate the prognosis and burden of disease, as suggested by the presence of certain morbidity clusters in patients with COPD." Globally, COPD is in fact an ecosyndemic. Research in Germany and China has shown that people living less than 325 feet (100 meters) from busy roads are significantly more likely to develop COPD than those living further away from the passage of heavy vehicular traffic. The increased concentrations of vehicular and other industrial air pollutants like particulate matter, nitrogen oxide, sulfur dioxide, and ground-level ozone can increase the risk of mortality in people with COPD. In recent years, ground-level ozone has become an increasingly important environmental pollutant affecting the mortality rate of patients with COPD. Additionally, exposure to wildfire smoke, which is increasing due to global warming, is associated with COPD mortality.

In sum, Yang et al. (2024) define a respiratory disease syndemic as "the concurrent presence and interconnectedness of multiple respiratory diseases within a population." Beyond interconnection, these diseases interact across variance pathways, including with nonrespiratory diseases, and increase the overall burden of disease in a population. Further, ecological conditions, which reflect dominant social relations, play a critical role in respiratory syndemics. The specific links among global warming, diminishing air quality, and respiratory health include (1) the direct adverse effects of air pollution generated by motor vehicles, industrial power plants, and industrial chemicals; (2) increased rates of intense and widespread wildfires that release great quantities of hazardous particulate matter, carbon monoxide, and polyaromatic hydrocarbons; (3) the formation of lung-damaging ground-level ozone when sunlight reacts with nitrogen oxides from car exhaust, coal power plants, and factory emissions; (4) spreading pathogenic diseases that infect the epithelial cells of the respiratory tract and cause oxidative stress; (5) toxic mold exposure promoted by changes in precipitation patterns, farmland restructuring, and more frequent flooding leading to water intrusion into inhabited buildings; and (6) warming induced expansions in both the range and quantity of pollen. For an increasing number of people on Earth, especially those from disadvantaged groups, gasping for breath, because of asthma, COPD, tuberculosis, lung cancer, or other environment-sensitive respiratory diseases, has become a painful daily experience.

For others, it has become a deadly one. These factors and pathways may also be significant in the COVID-19 pandemic, as discussed in the next chapter.

The Heart in Ecosyndemics

The ecosyndemic impacts of climate change and other environmental disarrangements extend beyond the exacerbation of respiratory diseases. Anthropogenic shifts in the global environment also affect cardiac health. The word heart traces back to *heorte* from Old English, and, in anatomy, refers to the muscle that circulates blood and oxygen. Beyond this, the term also has been used figuratively to label spirit, soul, will, desire, courage, and mind, usages that reflect cultural associations that revolve around the importance of the heart in human experience. Although drawn in anatomically inaccurate shape, the red heart symbol (a common emoji) and heart-shaped hand gesture of a heart often are used to represent the core of positive emotions. In turn, a heartless act is one with a complete lack of feeling or sensitivity to others. The heart, in short, is at the center of life and social relationship.

In medicine, the term heart disease (or cardiovascular disease, CVD) refers to a number of adverse heart conditions and related circulatory disorders, including heart disease, stroke, heart failure, and hypertension (high blood pressure). Heart disease is the leading cause of death in both the USA and globally. Reflecting syndemic interactions, the COVID-19 pandemic caused a significant rise in CVD-related deaths globally, reversing years of progress in reducing the human death rate due to this condition. In the USA, for example, the current mortality rate from heart failure is about 3% higher than it was 25 years ago. Fausto Pinto, co-author of the *World Heart Report*, notes: "The data doesn't lie. This report confirms the serious threat that cardiovascular disease poses all over the world, particularly in low- and middle-income countries" (World Heart Federation, 2023).

CVDs are the leading cause of death globally, taking about 18 million lives each year. In total, noncommunicable diseases (those not caused by infection) kill approximately 40 million people annually, about 74% of all global deaths, most of which are in low- and middle-income countries, and CVDs account for the majority of these lives lost.

The two major global health crises of our time, climate change and the epidemic of noncommunicable diseases like heart disease, are intertwined. Acting together they have eroded many public health gains and improvements in the quality of life, with their greatest impact on the poor and economically marginalized. Studies show that daily death rates linked to periods of both low and high temperatures, for example, are associated with rises in the rates of heart disease mortality. Available studies suggest that there is a growing risk from circulatory and heart disease because of climate change and, moreover, that there are syndemic links between cardiovascular diseases and other diseases (Al Mahmeed et al., 2021). Prolonged heatwaves, when temperatures reach at least 10 °F (5.5 °C) above the average high temperature for a region, produce heightened rates of heat stroke, the most serious of a range of health burdens associated with exposure to excessive heat. A 10 °F (5.5 °C) temperature increase from one day to the next is linked to an increased risk of hospitalization, ischemic heart disease, and ischemic stroke (conditions in which blood flow and thus oxygen are restricted in a part of the body). Heat strokes occur when the body's ability to control internal temperature fails, leading to a rapid jump in core body temperature. Normal core body temperature ranges from individual to individual, and is influenced by age, activity, and time of day, but tends to move between 97 °F (36.1 °C) and 99° (7.2 °C). People suffering heat stroke have hot, dry, and red skin but no perspiration, are confused, and may experience hallucinations. Suffering a heat stroke can cause severe and permanent damage to vital organs, prolonged disability, or even death. Among those at greatest risk upon exposure are people with heart disease because their internal body cooling systems may be damaged. Heat waves in several regions of the world are associated with increased cardiovascular mortality. Research suggests that adverse cardiovascular impacts are not only associated with extremes of temperature, but also with changes and variability in temperature.

In addition to the heart risks of rising temperature, there is the threat of air pollution. As noted, while exposure to particulate matter has been linked premature mortality due to respiratory diseases, between 70 and 80% of premature deaths due to such exposure are due to cardiovascular conditions. The unique vulnerability of the tissues of the cardiovascular system to air pollution is not yet well understood, but there is a considerable body of evidence documenting a rise in acute cardiovascular events with exposure to particulate air pollution. This evidence also shows that air pollution, especially smaller particulate matter, produces an inflammatory response and a chronic increase in CVD in individuals who are repeatedly exposed. Even short-term exposures to polluted air are linked to heart attacks, strokes, abnormal heartbeat, and abnormal heart rhythm. Further, existing evidence suggests that chronic and persistent exposure to air pollution increases the progression of lesions in the walls of arteries and negatively impacts blood pressure regulation, inflammation of the arteries, and endothelial function (which controls blood fluidity, blood platelet, and vascular tone) while playing a major role in the regulation of body immunology (Bhatnagar, 2017). In general, it appears that long-term exposure to tiny particulate matter enhances cardiovascular risk through a continuous buildup of plaque (fats, cholesterol, and other substances) on artery walls, whereas short-term exposure seems to trigger plaque rupture, clotting of the artery, and blood flow blockage. Reviews of multiple epidemiologic studies evaluating population-level acute triggers for heart attacks show that traffic exhaust was the single most serious preventable cause.

An identified pathway of air pollution-mediated cardiovascular disease involves the dysregulation of the body's internal circadian rhythms or biological clock. *These are natural physical, mental, and behavioral adjustments that follow a 24-hour sleep/wake cycle that are believed to confer an optimization of energy expenditure and the regulation of the internal physiology of the body.* Coordinated by a set of proteins in the brain, this system, which incorporates almost every cell type, prepares the body for wakefulness and sleepiness among other functions. Various factors, including stress, can disrupt the body's circadian rhythms. In humans, short-term disruption causes drowsiness, a drop in coordination, and difficulty with learning. Longer-term disruption can worsen existing health issues while increasing the risks of various diseases such as heart and blood pressure conditions. A growing body of evidence suggests that atypical circadian variations in blood pressure result in an increased occurrence of fatal and nonfatal CVDs. These understandings are supported by various animal studies, especially with hamsters and mice. This research shows that a breakdown in the synchrony between the external environment and the body's circadian rhythms is expressed as enlargement of the heart and the inadequate pumping of blood. It has been shown that particulate matter exposure impairs circadian rhythms, inducing obesity and diabetes. Importantly, studies of impaired circadian rhythm in shift workers or people with chronic sleep deprivation suggest that circadian disruption is a potent trigger of CVDs. This occurs, for example, in long haul truck drivers, a group with disproportionate rates of obesity and diabetes. Alertness while driving is a fundamental condition for road safety. The felt need for sleep grows stronger as a person's awake time increases. Demanding experiences like driving for long periods of time can increase sleep pressure and diminish cognitive functioning. Yet even when truck drivers take sleeping breaks, sleep interruption and insomnia are common because they have very stressful jobs and face pressing time demands (Lemke et al., 2016). An additional risk of truck driving is diesel fuel exposure. Breathing diesel fuel—a noxious cocktail of substances including diesel particulate matter, carbon dioxide and monoxide, nitrogen oxides, sulfur, formaldehyde, and benzene—has significant negative health effects. Long-term health effects of breathing diesel exhaust fumes for truckers include an increased risk of both cardiovascular and cardiopulmonary disease, respiratory disease, and cancer.

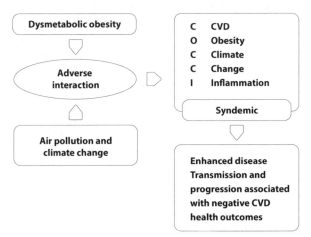

COCCI Syndemic

In light of the kinds of evidence described above, a group of osteopathic physicians at the Touro University College of Osteopathic Medicine in Vallejo, CA (Clearfield et al., 2018), have described the COCCI syndemic (involving CVD, obesity, climate change, and inflammation). Production of COCCI involves synergistic interactions between dysmetabolic obesity and atherosclerosis under environmental conditions of climate change and air pollution that enhance subclinical inflammation and subsequent CVD events. As these authors note, "The COCCI syndemic highlights the importance for the health care community to rise to the challenge to address this complex issue as both a social justice issue and a priority for overall public health and well-being" (Clearfield et al., 2014). Calling CVD in the twenty-first century part of a "new deadly quartet" involving obesity, metabolic syndrome, inflammation, and climate change, these physicians argue that "to complete this new quartet, the addition of increased exposure to elevated levels of particulate matter in the atmosphere may help elucidate why [the] cardiovascular pandemic continues, despite our concerted efforts" (Clearfield et al., 2014). COCCI is a social justice issue because this syndemic, they note, tends to be most common in ethnic minority and low-income populations. In the USA, COCCI is more prevalent in the Latino and Black populations than in the non-Hispanic white and populations of Asian descent. Globally, COCCI is linked with the concurrent environmental and socioeconomic stresses faced by low- and middle-income countries. Clearfield et al. (2018) note, "Wealthy energy-consuming nations are generally responsible for many, if not most, of these stresses, while many of the poorer countries may be the recipient of much of the increased risk."

A COVID-19 Ecosyndemic in Latin America

As noted earlier, while COVID-19 has impacted all regions and countries of the world, rather than constituting a single global syndemic involving environmental factors it is best understood as a set of complex and multilayered ecosyndemics under somewhat varying conditions of climate and other anthropogenic environmental changes. From this standpoint, Ramírez and Lee (2021) focus on climate factors and COVID-19 ecosyndemics in Latin America, including Brazil, Ecuador, but especially Peru. These countries have reported some of the highest incidence and death rates from COVID-19 in the wider region. They also face simultaneous synergistic threats from multiple other infectious diseases like dengue, malaria, leishmaniasis, and diarrheal and respiratory-related infections, especially during what are called El Niño-Southern Oscillation events that threaten Latin America every few years. El Niño (The Little Boy) is a colloquial Spanish term that expresses people's experience of the effects of recurring ocean–atmosphere interactions across the equatorial Pacific Ocean. Approximately every three to seven years, the surface waters of the tropical Pacific Ocean warm or cool several degrees, which is sufficient to have dramatic impacts. The occurrence and severity of El Niño-Southern Oscillation events is not predictable, but over the last 50 years highly impactful events occurred in 1972–1973, 1982–1983, 1997–1998, 2014–2016, and 2023–2024. Like a pendulum, an El Niño may be followed by a *La Niña (The Little Girl), which is a* cooling of the ocean surface. Usually, the stronger the La Niña event the cooler the ocean temperature. Peru, Ecuador, and Brazil are highly sensitive to El Niño-related hazards and subsequent disasters, including infectious disease epidemics because of the convergence and cascade of threats that often heighten health vulnerability.

Why are these weather oscillations called The Little Boy and The Little Girl? The pooling of warm water in the Pacific near South America commonly reaches its warmest point around Christmas time. The original colloquial name of the warming phase was El Niño de Navidad, which arose in the 1600s when Peruvian fishermen named the weather phenomenon after the baby Christ. Because El Niño caused fish to concentrate in the cold eddies near land, the change was viewed favorably as a heavenly gift. It made fishing much easier. La Niña was chosen simply to express the opposite conditions of El Niño. Of course a lot has changed since the 1600s. Most notably, the climate has changed, and ocean warming interacts adversely with Earth's weather oscillation patterns.

El Niño-Southern Oscillation is caused by changes in two belts of trade winds that encircle the planet. Typically, trade winds blow from east to west pushing warm surface ocean water and causing it to pile up in the Western Pacific near Indonesia. When these winds weaken, the warm waters push back toward South America, leading to the above average surface ocean temperatures that are characteristic of an El Niño event. When the trade winds strengthen, La Niña events occur. These oscillations are one of the most important climate phenomena that occur on Earth because of their ability to shift global atmospheric circulation, which, in turn, influences temperature and precipitation across the planet.

El Niño events often are associated with water, weather, and climate-related extremes and changes in seasonality that, in turn, influence local disease ecologies and the exposure of populations to infectious diseases. El Niño influence on disease transmission occurs through explicit ecological changes, including levels of rainfall and rising air and water temperatures. These weather shifts help propagate various infectious pathogens, while ushering in various environmental hazards, including floods, temperature extremes, windstorms, and droughts.

When it occurs, an El Niño complicates preexisting health burdens and heightens social vulnerabilities by disrupting access to drinkable water, sanitation, hygiene, adequate nutrition, and livelihoods. For example, in Peru, which is highly sensitive to El Niño events, people must cope with an ecosyndemic health burden that sharply rises during and following disruptive weather and extreme climate events. In El Niño-affected countries that were hard hit by COVID-19, a quarter of the healthcare facilities lack hand hygiene facilities, while Ecuador reports that several million residents are without basic handwashing facilities in their homes. In Brazil, one-third of schools lack facilities for handwashing. Further, many people work in informal sectors of the economy, and therefore, cannot minimize their exposure like those with the ability to remain at home. It is estimated that one in four persons in the region experienced severe health outcomes during the height of the spread of COVID-19 in 2020–2021 due to the growing prevalence of chronic underlying preconditions like diabetes and cancer. Together, COVID-19, other diseases that are disproportionately common among the poor like pneumonia, tuberculosis, and diabetes, and climate extremes have entwined magnifying adverse health outcomes for many Peruvians.

To examine this issue, Ramírez et al. (2018) used a computer system that analyzes and displays geographical information to assess an El Niño period in Piura, an area north of Peru's capital of Lima and adjacent to the Pacific Ocean. In 1998, Piura had a population of over 800,000 people. In this work, they used composite indices commonly employed in public health to characterize the well-being and vulnerability of populations and locations. In their effort, they mapped the geographic overlap of seven climate-sensitive infectious diseases (acute diarrheal diseases, cholera, acute respiratory infections, pneumonia, conjunctivitis, and two types of malaria) and used this information to construct an ecosyndemic morbidity index. They found there were over 80,000 reported cases of the targeted infectious diseases and an overall incidence rate of 9.5 per 1000 population during the initial study period (1982–1983). Prior to 1997–1998, the 1982–1983 El Niño was referred to as the biggest El Niño of the twentieth century. They then mapped and applied their findings onto a second El Niño event (during 1997–1998) as proof of concept. Their primary finding was that many of the districts they studied encountered multi-disease risks that were spatially clustered in 11 districts in western Piura. When they compared the ecosyndemic index in 1998 to 1983, they found a strong positive correlation, demonstrating the potential utility of their approach. Ramírez et al. (2018) also found that ecosyndemic disease burden correlated with urban density in low-lying areas affected flooding in Piura. Their research showed that urbanization (the percent of the population living in urban areas) and disaster damages (the number of people affected by floods) were significantly correlated with their ecosyndemic index. Ecological interactions with poverty also played a central role in disease exposures. In other words, multi-disease risk was contingent upon climate, which likely exacerbated social risks and heightened subsequent exposures to multiple infectious pathogens.

The Elder Health Ecosyndemics in the USA

Driven by the aging of the so-called Boomer generation, the US population is older in 2024 than it has ever been before. This population aging pattern is reflected in the fact that US Census Bureau data show that from 1980 to 2022 the median age of the population climbed from 30.0 to 38.9 years. The number of people aged 65 and older is projected to continue to increase, going from 58 million in 2022 to 82 million by 2050. This is a notable 47% increase. The percentage of people 65 and older is projected to rise from 17% to 23% by mid-century.

Furthermore, the overall profile of the elderly US population is changing. It is projected that between 2022 and 2050 the portion of the older population that identifies as non-Hispanic white will drop from 75% to 60%. Among adults aged 65 and older, about 17.5% of those identifying as Latino and African American lived in poverty in 2022. This is more than twice the rate of those who identified as non-Hispanic white (8%). Additionally, the share of divorced women aged 65 and older increased from 3% in 1980 to 15% in 2023, while for men it rose from 4% to 12% during the same period. Over one-fourth of women who are aged 65–74 lived alone in 2023. This share jumped to 39% among women aged 75–84, and to half among women aged 85 and older. This older population is increasingly alone and experiencing a care gap as their financial resources decline (Mather & Scommegna, 2024). In short, the group most often in need of help with basic personal care will nearly quadruple over the next 25 years and society is not ready.

The aging of the US population is unfolding in an era of significant climatic and other environmental change. A crisis is brewing as demographics and the environment meet in a disrupted world. Based on recognition of this dangerous trend, Janelle Christensen (2018) used an ecosyndemic framework to examine the consequences for elderly people in the USA during extreme weather events like hurricanes. The health conditions involved for this age group include underlying chronic diseases and disabilities common in older people, conditions that are especially present in the very elderly, including dementia. The social conditions in this ecosyndemic stem from the often poor economic status and geographic/social isolation of many elderly. Further, there is the social problem of reigning exclusionary "one-size-fits-all" disaster planning and limited support for the elderly during and after severe storms. According to critical disability theory, Christensen indicates that the social environment can be more disabling than actual physical impairment. This scenario played out during Hurricane Katrina where casualties were extremely high among the elderly. At the time of the hurricane, the elderly population of New Orleans, especially those in the Black community, was at more risk than any other social group, and greater numbers of elderly died during the storm and in the first year following the disaster than any other group. Society, in short, was not prepared for how to best deal with the special challenges faced by an aging population when the impacts of climate change hit hardest.

As an anthropologist, Christiansen approaches her study of how people with Alzheimer's disease and their informal (often family) caregivers prepare for hurricanes in Florida with a somewhat unique toolkit. Anthropology, she believes, is well situated to explore how a changing climate affects societies because of its holistic viewpoint. Anthropological researchers draw upon and inform not only the explanatory stories that provide humans meaning in their lives but they also investigate the relevant biological, ecology, and psychology factors, as well as social patterns and structures, political-economic, and historical contexts. In other words, in her work, Christiansen seeks to connect how the human body works biologically and socially within the context of its surrounding environment. During her research, it became clear to Christiansen that Alzheimer's disease is not the only chronic illness that affects older people during extreme weather events. The increasing loss of eyesight, which is part of the normal aging process, poses a significant challenge as intense storms make landfall. Experiencing chronic, long-term, progressive diseases makes evacuation particularly difficult and dangerous for the elderly. Furthermore, hurricanes are not the only threat older people face in a changing and increasingly chaotic climate. The combination of dense, largely elderly populations in coastal urban centers, as is the case in Southern Florida, risks creating "a perfect storm" of vulnerable situations. This perfect storm includes all the elements necessary to be labeled an ecosyndemic as vulnerability becomes adversely manifested as a cause of death.

Christiansen illustrates her argument through the presentation of a number of case studies. One such case is that of Lee and Lisa. Lee was 72 years old when he died in the aftermath of Hurricane Irma, which hit south Florida in 2017 and was the first Category 5 *hurricane* of an extremely active storm season. Lee had been admitted to Physicians Regional Hospital where he was treated for respiratory failure and internal bleeding. Years prior, Lee was diagnosed with heart disease and had poor circulation in his legs, which led to sores on his legs. The retired couple lived in a mobile home parked in a lower-income, fishing community. They knew from the news that they were living in a location predicted to be hit by Hurricane Irma; nonetheless they stayed and did not evacuate. Christiansen knew from her research, including many interviews and other data collection, that evacuating is expensive and physically difficult, especially for people like Lee with mobility limitations. Studies have shown that those who do not evacuate when hurricanes arrive tend to be older and have a past experience of successfully surviving a prior hurricane. These memories may have been on their minds as they considered the costs and benefits of staying or evacuating their home. To exacerbate their circumstances, the couple lacked the funds to insure their home although it was located in a climate-vulnerable area.

When Hurricane Irma arrived it tore through their community and damaged the couple's trailer. They survived but their trailer flooded, incurred extensive structural damage, and lost power. Still they remained. A few days after the hurricane hit, the local temperature reached 92 °F but the intense humidity made it feel even hotter. Their floors, walls, and bedding were damp, but they stayed in their trailer because there was no shelter or any temporary housing in town. Even if motel rooms had been available, they might not have been able to afford the cost. Instead, for five days, they tried to clean and sleep in their damp home. As the days passed, Lee had so much pain in his now blackened legs that they called an ambulance. He was taken to the hospital but by nightfall was in respiratory distress. He did not recover. Lee's death, in Christiansen's assessment, was likely the result of a complex interaction of emotional, physical, social, economic, and environmental factors that made him particularly vulnerable to certain diseases. Age, heat, underlying chronic illnesses, poor housing conditions, all amplified by the disaster, also contributed to Lee's cause of death.

Lee's death affirms that "[p]overty attracts an unfortunate abundance of risks. By contrast, the wealthy (in income, power, and education) can purchase safety and freedom from risk" (Beck, 1992). Disasters and associated ecosyndemics rarely have the same consequences for all people in a society in the same ways. The elderly, because of resource limitations, cognitive decline, physical ailments, and isolation, are disproportionately in harm's way and their vulnerability is magnified by the lack of societal preparation for their needs in a disaster. It is for this reason that archaeologist Jago Cooper (2012) titled a chapter in his book *Surviving Sudden Environmental Climate Change*: *"Fail to Prepare, Then Prepare to Fail."* Yet, it must be emphasized that the way age is measured and defined in Western societies is not shared in other places with different cultural traditions. How age and social roles are viewed differs across cultures, and also shapes the ways laws and policies are written and influence what is prioritized, including during disasters. Moreover, not all people over the age of 65 suffer from a disease or are cognitively or physically disabled. Some older adults, however, might be categorized as "frail," and it is these people who are particularly vulnerable during a disaster. Fernandez et al. (2002) define the frail elderly as "individuals aged 65 and older with physical, cognitive, social, psychological, and/or economic circumstances that will likely limit their ability to perform, or have performed for them, one or more" common activities of daily living. Frailty can be an overwhelming challenge in an era of ever more common ecosyndemics.

While the effort to develop an ecosyndemic lens on the health consequences of climate change is nascent, Christiansen's study suggests the value of the ecosyndemic approach for understanding and addressing the rapidly arriving and accumulating changes occurring as a result of human-wrought disruptions on Earth. While many components of a syndemic play out at the macrolevel (e.g., the actions of multinational fossil fuel companies), the adverse impacts are felt directly at the microlevel of human experience and misery, sometimes most intensely by those who face the dual challenges of being frail in an unprepared social world.

Adverse Pathogen–Pathogen Interaction in Ecosyndemics

Abu-Raddad et al. (2008) draw attention to one of the most theoretically challenging problems facing infectious disease epidemiology, namely "that of interacting strains of the same pathogen, such as influenza… or dengue…, or interacting diseases such as HIV/AIDS and malaria…, at both the population and intrahost levels." Co-infection by more than one disease-causing pathogen can be either simultaneous or sequenced. From a clinical standpoint, four primary patterns of such co-infection have been described:

- *Noninterference* occurs when co-infecting pathogens do not appear to interact. They are fellow travelers but do not affect each other. For example, influenza viruses primarily infect the upper and lower respiratory tracts, while human papillomavirus infection is mainly found on the skin, mouth, nasal cavity, and genitals. Found in different body tissues, the two viruses have no known intersection.
- *Interference* occurs when one pathogen competes to suppress the replication of another, or what has been termed a countersyndemic. For example, SARS-CoV-2, the virus that causes COVID-19, can effectively inhibit the replication of multiple respiratory viruses.
- *Synergy* occurs when one pathogen enhances the access, replication, or pathogenicity of other pathogens (or both are enhanced by the interaction). Synergy

complicates the symptoms and diagnosis of a disease and is the basis of infectious disease syndemics.
- *Dependence assistance* arises in viral cases where one of the involved viruses, such as hepatitis D (which causes potentially severe liver infection), has an incomplete genome and cannot complete its replication cycle by itself. Instead, it requires the assistance of a "helper virus," in this case hepatitis B virus, to complete its life cycle. Dependence assistance is considered a syndemic interaction because it enhances disease.

Various virulence factors in human infection may be significantly affected by interplay across strains and species of microorganisms during co-infection. Although a relatively new field, the study of pathogen–pathogen interaction (PPI) is emerging as a productive arena of new research and new knowledge in health and clinical care. The list of identified PPIs that contribute to the total health burden of human populations in specific times and locations has grown rapidly in recent years. The following four examples reveal the complexities and health consequences of this interaction.

Legionnaires' Disease

Examination of several examples of PPI opens a window on the similarities and differences in the pathways and outcomes of synergistic interactions among the diverse array of human pathogens that perpetuate disease. The first of these examples involves amoeba/bacteria interactions. Awareness has been mounting for some time about the role amoeba (unicellular organisms capable of altering their shape) play in facilitating bacterial infection. This interaction is seen in the case of Legionnaires' disease, a severe and potentially deadly form of pneumonia involving lung inflammation. People become infected by inhaling the bacteria *Legionella pneumophila* from water or soil. Upon transmission to humans, the bacteria enters and replicates inside amoeba-like macrophages, which are cells of the immune system that can be found in the lungs. This is possible because of a needle-like structure in the plasma membrane of *the bacteria* called Dot/ICM. This structure is used to inject bacterial proteins from the *Legionella* into an amoeba or a macrophage. These bacterial proteins interfere with normal cellular activities of both types of host, preventing them from consuming *Legionella* while creating the conditions that allow the bacteria to both survive and multiply.

Older adults and people with COPD, diabetes, and cancer, as well as people with weakened immune systems, caused by other infections are particularly susceptible to the disease. Eduardo Piqueiras (2021) in his ethnographic study of Legionnaires' disease among the working poor in the South Bronx, New York, found that another interaction involved depression. Participants in his study, which included 36 older adults ranging in age from 55 to 65, talked regularly about feelings of loneliness. These feelings centered on grieving the loss of loved ones, the loneliness of being housebound with few social interactions, the loneliness created by a rapidly changing cityscape due to gentrification, and the deep loneliness of feeling abandoned. Piqueiras presents the case of Ronald, who told him:

> when I first got sick and finally decided to go to the doctor, it was hard. I couldn't breathe good and I didn't have anyone to take me to the doctor, so I had to walk over to the subway stop which is only a couple of blocks away but it was under construction and closed, so I ended up walking a few more blocks to take the bus. The problem was that the three blocks between the subway stop and the bus were all under construction and the only way to get there was on the street along with the construction barriers with lots of traffic on the street and broken dangerous pavement which made it hard to navigate with my cane.

Ronald revealed the link between depression and Legionnaires' disease in his life, saying: "I've been depressed man, I haven't gone to a doctor about it or anything but that is because the last time I went to talk to someone about depression I was put on a waiting list for 3 months to talk to someone" (Piqueiras (2021). Depression and structural barriers on the way to and in healthcare settings cause people to delay treatment, seriously complicating their health problems.

Legionnaires' disease was discovered as the USA was celebrating the bicentennial in 1976 when an outbreak occurred among people attending a convention of the American Legion in Philadelphia. During the convention, 600 Legionnaires stayed at the Bellevue-Stratford Hotel, a frequent site for conventions. The cause of the outbreak was ultimately linked to the hotel's air conditioning cooling units. Medical authorities were baffled when over 200 convention-goers fell ill with what at first appeared to be very severe cold symptoms, including high fever, coughing, chest pains, and difficulty breathing. Ultimately, 34 American Legion members died during the outbreak. Based on epidemiological research it became clear that previous outbreaks by unknown pathogens were, in fact, what was now dubbed Legionnaires' disease. In an initial report on Legionnaires' disease, Timothy Rowbotham (1980) of the University of Leeds discussed the capacity of *Legionella pneumophila* bacteria, the causal agent of the disease, to multiply inside of an amoeba. He proposed that "an amoeba, full of legionellae, rather than free legionellae, could be the infective particle for man" (Rowbotham, 1980). This insightful idea was based on research findings indicating that both microorganisms can cohabitate in water cooling towers, evaporative condensers, and other man-made and natural water systems. While amoebas normally feed on bacteria by engulfing them, a process known as phagocytosis, Rowbotham reported that *L. pneumophila* bacteria can survive inside amoebas after being consumed. Consequently, they are called amoeba-resisting bacteria, a capacity acquired evolutionarily over millions of years of interaction. Amoebas, as a result, can serve as an environmental reservoir for bacterial pathogens enabling them to infect mammals, including humans. Bacteria grown inside amoebae exhibit changes in biochemistry, physiology, and virulence potential compared to those grown outside of amoebae. These changes include enhanced resistance to antibiotics and an increased ability to infect mammalian cells. In addition, amoebae can act as a "Trojan horse" or vector that carries bacteria into a human or nonhuman animal host. Further, horizontal gene transfer can occur in genetic material between the two organisms, which is, in this case, a bidirectional exchange where both partners have gained genes from each other.

This interaction is significant for health as over 100 human pathogens not only are able to survive but even to proliferate when in contact with various species of amoeba. The common bacteria, *Mycobacterium avium*, for example, a tuberculosis-related species, a common cause of systemic infection in people with AIDS, has a greater ability to cross through body tissues and to replicate when amoebae are present. Moreover, researchers have found that *M. avium* grown inside amoebae is more virulent than bacteria grown in a petri dish. There is, as well, evidence that the development of amoeba resistance in bacteria may enhance the disease-causing capacity in amoebae. In other words, the impact of the bacteria/amoebae interaction may be bidirectional with both pathogens gaining virulence through their interface. While it is clear that amoebae can play a role in the spread of bacterial diseases like Legionnaire's disease, social factors also appear to be at play as well. While Legionnaire's disease outbreaks have been reported in diverse indoor and outdoor settings, over time there has been an increase in outbreaks at automotive plants, plants that cool molded plastics with water, food manufacturing facilities, soap factories, wastewater treatment plants, and at prisons, settings disproportionately populated by poor and working people. The rise in Legionnaires' disease occurrence among working people in industrial settings, as well as among incarcerated people, highlights the importance of considering both biological and social relations in PPI, including sociopolitical issues in the passage of occupational health and safety regulations and their enforcement.

HIV/HCV Co-infection

The emergence in the early 1980s of HIV/AIDS dramatically magnified awareness of the major health implications of PPI. Since that time, it has become apparent that HIV interacts adversely with various other pathogens and that these connections helped to shape the global AIDS pandemic. Among patients with HIV/AIDS, a significant co-infection involves hepatitis C virus (HCV). Both HIV and HCV are viral, but from different virus families, and both are blood-borne (although HIV can also be transmitted through sexual contact, a rarer occurrence with HCV). HIV infects cells of the immune system, while HCV is a liver infection. Without treatment, HCV can cause liver cancer or severe liver damage that can proceed to complete liver failure.

In the USA, it is estimated that over three million people are infected with chronic hepatitis C, compared to about 1.2 million infected with HIV. Globally, it is estimated that 40 million people are infected with HIV compared to 180 million who are infected with HCV. Among these, approximately five million people are co-infected with HIV/HCV.

The origin of HCV in human infection remains unclear, but like HIV, it appears to have a zoonotic history. The closest viral relatives of HCV among nonhuman animals have been found in horses and donkeys (known as equine hepaciviruses). Genetic analysis of the several strains of HCV suggests it is at least 3000 years old and began with domestication and close human contact with these animals. In short, while both HIV and HCV spread from animals to humans, they have their roots in different parts of the world and only came together as a dangerous co-infection recently as a result of human behaviors and social patterns.

HCV spreads primarily through contact with the blood of a person who has HCV. A frequent route of this happening is through multiple-person use of syringes or other injection drug equipment (i.e., direct or indirect sharing syringes or other drug paraphernalia). Thus, in most cases, dually infected individuals are current or former injectors of illicit drugs. Among people who inject illicit drugs, HCV spreads much more rapidly than HIV, often during the initial phase of illicit drug injection. While new injectors are being taught by more experienced users how to inject successfully into a vein, the risk of co-infection stems from the marginalization and lack of access to treatment among injection drug users.

The negative health outcomes of co-infection appear to stem from the inability of the immune system to contain HCV after infection with HIV. It remains uncertain whether HCV accelerates HIV progression, but CD4 T lymphocyte cells, which are targeted by HIV, may be lower in a number in people who are co-infected with HIV and HCV compared to people who only have HIV infection (Lin et al., 2013). Both cirrhosis and liver cancer develop at a younger age among individuals who are dually infected with HCV and HIV. A meta-analysis of existing research found that patients with HCV/HIV co-infection have a three times greater risk of progression to cirrhosis or decompensated liver disease than people with HCV alone.

Tick-Borne Diseases

Tick-transmitted infections are the most common vector-borne diseases in the USA. They are also the most common vector-borne diseases in other locations not heavily impacted by malaria, which is also a very prevalent vector-borne disease. Already found throughout the USA, tick-borne diseases (TBDs) are increasing in geographic range as various tick species spread to new areas and cause significant outbreaks. The state of Indiana, for example, a long-time home to the dog tick, the vector of Rocky Mountain spotted fever, has experienced an intrusion of both Lyme disease caused by the black-legged tick (*Ixodes scapularis*) and the lone-star tick (*Amblyomma americanum*), both vectors of human ehrlichiosis. In recent decades, tick-borne disease epidemics have occurred in central and eastern Europe, India, Turkey, and Russia. Some outbreaks have produced high fatality rates or caused long-term morbidity and suffering raising considerable public health and popular alarm.

At first glance, ticks appear to be insects, but they are actually arachnids, relatives of spiders and scorpions. At least 12 species of ticks can transmit diseases caused by a range of pathogens including bacteria, rickettsia (a distinct group of bacteria), viruses, and protozoa. Some of the most common diseases caused by the pathogens spread by ticks are Lyme disease, Rocky Mountain spotted fever, babesiosis, ehrlichiosis, anaplasmosis, tularemia, Colorado tick fever, tick-borne relapsing fever, and Powassan disease (Rochlin & Toledo, 2020). The ability of the infectious agents of TBDs to infect, survive, and reproduce in ticks and animal/human hosts might, if disease was not the outcome, be admired as a celebrated wonder of evolutionary development.

Considerable attention has been directed at Lyme disease, which is caused in most causes by the bacterium *Borrelia burgdorferi*. Lyme disease is recognized as the most frequent tick-borne disease in both North America and Europe and is one of the most rapidly spreading infectious diseases across the USA. Epidemiological estimates suggest that almost half a million people are diagnosed and treated for Lyme disease each year in the USA. Lyme disease during pregnancy can lead to infection of the placenta. The spread of Lyme disease from mother to fetus is possible but quite rare. If untreated, Lyme disease can produce a wide range of symptoms, depending on the stage of infection. These include fever, rash, facial paralysis, an irregular heartbeat, and arthritis. In all, over a hundred different symptoms have been recorded, and symptoms change as the disease spreads to different parts of the body. Infection can spread to the joints, the heart, and the nervous system. Late-stage Lyme disease, which can occur in some people even after treatment, develops when the bacteria have spread throughout the body causing neurologic damage and cognitive impairment, difficulty sleeping, severe fatigue, swollen knees, and mental fogginess. The precise causes of persistent Lyme disease remain unresolved.

It has been confirmed that the black-legged *Ixodes* tick (or deer tick) that transmits *Borrelia burgdorferi* often carries and can simultaneously transmit several additional human pathogens, including *Anaplasma phagocytophilum*, the cause of immune-damaging granulocytic anaplasmosis, *Ehrlichia muris,* which causes ehrlichiosis, an infection with flu-like symptoms, and *Babesia microti*, a protozoan parasite that can trigger a malaria-like disease known as babesiosis. Transmission is through a tick bites, as seen in (Fig. 3.1). Furthermore, Ixodes ticks are known to transmit the Powassan virus. Illness linked to this pathogen, which derives its name from the Canadian town of Powassan, Ontario, although still rare, has been increasing in recent years. Most US cases are in the northeast and Great Lakes regions. Initially causing fever, headache, vomiting, and weakness, confusion, and seizures, Powassan virus infection can lead to severe disease, including encephalitis (swelling of the brain) and meningitis (inflammation of the membranes around the brain and spinal cord). In both Europe and Asia, Ixodes ticks transmit additional encephalitis-causing viruses.

Ticks transmit these pathogens during the process of feeding. To prepare for feeding, ticks pick a place to wait for a host on the tips of grasses and shrubs, a behavior called "questing." They identify potential hosts by detecting their breath and body odors, or by sensing body heat, moisture, and vibrations. When they come in contact with a potential host, namely an animal or human body, ticks crawl aboard and seek a feeding spot (often where the skin is thinnest), grasp the skin, and cut into it. Into this opening, the tick inserts its feeding tube. Many tick species secrete a cement-like substance that helps keep them firmly in place during their blood

Adverse Pathogen–Pathogen Interaction in Ecosyndemics

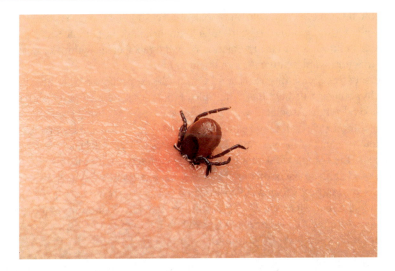

Fig. 3.1 Embedded tick

meal. Some feeding tubes are armed with barbs which also help keep the tick securely in place. Moreover, ticks can secrete small amounts of their saliva, which contains anesthetic properties so that the animal or person does not feel the tick. Tick saliva also contains biochemical compounds that increase blood flow, prevent clotting, and suppress the host's immune response. Depending on the species and stage of development, ticks suck in blood for anywhere from minutes to days. If the host already has a blood-borne infection, the tick will ingest the pathogens with its blood meal. If the tick picked up any pathogens from the host, it is able to transmit them to a new host at its next feeding. It is the tick's saliva that transmits pathogens to the host. The host, however, suffers the consequences of pathogen damage to body organs and tissues, patterns that vary based on the pathogens involved. For example, pathogens in the *Rickettsia* genus initially target endothelial cells, which cause severe vascular injury, while pathogens in the *Babesia group* infect red blood cells, where they reproduce asexually. *During their evolutionary journey, tick-borne pathogens have developed* mechanisms to manipulate the immune systems' protective responses of both their tick vectors and animal/human host to facilitate the infection and transmission of the disease.

Co-habitation of ticks by several different human pathogens has been observed in the laboratory and in one field study of tick populations over 70% of collected ticks were found to be co-infected with both *B. burgdorferi* and *B. microti*. A study of the *Ixodes persulcatus* tick in Mongolia found that the frequency of co-infections was very high, with about one-third of all infected ticks being co-infected with two or more pathogens. The vast majority of co-infections were caused by two pathogens, and no ticks were found to be infected with more than three pathogens (Lagunova et al., 2022). Feng et al. report (2023), "With ticks able to transmit several pathogens in one bite, co-infections may be 'the rule, not the exception.'

Comorbid human infection with more than one tick-borne pathogen is often detected worldwide. Co-infection is of particular human health importance and is getting increased attention due to the interaction of pathogen species within the host, which makes diagnosis and treatment more challenging."

In discussing Lyme disease, David Owen (2006) proposed what he called "the jigsaw hypothesis," namely that "multiple coinfections are invariably present in the clinical syndromes associated with Lyme disease and … that these act synergistically in complex ways. It may be that patterns of coinfection and host factors are the main determinants of the variable clinical features of Lyme disease" and the source of some of the complexities that have been encountered with this disease. In other words, the health impacts of Lyme disease are the result of syndemic interaction among two or more pathogens in co-infected ticks (Singer & Bulled, 2016). This is the understanding espoused by TBD-sufferer Pamela Weintraub, author of *Cure Unknown: Inside the Lyme Epidemic*, based on her own illness experience and that of other family members. In Weintraub's view:

> [In the] community of [tick-borne disease] patients are the coinfected: those with babesiosis, anaplasmosis, ehrlichiosis, or some other tick-borne infection. Surveys around the country report that ticks can transmit these well-known human diseases, yet primary care physicians almost never consider or test for them, even if they seriously consider Lyme disease. I think they need to determine the suite of possible diseases Lyme disease patients may be carrying because … those patients can be very sick and resistant to treatment specifically because their illness isn't just Lyme disease (Weintraub, 2011).

This raises the issue of the role of pathogen–pathogen syndemic interaction across the multi-disease TBD spectrum. Are syndemics a key driver of illness among people bitten by ticks? If this is the case, are there key environmental issues propelling the spread of what would appropriately be called TBD ecosyndemics?

It has become increasingly clear that changing weather conditions are providing disease-carrying ticks additional time to reproduce, opportunities to expand their habitats, and conditions that favor the spread of diseases. Because of the warming of once cooler areas, the geographic ranges where the ticks that cause Lyme disease, anaplasmosis, ehrlichiosis, and spotted fever rickettsiosis have expanded. Researchers predict that because of climate-related changes in weather, TBD frequency will continue to increase (Singer & Bulled, 2016). Overall, vector-borne diseases like those initiated by ticks have been identified as one of the biggest health threats produced by climate change. For example, the rapid expansion of cases of Lyme disease cases reported in the USA since the 1990s led the Environmental Protection Agency to track this TBD as one of their key health and society climate change indicators. Because ticks spend much of their lives on the forest floor—where prevailing temperature and humidity levels shape their survival—they are highly sensitive to changes in the climate. The CDC reports that Lyme disease "hotspots" in the Northeastern and upper Midwestern regions of the USA increased by more than 320% between 1993 and 2012. During this time, the number of counties in the USA reporting black-legged ticks has more than doubled. Explains Frank Curriero, a professor of epidemiology at the Johns Hopkins Bloomberg School of Public Health and director of Spatial Science for Public Health, "Your home—and by that I mean the surrounding geography, including the environment, demographics, and your behavior—all can have an impact on exposure to Lyme" (quoted in Cimon, 2022).

Over time, the surrounding environment in the places people live and the hospitality of that environment to ticks has changed significantly. In the Northeast USA, for example, during the nineteenth century, people cut down millions of trees for timber and to facilitate deer-hunting for food. As a result, deer populations collapsed across the region as there was nowhere for the deer to hide or raise their young. Beginning in the 1920s, as people left their farms for the city, a reversal occurred. While the trees were not the native species but imported species, reforestation of cut-over places occurred and continued for the next 50 years. The deer population bounced back, and people started getting Lyme disease, including in Lyme, Connecticut, which gave the disease its name. As they came back, the deer ventured closer to the appealing lawns and shrubbery of the suburban housing developments that also brought people back to less urban areas. Deer, considered the keystone host for the black-legged tick, brought the disease-bearing arachnids with them, ever closer to people. Another tick host primary pathogen reservoir that proliferated was the white-footed mouse. Its abundant population growth occurred because when the remaining areas of forest were cut to build housing or roadways, ecosystems were fractured and could not support the fox, owl, and other predator species that feed on mice. For many larval or nymph ticks, their first host is a mouse. Mice bring ticks near to and inside of homes, where they can drop from mice and move to a human host.

In other research, Solveig Jore et al. (2014) found that the disease-carrying black-legged ticks have spread to an ever wider geographic range and at higher altitudes in mountainous areas because of climate change. Jore and colleagues examined the relationship between the distribution of infected ticks and microclimatic conditions at a series of data collection points situated along the southern coast of Norway. They reported that the level of humidity has a substantial impact on the ability of the tick-borne encephalitis virus to survive and reproduce in ticks and be transmitted to humans in areas where the tick previously was absent. These researchers conclude that "Expected climate changes accentuate ... the need for considering climate variability effects upon ticks and tick-borne pathogens" (Jore et al., 2014). Supporting the finding of Jore and co-workers, Munderloh and Kurtti (2011: 148) report that "areas that are likely to experience increased or prolonged seasonal tick activity are ... those located at the current extremes of the current range of distribution, areas where climate change will be felt most acutely." Of critical importance, in other words, is climate warming along the cold boundaries of a species' existing distribution, such as the changes that are now promoting the movement of *Ixodes scapularis*, a Lyme disease tick vector, from the USA into Canada and tick-borne encephalitis in higher altitudes in Slovakia (Ogden et al., 2013).

In Canada, Lyme-carrying ticks have tended to be concentrated in southern areas along the US border, especially in New Brunswick, Nova Scotia, southern Ontario, southern Quebec, southern Manitoba, and some parts of British Columbia. Rising temperatures and changing landscape ecology are beginning to change this pattern.

Tick populations are increasingly migrating northward, to areas they could not survive in the past. The number of Lyme cases in Canada grew by ninefold between 2012 and 2021. Theresa Tam, Canada's chief public health officer, highlighted Lyme disease as a condition to monitor in her 2022 report on the state of public health in the country, writing: "There are more ticks, more infected ticks and more people getting in contact with them" (quoted in Rehman, 2024).

This body of research and other findings indicate, as the US Department of Health and Human Services (2024) affirms:

- Increasing temperatures due to climate change can influence tick life cycles and increase the ability of ticks to reproduce. This change, in turn, can lead to bigger tick populations and greater risk of tick-borne pathogens spreading from tick bites to people.
- Milder winters and warmer early spring temperatures expand the seasonal frame during which ticks are active, resulting in more weeks of the year that people are at risk of tick bites.
- Changing climate patterns alter the natural environment and historic ecological relationships. The distribution and density of the wildlife ticks feed on (such as deer and small rodents) is changing, which can lead to an expanded geographic distribution across latitudes, longitudes, and altitudes of the diseases and associated with ticks.
- Expanding tick ranges and increasing cases of TBDs are also linked to changes in human land-use patterns, such as forest fragmentation and suburban housing development, which can increase the opportunities for humans to be exposed to ticks and the diseases they spread.

Malaria and Intestinal Parasites

Malaria is an infectious disease that is spread when a female mosquito bites an infected person sucking in their blood (to nourish her eggs), and the infected mosquito subsequently bites a noninfected person and injects in the pathogens that are floating in the mosquito's saliva. When this happens, malaria parasites enter the second person's bloodstream and travel to the liver. When the parasites reach maturity, they leave the liver and infect red blood cells. The most common parasites causing malaria in humans are from the species *Plasmodium falciparum*. This is the most virulent malaria parasite and is responsible for the majority of malaria deaths globally. *Plasmodium vivax* is a related cause of malaria. In infections with the latter parasite, the pathogen can lie dormant in the liver and be reactivated at a later date without any subsequent mosquito bites, leading to what is called relapsing malaria. Three other members of the *Plasmodium* genus, namely, *P. ovale*, *P. malariae*, and *P. knowlesi*, also cause malaria.

It is estimated by the World Health Organization (WHO) that in 2022 about 250 million cases of malaria occurred in 85 malaria-endemic countries (Venkatesan, 2024). This translates to 58 cases of malaria per 1000 population risk. This is a jump from 2019 when there were an estimated 233 million global cases. Of the cases of malaria in 2022, approximately 94% were in Africa, with Nigeria (27%), the Democratic Republic of the Congo (12%), Uganda (5%), and Mozambique (4%) accounting for nearly half of all cases. However, the largest increase in cases from 2021 to 2022 occurred in Pakistan, which saw about 2.5 million cases in 2022 compared with 500,000 cases the year before. What changed? Most of the cases in Pakistan in 2022 were the result of the devastating floods that hit the country between June and October of that year. Linked to climate change, flooding caused a fivefold increase in the malaria case load. Nearby countries that had not reported locally transmitted cases for several years, such as Iran, suffered more than 1000 cases in 2022. The WHO highlights climate change as a substantial risk to progress in controlling and reducing rates of malaria. Extreme weather events such as flooding and heatwaves are linked to malaria outbreaks and increased transmission. It is estimated that over 600,000 deaths occurred globally due to malaria in 2022, a mortality rate of over 14 deaths per 100,000 population at risk for infection. Over half of all malaria deaths occurred in four countries: Nigeria (31%), the Democratic Republic of the Congo (12%), Niger (6%), and Tanzania (4%).

Symptoms of malaria range from mild to life-threatening. Mild symptoms, most common in people who have had malaria before, include fever, chills, and headache. Severe symptoms include extreme fatigue, confusion, impaired consciousness, seizures, jaundice, dark or bloody urine, and encumbered breathing. Symptoms usually set in within 10–15 days of being bitten by an infected mosquito, as seen in Fig. 3.2. Malaria is associated with a decrease in body iron levels, destruction of infected red blood cells, a shortened lifespan of blood cells that are not infected, and decreased production of blood cells in the bone marrow, all of which lead to anemia. Our bodies need iron for growth and development. It is used to produce both

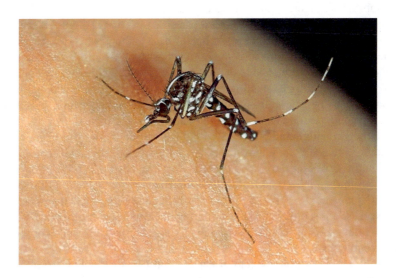

Fig. 3.2 Biting mosquito

hemoglobin, a protein found in red blood cells that carries oxygen from the lungs to all parts of the body, and myoglobin, another protein, which supplies oxygen to our muscles. Iron is also used to make some needed hormones.

Those who are at highest risk of getting very sick and dying from malaria include:

- People with little or no recent exposure to malaria parasites. This can include young children under five years of age (claiming a child's life every 30 seconds) and pregnant women (who may suffer premature delivery or delivery of a baby with low birth weight), as well as travelers coming from areas without malaria.
- People with a preexisting disease that compromises the immune system like HIV/AIDS.
- People who have been frequently exposed to the bites of infected mosquitoes.
- People who live in rural areas with limited access to health care.
- The poor endure the largest toll from malaria as they are the least able to afford preventive measures like insecticide-treated bed nets and often cannot afford medical treatment. Hence malaria is often referred to as "a disease of the poor."

In addition to its health impacts, malaria impoverishes individuals, families, and households, and damages national economies by lowering worker productivity. Countries with high rates of malaria transmission have historically had lower economic growth than countries without the disease. It is estimated the disease has slowed economic growth in sub-Saharan Africa by 1.3% a year as a result of lost life and lower productivity. Consequently, economists refer to malaria as a "growth penalty." In Tanzania, for example, malaria accounts for 30% of the country's national disease and for 43% of under-five outpatient attendance, 35% of under-five hospital admissions, and 37% of under-five hospital deaths (European Alliance Against Malaria, 2008).

In sub-Saharan Africa, malaria has overlapping distribution with another prevalent infectious threat to health: intestinal parasitic infections (IPIs). IPIs are caused by helminths (worms) or protozoa, or both. These pathogens rely on human hosts (particularly their guts) to hatch, grow, and flourish. Once inside the host's body, helminths like hookworm, a kind of round worm, attach themselves by their mouth to the lining of the upper small intestine, where they feed on blood and produce substances that keep blood from clotting. They spread from person to person when an unsuspecting person unknowingly and unintentionally ingests their microscopic eggs. Infection with helminths (which is called helminthiasis) is a major cause of morbidity, especially in impoverished social groups. The incidence of IPIs is approximately 50% in developed countries but reaches up to 95% in developing nations, with the highest burden of these infections globally being in sub-Saharan Africa (Njunda et al., 2015). IPIs are most common in the tropical parts of Africa because these areas often are characterized by the conditions that support transmission, including a humid climate, unsanitary living environments, and poor socioeconomic conditions.

Due to the geographic overlap in malaria and IPIs distribution, co-infection is common. Co-infection produces various effects in the host. Children suffering from dual infection exhibit developmental and learning problems, as well as increased susceptibility to other infections. Individuals co-infected with more than one parasite species are at heightened risk of morbidity as well as an increased risk of developing more frequent and more severe disease. Concomitant infection with malaria and IPIs also is associated with anemia. Independent of malaria, both hookworm and whipworm cause anemia by promoting blood and iron loss in the intestinal tract. Co-infection with malaria magnifies the severity of anemia. In other words, malaria and some IPIs interact adversely, thereby increasing the health burden of an infected population.

In the Southwest region of Cameroon in Central Africa, Anna Njunda et al. (2015) in the Department of Medical Laboratory Sciences at the University of Buea implemented a cross-sectional study to determine the prevalence of co-infection with malaria and intestinal parasites. Their goal was to assess the association of co-infection with anemia in children ten years old or younger who were not on any antimalarial or antiparasitic drugs for at least two weeks prior to enrollment. Participants were children with fevers who were admitted to the district hospital between April and October of 2012. Blood and stool samples were collected from 411 participants. Hemoglobin concentration was determined and a complete blood count was performed for each child. Samples were screened to detect malaria parasites and intestinal parasitic infections. They found a prevalence of malaria in almost all the participants (98.5%). Only six children were not infected with malaria. IPIs occurred in 11.9% of participants, and there was co-infection of malaria and IPI in 11.9% of participants. In other words, almost all of the children infected with intestinal parasites were also co-infected with malaria. The rate of IPI was lower than comparable studies elsewhere, including Cameroon, Ethiopia, and Thailand, which might be attributed to regular deworming campaigns run by the Ministry of Public Health in study areas. The children were found to be infected with several different intestinal parasite species, including *Ascaris lum bricoides* (a roundworm) (73.5%), *Entamoeba histolytica/dispar* (18.4%), and hookworm (8.2%). Infection with more than one intestinal parasite was not observed in the study. Meanwhile, anemia was observed in 44.8% of the children. The prevalence of severe anemia was 13%, 14.8%, and 14.8% among those participants with malaria, IPIs, and malaria and IPI co-infection, respectively. Anemia and IPIs were significantly associated with age. Anemia was most prevalent in children under five years of age, while IPIs were more prevalent in children between five and 10 years of age. A significant adverse correlation was found between density of malaria parasites and hemoglobin. This is because as the parasite density increases, there is an increasing destruction of red blood cells and an eventual decrease in hemoglobin. While the findings are suggestive, because malaria, which on its own can cause anemia, was so high and IPIs so low, it was not possible to establish definitively an ecosyndemic pattern in this population.

In a study of hookworm and malaria co-infections among early twentieth-century colonial plantation workers in British Malaya, James Webb (2002), a historian, investigated another possible ecosyndemic involving these pathogens. As noted in Chap. 2, the newly formed Rockefeller Foundation initiated a campaign to eradicate hookworm disease, malaria, and yellow fever. To begin this effort, the Foundation began an overseas survey of hookworm infections through correspondence with American representatives abroad. They sought to determine if hookworm disease in tropical and subtropical environments was the source of a significant economic burden for colonial regimes. In 1913, the Foundation created an International Health Commission to extend its hookworm initiative. At the time, the colonial government and its economic partners in British Malaya were in the midst of massive ecological conversion to enhance profits from Malayan soil. British, Chinese, and Indian capitalists in Malaya organized workers to cut down both highland and lowland rainforests in order to establish rubber plantations. The laborers initially worked under difficult conditions, with poor housing and nutrition, and were soon subject to intense malarial infections. The death rates on some plantations rose as high as 10% of the workforce. This environmental transformation was a response to the demand for rubber during World War I. During the war, motor vehicles gained a key role as transport facilities for troops and equipment. These vehicles needed tires made of rubber, which consequently became a raw material of strategic importance. The plantation economies of the British colonies of Malaya and Ceylon dominated the profitable rubber market. While the term had not yet been coined, Rockefeller personnel discovered what today would be called an anemia syndemic among Tamil and Chinese laborers involving hookworm and malarial co-infection. Confronted with several failures in its effort in Malaya, including continual re-infection with hookworm after treatment and realization that hookworm was not acting alone in causing illness but in concert with malaria, the Rockefeller Foundation dropped its hookworm initiative and avoided identifying an intervention against ecosyndemic anemia. According to Webb (2022), "As historians engage with [the syndemics] paradigm to understand disease patterns, they will play an important role in unveiling and interpreting the history of the biosocial contexts in which syndemics occur."

The Ecosyndemics of Childhood Diarrhea

Globally, diarrhea is the third leading cause of death in children under 5 years of age. Children from poor and marginalized communities are particularly at risk. During childhood, frequent and prolonged episodes of diarrhea—lasting several days—have deleterious and irreversible effects on physical and cognitive development by directly diminishing the intestinal absorption of nutrients that are necessary for optimal growth and development of the body, brain, and neuronal synapses that influence a child's future potential. During the early postnatal years, a child's developing brain increasingly needs critical nutrients, including zinc, iron, and fatty acids. Repeated diarrhea infections, however, contribute to long-term intestinal damage that diminishes nutrient absorption. Research has identified a link between repeated episodes of diarrhea and cognitive deficits amounting to a loss of up to 10 intelligence quotient points and 12 months of schooling by age nine. Ten points on a 100-point standardized cognitive test are generally considered to be an important difference in cognitive performance. A study of a cohort of children from 0 to 24 months living in a shantytown in the state of Ceará (population approximately six million) in northeast Brazil found early childhood diarrhea had effects on children's intellectual function well into later childhood (Pinkerton et al., 2016). Growth deficits (stunting or reduced height for age) also have been shown to be a consequence of childhood diarrhea (Troeger et al., 2018).

Diarrheal disease is defined as the passage of three or more loose or liquid stools per day (or more frequent passage than is normal for the individual). Diarrhea can cause severe dehydration, leaving the body without the water and salts (sodium, chloride, potassium, and bicarbonate) that are necessary for survival. Children are especially vulnerable to the various infectious diseases that cause diarrhea because of the immaturity of their immune systems, as seen in Fig. 3.3. This biological vulnerability is enhanced by the common impacts of long-term poverty, such as reduced nutrition, poor hygiene, and deprived home environments. There are indications in the existing literature that an important factor in childhood diarrhea, and thus a profound risk to the health of children, is an adverse interaction between biosocial and bioenvironmental disease, or an ecosyndemic.

Annually, diarrhea is directly responsible of the deaths of around 450,000 children under 5 years plus an additional 50,000 children aged 5–9 years. Around the world, there are over 1.5 billion cases of childhood diarrheal disease every year. Moreover, it is a leading cause of malnutrition in children before their fifth birthday (World Health Organization, 2024a). Moreover, research by Christopher Troeger et al. (2018) quantified the global impact of diarrhea and diarrhea-induced outcomes on child health. To assess the impact, these investigators used disability-adjusted life-years (DALYs, as noted in Chap. 2, is a sum of the years of life lost due to premature mortality and the years lived with a disability due to disease) as a measure of disease impact. They found that in a single year diarrhea cases and deaths in children younger than five years were responsible for more than 40 million DALYs and that the expanded effects of diarrhea were responsible for almost 16 million additional DALYs. Further, they found that about 84% of long-term DALYs were due to the increased risk of infectious diseases stemming from diarrhea-induced undernutrition.

Diarrhea is usually a symptom of an infection in the intestinal tract, which can be caused by a variety of bacteria, viruses, and parasitic organisms like worms. Infection

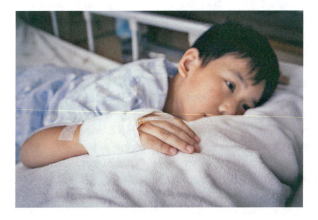

Fig. 3.3 Childhood diarrhea

is spread through contaminated food (that has been prepared or stored under unhygienic conditions) or drinking water, or from person to person as a result of poor hygiene. Unsafe drinking water storage and handling is also an important risk factor as are fish and other seafood taken from polluted water. Worldwide, it is estimated that 780 million people lack access to safe drinking water (i.e., water that is not polluted by feces or toxins) and 2.5 billion lack adequate sanitation. The World Health Organization estimates that over 1.5 billion people lack basic sanitation services, such as private toilets or latrines. Of these, about 420 million are forced to defecate in the open, for example in street gutters, behind bushes, or into open bodies of water, actions that promote the spread of diarrhea-causing pathogens. Open defecation helps perpetuate a vicious cycle of disease and poverty in which poverty promotes disease and disease promotes poverty. The countries where open defecation is most common also have the highest number of deaths of children under 5 years as well as the greatest levels of malnutrition and poverty. They also tend to have big disparities in wealth between the top and bottom of the social hierarchy. Further, at least 10% of the world's population is believed to consume food that has been irrigated with wastewater. This threat is particularly high in urban areas, particularly in densely populated, low-income, and shantytown or squatter areas of cities where sewerage management is precarious or nonexistent, space for toilets is limited, pits are poorly designed and managed, septic tanks contaminate open drains, and groundwater and services for fecal sludge removal are nonexistent or unaffordable. Such inequalities are compounded when sewage discharged into storm drains and waterways from wealthier parts of a city pollutes poorer and lower-income areas.

The effects of climate change, including floods, water scarcity and droughts, and sea level rise, further exacerbate these problems and create conditions that promote the spread of infectious pathogens. In a study evaluating monthly reports of diarrheal disease among patients who sought care at health facilities in Botswana, an arid country located in Southern Africa, for example, Alexander et al. (2013) found that diarrheal case incidence was highest in the dry season. Their analysis suggests that forecasted climate change increases in temperature and decreases in rainfall may increase dry season diarrheal disease incidence with hot, dry conditions starting earlier in the year and lasting longer. The study identifies significant health/climate interactions and suggests similar patterns will emerge in other arid countries in Africa where diarrheal disease remains a persistent public health problem. The reasons for the connection between a drop in rainfall and diarrhea are not fully clear, but may be influenced by changes in water quality, hygiene related to water economizing, sanitation, sharing of water utensils, and food spoilage. At the opposite end of the spectrum are countries that face increased precipitation because of climate change. Dhimal et al. (2022) implemented a national ecological study in the South Asian country of Nepal to assess the relationship of weather and climate with diarrhea incidence. Using monthly diarrheal disease counts and meteorological data from all districts of the country, they found that diarrheal disease incidence significantly increased with a 1.8 °F rise in temperature (1 °C). Moreover, the effects of temperature and rainfall were highest in the mountainous regions of the country. This suggests that additional climate change could increase diarrheal disease incidence across the nation but that mountain areas are the most sensitive to climate variability and consequently to the burden of diarrheal diseases.

Climate change also impacts food availability, reduces access to food, and affects food quality. Projected increases in global temperatures, changes in precipitation patterns, intensification of extreme weather events, and reductions in water availability may all result in reduced agricultural productivity and the nutritional value of certain grains and legumes while decreasing food affordability. For example, in studies conducted in southern Africa, climate is one of the most frequently cited drivers of food insecurity. An immediate consequence is undernutrition in young children. Undernutrition is a well-recognized and widespread health problem, which accounts for over half of deaths in young children worldwide. The impact of undernutrition is magnified by its damaging interaction with pathogen-caused diarrheal disease. Diarrheal disease and malnutrition interaction triggers a vicious cycle. Children who endure repeated bouts of diarrhea are vulnerable to chronic infections that can contribute to undernutrition. Undernutrition, in turn, makes children vulnerable to new diarrhea infections.

Because intestinal co-infections are frequent, diarrhea-causing pathogens also can interact with each other in ways that increase the severity of disease symptoms (Bulled et al., 2014). The Global Enteric Multicenter Study (Kotloff et al., 2013), a three-year, case-control research project involving 22,000 children conducted at seven sites in Africa and Asia, investigated the cause, incidence, and impact of moderate-to-severe diarrhea. The study found that four pathogens were responsible for the majority of diarrhea cases. *Rotavirus* was the leading cause of diarrheal disease during infancy across all study sites. *Cryptosporidium*, a parasite, was the second leading cause at five sites. *Shigella*, a type of bacteria, was the first or second leading cause among children 12–59 months of age at most of the project sites. Finally, the bacteria *enterotoxigenic E. coli* was a significant factor in at least one age group at every site. Co-infection with multiple diarrhea-causing pathogens was common. Two or more intestinal pathogens were present in 45% of cases. The nature of the interactions between pathogens that cause diarrhea are not yet fully clear. Research, however, is beginning to suggest possible synergistic effects of co-present pathogens in promoting disease (Bulled & Singer, 2016). Observational studies note that molecular interactions may occur as a result of co-infections exacerbating disease symptoms. For example, a study of children hospitalized for acute gastroenteritis in Rome, Italy, identified co-infection in 18% of patients (Valentini et al., 2013). Co-infected patients also suffered more severe clinical outcomes. A case-control study of 22 communities in Ecuador found evidence of *rotavirus/Giardia* and *rotavirus/E. coli* co-infections (Bhavnani et al., 2012). Researchers reported that during co-infection the pathogenic potential of each infectious agent was enhanced. Together, these studies suggest that moderate-to-severe diarrhea in children may be the result of syndemic microbial interactions. Likely, these interactions are promoted and accelerated by the adverse impact of poverty and related social conditions.

Antimicrobial Resistance Syndemic

In microbiology, there is a well-known story about Alexander Fleming, the Scottish physician who stumbled onto the discovery of penicillin in 1928, an event that launched the golden age of antibiotic exploration. Upon returning from a holiday, Fleming went to his lab and found that a known fungus, *Penicillium notatum (since re-identified as Penicillium rubens)*, had contaminated a cultured petri dish of *Staphylococcus* bacteria that he accidentally left uncovered. Fleming isolated and grew the mold in pure culture. He soon realized that *the mold* was extremely effective, even in very low concentrations, in preventing *Staphylococcus* growth. He hypothesized that the mold produced a substance (an active metabolite) that killed the bacteria. Fleming was awarded the Nobel Prize for his contribution. Penicillin changed the entire direction of medical approaches to treating infectious diseases.

During the 1950s and 1960s, about 150 classes of antibiotics were introduced, and were heralded as chemical miracles. Before antibiotics, if a person received a cut or similar minor injury, the chances of a serious infection or death were high. During the American Civil War, for example, where open wounds were very common, two-thirds of the approximately 660,000 deaths of soldiers were caused by uncontrollable infectious diseases, not cannon balls or bullets. After the introduction of antibiotics, everything changed, at least for a while. The introduction of antibiotics led to a climate of optimism during the second half of the twentieth century that infectious diseases, in the Global North at least, would soon be under control, and medical attention could shift to noncommunicable diseases. Increasingly in recent years, however, a period during which antibiotics have been heavily prescribed, some bacteria and fungi have developed effective resistance. In fact, the earliest sign of antibiotic resistance was observed soon after the discovery of penicillin. *E. Coli* was found to be able to inactivate penicillin by producing the enzyme *penicillinase*. It is estimated that in the USA alone more than 2.8 million infections and 35,000 deaths now occur each year because of antibiotic-resistant pathogens, and these numbers are projected to rise as resistance spreads across pathogenic species, creating what are informally called "super bugs." The problem is not limited to the USA but is a global phenomenon accounting for 1.3 million deaths worldwide each year.

The World Health Organization's Global Antimicrobial Resistance and Use Surveillance System report (World Health Organization, 2022) documents alarming rates of resistant infections across a broad range of microorganisms. An assessment in 76 countries found median rates of 42% for third-generation cephalosporin-resistant *E. coli* and 35% for methicillin-resistant *S. aureus,* indicating a serious threat to human, animal, and environmental health. For urinary tract infections caused by *E. coli*, one in five cases show reduced susceptibility to frontline antibiotics like ampicillin, co-trimoxazole, and fluoroquinolones. Murray et al. (2022) estimated that almost five million deaths were associated with bacterial antibiotic resistance in 2019.

Several super bugs are of special concern. One of these is a new strain of a hypervirulent bacteria species called *Klebsiella pneumoniae* which is found in 16 countries, including the USA. It causes rapidly progressing deadly infections, even in people whose immune systems are heathy. *K. pneumoniae* is found in the environment, including soil and water, but also in the upper throat and gastrointestinal tract of various animals, including humans. In recent years, the bacteria has developed resistance to an ever growing list of drugs. Some strains now show resistance to carbapenems, a class of last-resort antibiotic drugs used against multidrug- and extensively drug-resistant pathogens. Combining drug resistance and hypervirulence makes this a particularly worrisome bacteria. Another pathogen of great concern is methicillin-resistant *Staphylococcus aureus* (MRSA), which is the leading cause of resistance-related deaths in Global North countries. In 2019, MRSA caused more than 100,000 deaths worldwide making it one of the top ten threats to global health (Piewnam & Otto, 2024). It can be spread through direct skin-to-skin contact or by touching contaminated items like clothing. A third high priority concern is *Mycobacterium tuberculosis*. Globally, multidrug-resistant *M tuberculosis* caused an estimated 160,000 deaths in 2022. The countries with the largest number of people estimated to have developed multidrug-resistant *tuberculosis* in 2022 were India, the Philippines, and the Russian federation.

Drug resistance-conferring mutations have occurred in many pathogens. Resistance is facilitated by the ability of bacteria to move genes across microbial species through horizontal gene transfer (Ventola, 2015). In human intestines, for example, a large number of species of gut bacteria are constantly in close proximity, a situation ripe for genes to jump from one microbe to another. As food, people, and goods move across borders, they bring with them their bacterial arrays. As a result, antibiotic-resistant bacteria that develop anywhere in the world can be quickly transported to other regions.

Beginning in the late 1960s through to the early 1980s, the pharmaceutical industry introduced a number of new, more powerful antimicrobials to address the resistance problem, but since then few new antibiotics have been produced. Most of the largest pharmaceutical companies that once produced antibiotics have ended their production and the research that supported it. Antibiotic production is not seen by Big Pharma as a lucrative business. Adding to the development of resistance is the widespread use of antibiotics in livestock raised for human consumption. In fact, about 80% of antibiotics sold in the USA are used in animals to both prevent infection and promote growth. Antibiotics used in livestock, including those that have developed resistance, however, are eventually ingested by humans when the animals are consumed. The transfer of resistant bacteria to humans by farm animals has been known for more than 40 years. The end result of these various factors is what some scientists refer to as a "nightmare scenario" for health in a world of infectious microbial agents.

Complicating this threat is the syndemic interaction of drug-resistant pathogens and other infectious and noninfectious diseases. Research, in fact, suggests that antibiotic drug resistance may be a component of several syndemics. A deadly example involves the interaction of multidrug-resistant tuberculosis and HIV, which has emerged as a major challenge facing disease control programs worldwide, especially in Asia and Africa. Findings from several studies on the association of HIV and drug-resistant TB indicate significantly increased risks, although this has not been found in every case. A systematic review and meta-analysis of the literature on the association between HIV infection and multidrug-resistant tuberculosis by Mesfin et al. (2015), for example, found a moderate association in population-based studies. No significant association was identified, however, among patients in institutional settings. HIV/multidrug-resistant TB interaction is particularly prominent in South Africa, where over 300,000 new cases of TB are reported every year and 4.4% of cases are drug resistant. About 60% of patients with TB also are infected with HIV. Many co-infection cases in South Africa involve nosocomial (hospital) transmission (Gandhi et al., 2013). Overall, there is an extremely high mortality among individuals with multidrug-resistant TB, especially among patients with HIV co-infection.

The bacteria *Neisseria gonorrhoeae*, the pathogenic agent of gonorrhea, has developed antimicrobial resistance to every major class of antimicrobials that has been used to treat it. It is estimated by the World Health Organization (2024a, b) that there were over 82 million new adult cases of this sexually transmitted infection (STI) in 2020. There is growing epidemiological and medical concern that in the near future gonorrhea may be untreatable with all available antimicrobial drugs. One aspect of this concern is bystander selection, the inadvertent pressure placed on antibiotic treatment of microbes other than the targeted pathogen. It is hypothesized that bystander selection may be an important factor in the propagation of antibiotic resistance. Because gonococcal infections cluster with other STIs, Kenyon et al. (2020) used data from the European Antimicrobial Resistance Surveillance Network to investigate the significance of bystander selection in producing antimicrobial resistance in gonorrhea. They concluded that people with gonorrhea are exposed to multiple drugs used to treat other STIs and that gonococcal resistance is part of a syndemic of resistance that would benefit from antibiotic stewardship campaigns to reduce the total consumption of antibiotics.

Beyond STIs, populations like those over 65 years of age that tend to suffer from comorbidity and multimorbidity are at risk for the development of antibiotic resistance. Resistance is quite prevalent among elderly nursing home residents, for example, but is associated with the total burden of comorbidity but not with individual diseases. In a retrospective study of 299 patients with culture-positive UTIs who were consecutively admitted to a nursing home in Taranto, Italy, resistance was detected in 162 (54%) of study participants. In logistic regression, the presence of antibiotic resistance was independently associated with a higher Charlson score, a 19-item tool used to predict risk of death within one year of hospitalization for patients with comorbid conditions (Laudisio et al., 2017).

Nursing homes, in fact, are associated with the emergence not only of antibiotic-resistant species but of multiple multidrug-resistant microorganisms (MDROs). Thus far, there has been limited examination of synergistic interactions among different MDRO species. A study of catheter-associated UTIs caused by various bacteria, including *E. coli, Enterococcus*, and *S. aureus,* revealed a complex pattern of interactions. Antibiotic use was a risk factor for primary MDRO colonization, which, in turn, was a pathway for colonization and infection by other MDROs. Co-colonization with specific pairs of MDROs increased the risk of UTIs, indicating the adverse involvement of microbial interactions in UTI pathogenesis. Thus, preexisting *P. mirabilis* colonization increased the risk of acquiring *A. baumannii*, and preexisting colonization with *A. baumannii*, *E. coli*, and *P. aeruginosa* increased the risk of acquiring *P. mirabilis*. The colonization of bacterial pairs, including *E. coli*/*Enterococcus*, *P. mirabilis*/*E. coli*, and *P. mirabilis*/MRSA, was found to synergistically increase the risk of developing a catheter-associated UTI (Wang et al., 2017).

Accumulating research highlights the fact that the response of bacteria to antibiotics is significantly affected by the presence of other interacting microbes living together in multi-species communities. This component of bacterial ecology often is not considered in determining pathogen sensitivity to antibiotics. The evolution of antibiotic resistance therefore should not be considered only with reference to individual bacteria species but also as an emergent property of the particular microbial community in which pathogens are embedded. In such communities, like biofilms (cells that stick together and to a surface, like dental biofilm on teeth), interspecies interactions may shape responses to antibiotic exposure and change the trajectory of resistance evolution. Bottery et al. (2021) describe three potentially overlapping forms of such interaction: (1) *collective resistance*, interactions that elevate the ability of community members to resist an antibiotic; (2) *collective tolerance*, interactions that alter cell state, such as slowing down metabolism, and cell death during transient exposure; and (3) *exposure protection*, interactions within a community that protect its sensitive members during antibiotic exposure by reducing the concentration of the antibiotic. In that the outcome of any of these forms of cross-species interaction may promote disease, they are all syndemic in nature.

Microbial interactions can occur across pathogenic types. Acute otitis media, for example, a disease that leads to frequent antibiotic use in pediatric patients worldwide, is a polymicrobial disease. It commonly occurs as a complication of viral upper respiratory tract infection. While respiratory viruses alone can cause acute otitis media, they also can syndemically increase the risk of bacterial middle ear infection and worsen clinical outcomes of bacterial ear infection. Research on the bacterial pathogens involved in acute otitis media shows increasing rates of antibiotic resistance.

The threat of antibiotic resistance was amplified by the COVID-19 pandemic during which progress made in controlling resistant infections was lost. In the USA, for example, during the first year of the pandemic, over 29,000 people died from antimicrobial-resistant infections commonly associated with healthcare settings. Of these, almost 40% were infected while they were in the hospital with COVID-19. As a result of the pandemic, hospitals treated sicker patients who needed more frequent and longer use of catheters and ventilators. Resistant hospital-onset infections and deaths both increased at least 15% from 2019 to 2020 among seven bacterial and fungal pathogens (Centers for Disease Prevention, 2024b). In short, Ferrinho et al.

(2023) note, "The multidimensionality of antimicrobial resistance determination and its synergy with concurrent or sequential epidemics or disease clusters in the most diverse populations, which exacerbate the prognosis and burden of disease argues, in favour of considering it as a syndemic. The lack of consideration for this syndemic nature of antimicrobial resistance has been one of the limiting factors for the effectiveness of measures taken so far."

Case Study: Ecosyndemics in the Context of Planetary Health
We still have much to learn about the nature and pathways of ecosyndemics. Research in this arena is young and still somewhat limited. However, the broader body of work on syndemics, characterized by a focus on social structural factors in adverse disease interactions rather than environmental ones, can serve as a guide pointing the way forward. Moreover, with the full impact of climate change becoming increasingly clear, syndemic researchers recognize that social factors drive climate change and climate change is a massive existential threat to health across species. Incorporation of the ecosyndemic conceptual framework into planetary health-focused research, intervention, and policy will strengthen the comprehensive and integrated response sought by its advocates to the rising health challenges we face. Seeing health through an ecosyndemic lens reveals a key mechanism through which adverse environmental changes increase the health burden in affected populations. Many anthropogenic environmental alterations, including climate change, air pollution, biodiversity loss, freshwater depletion, ocean acidification, deforestation, land-use changes, desertification, and exposures to toxic chemicals, create the conditions that spark ecosyndemic interactions. These disruptive shifts reduce the habitability of ecosystems for humans and nonhuman species alike while increasing vulnerability to disease, disease clustering, and adverse disease interaction.

Both ecosyndemics and planetary health require a systems thinking approach to health issues. Three key concepts that undergird such thinking are critical to both ecosyndemics and planetary health. These are: (1) having a "big-picture" or holistic orientation (seeing the forest and the trees); (2) drawing distinctions (heuristically isolating intertwined system components); and (3) seeing relationships (discovering kinds and degrees of associations, convergences, and interactions). This systems-based approach to actionable knowledge and understanding serves as a foundation for the enmeshing of ecosyndemic theory in planetary health. Staff members of the World Health Organization (Hunter et al., 2024), for example, have identified the benefits of addressing interacting noncommunicable disease syndemics (such as those involving diabetes and cardiovascular disease) within planetary health initiatives. Their holistic vision emphasizes the importance of multiple causal loops between climate change, other environmental crises, and interacting noncommunicable diseases.

Complex health crises and syndemics require "whole-of-society responses" (Tweed et al., 2023). Indeed, in an interconnected world in which diseases and people are mobile and the environmental degradations and disruptions produced in one region impact other regions, and even the whole planet, whole-of-all-society and multinational responses are required. This necessitates subordination of private interest for the public good. A whole-of-society approach involves both formal and informal institutions, and civic society, including social movements, in seeking a basic agreement across society about policy goals and the means to achieve them.

The emergence of planetary health, especially since it evolved to be more sensitive to Indigenous participation and leadership, offers an umbrella to rally scientists, policy makers, and populations around a common forward-looking, collaborative framework. This explicit effort to adopt perspectives across scientific and community domains allows for broader buy-in from scientists across academic fields, physical and social, and diverse communities around the globe. Planetary health encourages thorough examination of the interplay between human (especially corporate) economic activities and natural systems changes. Evidence supporting a specific policy compiled across multiple fields of study, varied ways of knowing, and varied human experience provide compelling support for meaningful action in troubled times.

The following chapter discusses grassroots efforts to build an effective and united fightback against the growing ecocrises we face and how the unified ecosyndemics/planetary health framework can inform those efforts.

Case Study: Digging Up Syndemics
Emily Mendenhall et al. (2022) comment: "Everyone concerned with past health would gain considerably by viewing epidemic clusters through the lens of syndemic theory." Accordingly, in recent years, the fields of paleopathology and bioarchaeology have begun to provide long-term perspectives on the biocultural patterns and complexities in disease interactions in historic contexts. Bioarchaeologists, moreover, have emphasized the need for understanding the sources of inequity that create heterogeneous experiences, risks, and outcomes of disease within and across social groups. Fabian Crespo (2022), for example, discusses the sensitivity of the human immune system to ecological and social factors during the first 1000 days of life and the impact of this sensitivity for longer-term inflammatory responses. Further, Crespo (2021) highlights the utility of a syndemic perspective for interpreting inflammatory responses in skeletal remains (which are evident in structural changes in bone architecture). With this approach, DeWitte and Wissler (2022) analyze the fourteenth-century Black Death pandemic in England as a syndemic. Prior to this deadly outbreak, some communities were disproportionately impacted by an acute agricultural crises and resulting malnutrition. This disparity and the vulnerability it created in some social groups and not others could have led to intergenerational health inequalities that continued until the Black Plague epidemic, syndemically causing a disproportionate level of mortality among individuals of lower socioeconomic statuses.

In this light, Perry and Gowland (2022) proposed the occurrence of a rickets–tuberculosis syndemic in the context of poverty. The key mechanism behind the relationship of these two diseases, one caused by a deficiency of a vitamin needed by the body to help absorb calcium and phosphorus, the other a respiratory infection, is vitamin D. Vitamin D deficiency adversely impacts the immune system, particularly the cells involved in fighting respiratory infections. Both of these health conditions can affect the human skeleton and have been reported on extensively in the paleopathological literature. They have been found to co-occur in some historical and archaeological contexts, especially during the eighteenth- and nineteenth-century England during the Industrial Revolution.

Infection with the pathogen *Mycobacterium tuberculosis* causes the development of skeletal lesions in about 3–5% of untreated cases. *M. tuberculosis* travels to bones through the circulatory system favoring areas with red bone marrow producing blood cells, such as the main weight-bearing portion of a vertebra, as well as the expanded end of the long bones in adults and the flat bones of the crania and the shaft of long bones in children. The common diagnostic lesions of skeletal infection appear on the vertebra and joint regions. The extraction and identification of *M. tuberculosis* DNA in skeletal remains provides an additional means of diagnosis in skeletal remains. Vitamin D deficiency is a risk factor for tuberculosis infection. Inadequate access to vitamin D also triggers the release of stored calcium from the skeleton which causes the poor bone density and bone shape deformities known as rickets. Vitamin D primarily is obtained through exposure to UVB (ultraviolet B radiation) in sun rays.

In addition to the synergistic impacts of rickets and tuberculosis on the immune system and the development of lesions on the bones, environmental and social risk factors help explain why these two diseases cluster in the same contexts. Tuberculosis, referred to as a "disease of poverty," is linked to poor living conditions and economic inequity, usually including crowding, unsanitary housing, and poor nutrition. Perry and Gowland (2022) note: "The combined effects of low UVB exposure due to living and working conditions, other metabolic deficiencies, and comorbid diseases created a 'perfect storm' for high rates of rickets in working class urban industrial communities in Britain…." Domestic coal fires for heating and cooking contributed to extensive air pollution that blocked UVB radiation and the poor air quality outdoors kept many individuals indoors. These conditions produced a rickets–tuberculosis ecosyndemic that left its indelible mark on excavated skeletal material.

Discussion Questions

1. Why is identifying and understanding syndemics an important aspect of population health?
2. What are the primary components of syndemics and ecosyndemics?
3. How did SIV become HIV and why was this evolution important?
4. What is SAVA and its role in the development of syndemic theory?
5. Why are human lungs a site for the development of ecosyndemics?
6. What is the El Niño-Southern Oscillation and why is it important in modulating climate change health effects?
7. Discuss Janelle Christensen's work on elder care and ecosyndemics.
8. Why do both ecosyndemics and planetary health require systems thinking and what are the three key approaches shared by ecosyndemics and planetary health?

Class Projects

1. Put together a slide show on ecosyndemics and student health.
2. Create a set of "Did You Now" posters on syndemics and health for display around campus.

Fighting Back: Uniting the Health and Environment Movements

4

Abstract

Having laid out the severe challenges that threaten the sustainability of many species, including our own, Chap. 4 addresses grassroots efforts to build an effective and united fightback against the growing ecocrises that are occurring globally. The chapter addresses a simple question about an enormously complex problem. In the face of the staggering threats facing health and environmental sustainability, what is to be done? The dominant characteristics of grassroots heath activism are analyzed and an array of health activist groups, their goals, successes, and limitations are discussed. Subsequently, beginning with Love Canal the evolution of the environmental health movement is examined, followed by an exploration of the lessons of COVID-19.

Keywords

Grassroots health activism · Environmental activism · Climate activism · Disability activism · Breast cancer activism · Harm reduction · Women's health movement · Long COVID · Love Canal · Greta Thunberg

Planetary Health, Ecosyndemics, and Activism

This chapter addresses a simple question about an enormously complex problem. In the face of the staggering threats facing health and environmental sustainability, what is to be done? As noted in Chap. 2, the founders of the modern planetary health effort defined it as a social movement focused on analyzing and addressing the impacts of human disruptions to Earth's natural systems on human health and all life on the planet. In this regard, Arpit Mago and co-workers (2024) stress, "[b]y building a foundation for understanding the interconnections between environmental, social, and health crises and searching for solutions to the shared challenges that the globe faces today, planetary health has become more important than ever." This orientation toward connectedness jibes with the call by social activists for direct political action regarding climate change and other pressing environmental issues. At least since Earth Day 1970, the climate and environmental movements have embraced the goal of protecting all life on Earth. In this regard, physicians have been encouraged to move beyond a focus on individual patients and work with community groups and others to build a social movement to pressure the policy and private sectors to significantly accelerate action to protect Earth's natural systems. There is evidence that increasingly physicians are becoming engaged in activist efforts to safeguard a livable future for humanity and all species (Myers, 2022). In the Netherlands, for example, students and medical residents have begun organizing planetary health webinars, which have attracted large audiences. Flowing from this work, a manifesto signed by over 1000 healthcare professionals called for climate action and integration of the topic into medical education curricula. Part of this momentum was the formation of the GREENER collective in November 2020, after a virtual network meeting about research in climate and health. The GREENER collective, a diverse multidisciplinary group of medical students, health professionals, scientists, and policy advisors, urges immediate reform of the medical school curricula to educate students and young professionals about planetary health (Mattijsen et al., 2023). A core message of climate activism is that we are running out of time, see Fig. 4.1.

Claudia Magistretti, a professor at the University of Applied Sciences and Arts Northwestern Switzerland, and her colleagues (2021) argue that grassroots environmental and climate groups have both the willingness and potential to bring about planetary health. To help them do so, these academicians call on health promotion practitioners to support grassroots actions, contributing to a participatory process in

Fig. 4.1 Climate activists

the creation of planetary health. In their assessment, planetary health challenges traditional anthropocentric thinking on sustainability and seeks to re-center life and health as dependent on the well-being of Earth. They further argue that:

> Across the globe, local grassroots initiatives are undertaking actions directed towards sustainability and planetary health. These groups do not value the environment as an object to be influenced, owned or shaped, but rather understand it as a co-environment with which they interact in the interest of commanding greater quality of life for local people, and continued vitality of ecosystems (Magistretti et al., 2021).

Consequently, planetary health scholar-activists are urged to create alternative systems grounded in principles of relational well-being and engagement in community-driven climate/environment and social justice actions.

This is the perspective as well of the originators and advocates of ecosyndemics theory, who see the community and the academy as interlinked sites of struggle for health, environmental sustainability, and social justice (Baer & Singer, 2024). Willen et al. (2017) see syndemics as both a field of health research and an idiom of social justice mobilization for health. They compare the domains of syndemics and health and human rights with the intention of identifying their complementarities and advocating for a unified syndemics/health and human rights approach. In their view,

> By mapping the links between widespread human rights violations and specific forms of syndemic suffering, a combined syndemics/health and human rights approach can help clinicians, health researchers, and other stakeholders expand their field of vision and better understand how power asymmetries and complex contexts—social, political, economic, historical, even environmental—shape and constrain the lives of … vulnerable groups. Similarly, this approach can help identify potential partners in collaboration, potential points of political leverage, and ripe opportunities for upstream intervention (Willen et al., 2017).

Prelude to Activism

A starting place for thinking about how to address this question can be found in the journey taken by Andy Hix (2020), a mindfulness coach based in North London, England. When Hix was a university student, he encountered the book *How We Can Save the Planet* by Mayer Hillman et al., (2008). In the book, Hillman argues that climate change is the single greatest problem that humankind has ever had to face. It is a point others also have made, increasingly so over the years. As Hix read the book his world was shattered. He became totally convinced if he did not act urgently and drastically to curb carbon emissions, the world would become unlivable. Once this idea sunk in, no other issue really mattered to him. He literally asked himself: why worry about doing anything to end homelessness, mental health problems, the burgeoning prison population, and even poverty if the world is going to fall apart in a few decades? As a result, he became a passionate and single-minded climate activist. In his personal life, he tried to walk the talk by becoming a vegan and boycotting air travel. While still at university he became president of his campus' environmental society and frequently participated in climate marches in London. Twice he went to the UN climate negotiations.

But all the while, Hix grew increasingly frustrated and did not understand why other people did not care as much about climate change as he did. Before long even his activist friends began to see him as incredibly judgmental. To him, the world looked like a dark, unfriendly place. In his yearbook, a friend wrote "Andy, I admire your one-man mission to save the world." But Hix had not meant to be a one-man mission; he expected others to join him. He could not understand why they did not feel and act like he did. He found that, in fact, his attitude and actions isolated him. After several years of being obsessed with halting climate change, and in the aftermath of the UN Climate Summit in Copenhagen failing to chart a clear path toward a global treaty with binding commitments on carbon emissions, Hix became disillusioned and despairing, and put everything about climate change out of his mind. In his heart he still knew it was the number one issue facing humanity, but he had run out of energy to do anything about it. Hix suffered from burnout, a form of exhaustion and emotional depletion usually associated with work but also possible in other areas of someone's life. As a result, Hix's climate change activism ended and he eventually focused on wellness issues.

Hix's journey can be read as a cautionary tale. And he is not alone. Interviews conducted by staff of the USA Today newspaper (Fulton, 2022) found that many climate activists expressed frustration that the challenges and distractions they face keep piling up. Some reported that they worry that their annoyance could one day turn to apathy. In the words of one interviewee, Sarah Goody, who began climate work in the sixth grade and was a senior in high school at the time of the interview, "There's just so many other things to focus on, and they're taking our attention away from climate organizing." Goody reported that she watched burnout take its toll on the enthusiasm that initially brings young people into climate work. Goody went on after high school to enroll at the University of California Berkeley with a double major in legal studies and society and environment. She did not succumb to burnout, however, but rather has remained a climate activist and public speaker, helping to found Climate NOW, an international youth-led organization committed to educating and empowering young people to participate in climate action and provide them with the skills needed to launch community-based initiatives.

But Goody was not always so focused and motivated. In the 5th grade, she was diagnosed with clinical depression. She was extremely lonely, lacked motivation, and had a deep sense of sadness. By the time she was a freshman in high school, however, her life had turned around, and she thanks activism for this. She says, "In fact, I think it saved me." She adds, "activism can give young people confidence and a sense of purpose in their lives" (NBC Nightly News Kids Edition, 2020). As Goody learned, the fight to "save the planet" or at least life as we know it is not a sprint but a marathon strewn with numerous obstacles, one after the other. Long-term activism is absolutely vital. Consequently, learning how to remain active for the long haul and avoid burnout is essential. In Goody's case, the comradery of other activists, the profound nature of the goal, the inspiration of activist leaders, and the ability to maintain a sense of balance proved to be critical.

Kaethe Weingarten (2023), Director of the Witness to Witness Program of the Migrant Clinician Network, comments, "I have been an activist since I was nine years old, and, 65 years later, I can truly say that following my own tips has contributed to the longevity of my activism. I may never enjoy the gratification that comes from solving a massive problem, but I do enjoy the satisfaction of working with others toward changes that matter." Among the tips to which Weingarten refers are:

- Remember that you are one person. It is important to set an expectation of yourself that is neither too modest nor too grandiose. Ask yourself this question: What is within my scope to achieve? Or this question: What can I do myself directly, and what should I advocate for world, national, state, and/or local leaders to address?
- Monitor your body for signals that you have taken on too much.
- To stay active for the long haul, it is necessary to monitor your own well-being. No matter what you care about, if you do not care about yourself, ultimately your efforts crumble.
- Working with like-minded people. Effective activism is not an act of individual effort, but emergencies from community. Weingarten, for example, is involved in 1000 Grandmothers, a group focused on the climate justice/environmental crisis that is committed to doing whatever they can, at this moment in history, to expose, impede, and shut down the fossil fuel industry. The group is based on collective action, and building the capacity to act collectively. In other words, as an activist, you are not alone. While we may hear a lot about the dangers of climate change in the media, we hear far less about the millions of people around the world taking part in climate actions every day, including uplifting stories about their local victories. For example, there is the case of Ghanaian environmental activist Chibeze Ezekiel who has walked the streets of the capital city of Accra to raise awareness about environmental issues. In 2020, Ezekiel won the Goldman Environmental Prize in recognition of his successful efforts in steering his nation away from coal use. Similarly, Murrawah Maroochy Johnson, an Indigenous Wirdi activist from the Birri Gubba Nation, won the prize for helping block development of a massive coal mine that would have destroyed the Bimblebox Nature Refuge in Queensland, Australia, while adding 1.58 billion tons of CO_2 to the atmosphere over its lifetime.
- Help children become activists. Children are curious and energetic. It is critical to design ways to include children in intergenerational activism. Both children and the climate change action movement benefit when children are actively involved in the process. Research indicates that activities that build an appreciation of nature, like hiking and nature photography, are positively associated with children's connection to nature. These activities also are positively linked to children's environmental-citizenship behaviors.

The groundbreaking community activism of the esteemed Brazilian educator and philosopher Paulo Freire suggests an additional tip.

- Value purposeful reflection. It is necessary to reflect on the theory and philosophical underpinnings of activism. The urgency of the desire for significant social change often hinders efforts to find a critical space needed for reflection to occur. Freire stressed that people must reflect collectively about their world in order to transform it. This book is intended as a starter tool for the reflexive thinking that is needed.

A related issue that warrants consideration is why some people, especially those who are aware of the threat, do not become active. One of the barriers that blocks some concerned people from becoming activists is climate or environmental anxiety. Every day we are hit by news about and images of climate-related disasters, like death from sizzling heatwaves or the melting of the doomsday glacier. As the last sentence was being written came news that *Earth just experienced its warmest day since 1940 when the Copernicus Climate Change Service data collection began. In the face of dreadful news overload, many people have grown* increasingly anxious about the perilous state of our planet. Mental health clinicians report seeing more patients with symptoms of this emergent condition, and they are not sure what to do about it. It is a trend that is mirrored in public surveys and Internet search data: Yoder (2021), for example, reported that Google searches for "climate anxiety" soared by 565% in 2021. This rise in existential fear signals a shift in awareness of the crisis from an abstract idea to a concrete and inescapable reality. This has led to a sharp growth in the number of people trying to grapple with what the environmental crisis means for their own lives and the lives of their relatives, friends, and communities. It has led some people of childbearing age to question whether it is right to bring new children into the world. This response is predicated on the fact that if the planet continues to warm on its current trajectory, the average 6-year-old living today will probably witness about two to seven times as many climate-enhanced disasters as someone born in 1960 (Thiery et al., 2021).

The largest survey of its kind, involving 10,000 young people (16–25 years of age) in ten countries (Australia, Brazil, Finland, France, India, Nigeria, the Philippines, Portugal, the UK, and the USA), found that the climate crisis was causing significant psychological distress (Marks et al., 2021). Forty-five percent of teens and young adults who participated in the survey stated that climate anxiety was affecting their daily lives and ability to function, over 50% indicated that they feel sad, anxious, angry, powerless, helpless, and guilty, while 56% said they thought that "humanity is doomed." Caroline Hickman, a researcher at the University of Bath in the UK who worked on the survey, noted that "[t]his study paints a horrific picture of widespread climate anxiety in our children and young people" (quoted in Yoder, 2021).

Researchers at Yale University, including Anthony Leiserowitz and Sarah Lowe, have been at the forefront of studying the rising tide of climate anxiety as well as ways to ameliorate it. In a Q&A session held on campus, Leiserowitz and Lowe discussed the nature of climate and why some amount of worry can be a good thing (Yale Office of Sustainability, 2023). According to Lowe, greater climate anxiety can manifest as intrusive thoughts or feelings of distress about future disasters or the long-term future of human existence and the world, including one's descendants. This can include a physiological component, such as a racing heart and shortness of breath, and a behavioral component, which is seen when climate anxiety interferes with social relationships or functioning at work or school. Another expression of anxiety is "solastalgia," which is feelings of nostalgia for one's home environment and the way it used to be. Glenn Albrecht (2005), who coined this term, defined it as "the homesickness you have when you are still at home" because your local environment is changing in ways you find upsetting. Inherent in solastalgia is a sense of powerlessness.

Leiserowitz differentiates worry and anxiety. Many people worry about climate change, which is a healthy thing because concern is a motivator of action. Worry becomes a problem when it is overwhelming and debilitating, the opposite of action. Additionally, Lowe believes that engaging in collective action can have numerous life benefits, including experiencing social connectedness with people who share similar goals and values. A large body of research shows that social support is one of the strongest predictors of mental well-being.

Case Study: Greta Thunberg Strikes
Greta Thunberg was born in the Swedish capital of Stockholm in 2003. Her mother, Malena Ernman, is an opera singer, and her father, Svante Thunberg, is an actor. Young Thunberg first learned about climate change when she was eight. It made a deep and lasting impression on her. Although quite intelligent and articulate, at 11 years old she was diagnosed as neuroatypical (a condition previously known as autism). This added to a prior diagnosis of depression.

On August 20, 2018, 15-year-old Greta Thunberg began a school strike to call attention to the mounting risk of climate change. In the three weeks leading up to the Swedish election, she sat outside Swedish Parliament every school day with a homemade sign that read in Swedish "Skolstrejk för klimatet" (school strike for climate), and demanded her government take urgent action on the climate crisis. She was tired of the government's unwillingness to see the climate crisis for what it really is: a major existential threat. Initially, she was all alone, but within a week, she was joined by fellow students, teachers, and parents and began attracting media attention for her climate campaign. On the 8th of September, she and her schoolmate strikers decided to continue their strike every Friday until the Swedish policies were committed to a reduction in greenhouse gas emissions that was in line with the Paris Climate Accords signed in 2016. These students created the hashtag #FridaysForFuture and encouraged other young people all over the world to join them through walk-outs at their own schools. In November 2018, over 17,000 students in 24 countries took part in Friday school strikes. This marked the beginning of the global school strike for climate. In February 2019, protests inspired by Thunberg were held across more than 30 countries, from Sweden to Brazil, and

India to the USA. The next month, the number of students taking part in school strikes grew to more than 2 million people across 135 countries.

Between 2019 and 2020, Thunberg took a year off of school (although not from learning) to concentrate on activism, and became famous for her impassioned speeches to world leaders. Beyond a number of fierce speeches to people with the power to limit greenhouse gas emissions, Thunberg has been arrested several times for her participation in environmental protests around the world and fined by the Swedish courts for disobeying police orders and blocking an entrance to parliament on two occasions in March 2024. Meanwhile, Malena Ernman reported that her daughter became a much happier person after she started her campaign. Thunberg adds: "I know lots of people who have been depressed, and then they have joined the climate movement or *Fridays for Future* and have found a purpose in life and found friendship and a community that they are welcome in." She considers the best things that have resulted from her activism to be friendships and happiness. On the question of solidarity among activists, she says: "Definitely. We have daily contact. We don't just campaign together, we are also friends. My best friends are within the climate movement" (quoted in Hattenstone, 2021).

Thunberg is credited with raising public awareness of climate change across the world, especially among young people. In 2023, she posted on her Instagram account: "For five years now we have been striking from school every Friday to protest and demand climate justice. We were born into a crisis that we did not create. It is shameful that the responsibility to act falls so disproportionately on children and youth because the people in power and adults fail to step up" (quoted in Neil, 2023). Since then, she has continued her activism and has broadened her focus to include other humanitarian issues.

In honor of her defense of nature, scientists have named a number of newly discovered species after her, including *Pristimantis gretathunbergae,* a species of frog native to Panama.

Bottom-Up: Grassroots Heath Activism

In considering the way health is conceived and treated, Beatrix Hoffman (2008) differentiates grassroots health activism, including movements that are led by patients or potential healthcare consumers, from elite health reform, which relies on formal research and medical expertise and is directed by empowered political sectors and institutions. Health social movements have been "an important political force concerning health access and quality of care, as well as broader social change" (Brown & Stephen, 2004). As defined by Brown and Stephen (2004), health social movements provide "collective challenges to medical policy, public health policy and politics, belief systems, research and practice." Susi Geiger (2021) proposed using the term "healthcare activism" rather than "social movements" to label "the sometimes precarious state of the collectives that carry out the 'activist' activities," as opposed to the larger and relatively well-organized networks that the term 'social movement' implies. What unites healthcare activism according to Geiger is a guiding vision of what she terms the collective good, namely a vision of what is moral or right. However, "activism" as Greiger uses the term can transition into well-organized entities with national and even international reach.

Hoffman notes that grassroots health activism, which wells up from below, from those most affected, has tended to focus on a single issue or demand specific benefits for a particular group (e.g., AIDS patients demanding AIDS care). A core strength of such self-advocacy groups in health is having individuals with the courage and willingness to publicize and politicize their own health problems, a process that often empowers other affected individuals to overcome their hesitation and join the cause. The specific health changes grassroots efforts have advocated for, and in some cases (and to varying degrees) won, have made important changes in the conception of health in society and in the functioning of healthcare systems. Further, participants often have taught themselves to read and understand the scientific and policy literatures on their health concerns, becoming quite well-informed in the process, which has added credibility to their inclination to tell the stories of their own lived experiences. These efforts have challenged the scientific and medical establishments as well as policy makers, [comma] while also raising public awareness. Additionally, Hoffman (2008) emphasizes that "Through their experiences in the medical system and also their experiences with activism, members of social movements for health reform [have] repeatedly concluded that their demands could be fully realized only with universal access to health care. A recurring theme of health care activist movements has been the broadening of their single-issue and particular demands to include fundamental change in the US health care system." Together, such initiatives underscore the fact that "health policy is often a power struggle, in which divergent interests, values, and financial concerns compete with and at times trump epidemiological evidence" (Lane et al., 2016). Some noteworthy health-linked social activist initiatives are discussed below.

AIDS Activism

The profound impact of grassroots activism on health issues was on full display during the height of the AIDS epidemic. The mobilization of people suffering from diagnosed AIDS, infected with HIV, or at high risk for infection achieved unprecedented changes in the healthcare system, including accelerated clinical drug trials, reductions in pharmaceutical pricing, major increases in AIDS research, and expansion of Medicaid benefits to include needed AIDS services and treatments. Steven Epstein (1998) documented how nonscientist AIDS activists gained a critical voice in the scientific world which helped shape government-sponsored AIDS research to a remarkable extent. Central to this effort was a grassroots organization called AIDS Coalition to Unleash Power (ACT UP) which formed on March 12, 1987, at the Lesbian and Gay Community Services Center in New York City. Two weeks later, 250 ACT UP members demonstrated at the intersection of *Wall Street and* Broad *Street*, one of the most heavily visited corners in New York City, to demand greater access to experimental AIDS drugs and for the development of a coordinated national policy to fight the disease. Seventeen ACT UP members were arrested for engaging in civil disobedience, but the event established radical social action as a core strategy of AIDS activism. In October 1988, about 1500 ACT UP protesters marched on the US Food and Drug Administration office building in suburban Rockville, Maryland. Their intent was to call national attention to the failure of the agency to approve new medications to fight AIDS. The marchers held signs that read: "The government has blood on its hands; one AIDS death every half hour." One protestor unfurled a banner with the ACT UP slogan: "Silence=Death" and taped it across the glass doors of the building. The day after participating with 200,000 activists in the Second National March on Washington for Lesbian and Gay Rights in October 1987, members of ACT UP organized civil disobedience at the US Supreme Court Building. On September 14, 1989, seven ACT UP members snuck into the New York Stock Exchange and chained themselves to the VIP balcony to protest the high price of azidothymidine (AZT) ($10,000 per patient per year), the only federally approved AIDS drug. In response, Burroughs Wellcome, the pharmaceutical company that produced AZT, dropped the price by 36%.

Inspired by this new approach to direct action, activists in multiple cities formed local ACT UP chapters and eventually ACT UP spread internationally. At its peak, ACT UP reported it had 148 chapters. Whether holding marches, rallies, blocking rush-hour traffic, taking over public spaces with "die-ins," dumping a coffin filled with the cremated ashes of friends who had died of AIDS in a public place, interrupting CBS Evening News and the MacNeil-Lehrer NewsHour by chanting slogans like "Money for AIDS, Not for War," or by disrupting scientific conferences and political affairs using foghorns, fake blood, and smoke bombs, ACT UP kept their demands in the media and on the minds of politicians and researchers alike, as seen in the ACT UP demonstration in Fig. 4.2. Anthony Fauci, who became the director of the National Institute of Allergy and Infectious Diseases in 1984, and was often the target of ACT UP frustration, recalls: "I was saying to myself, 'I would be doing exactly what they were doing if I were in their shoes,'… One of the best things I've ever done in my life was to say, 'Let me put aside the theatrics, the confronted behavior and the iconoclastic behavior, and listen to what they were saying. And once I listened to what they were saying, everything got better. Better for medicine, better for science, better for regulation" (quoted in Schumer, 2024). Fauci allied himself with ACT UP and other AIDS activists. Based on their recommendations, he convinced others at the National Institutes of Health to alter clinical trial requirements and allow an increase in the number of patients who could access HIV/AIDS treatments. Fauci also arranged for activists to sit at the table as patient advocates, a practice that continues today in all NIH drug-testing committees (Wynn, 2021). This practice was revolutionary at the time but it helped move the process of patients gaining access to AIDS treatment.

Bottom-Up: Grassroots Heath Activism

Fig. 4.2 ACT UP Demonstration in New York

Disability Mobilizing

The discipline of disability studies makes an important distinction between "impairment," the bodily obstacles that a disabled person experiences, and "disability," the social and political components of disability (Clare, 1999). This distinction has been a central tenant in the anthropological study of disability (Hartblay, 2020). This work emphasizes the "social model of disability," which holds that it is the surrounding social environment (i.e., ableism), and not something inherently wrong with disabled people, that creates disability. Disability, in short, is the disadvantage or restriction of activity caused by a society which takes little or no account of people who have impairments and thus excludes them from mainstream activity. The social model has been presented as a challenge to the medical model, which focuses on impairment and rests on the social standing of medical authority (Ginsburg & Rapp, 2013). Disability activism, in turn, has focused on changing the social environment of the disabled including exposing discrimination, shaping the human built environment, and supporting the rights of people with disabilities.

The environment of the disabled reflects historic developments. As US cities expanded and public spaces became more crowded during the latter half of the nineteenth century, there emerged a growing emphasis on maintaining not only order but also the aesthetics of urban streetscapes. Under a local ordinance passed by the city's Board of Supervisors in 1867, San Francisco led the way in making it a crime for "any person who is diseased, maimed, mutilated, or in any way deformed so as to be an unsightly or disgusting object... to expose himself or herself to public view" (Board of Supervisors, 1897). This type of legislation targeting people with visible disabilities was quickly embraced by many other cities and states—from California to Pennsylvania. These laws appeared alongside restrictions on racial integration, immigration, and vagrancy (Schweik, 2010). Some of the supporters of the "ugly laws" believed that if disabled people were moved from the streets into almshouses, they would receive better care. However, placing them in almshouses only led to further marginalization by stripping disabled people of their right to self-determination and isolating them from society. In the end, however, disabled people helped to fuel the disability rights movement.

The disability activist struggle can be traced to before the turn of the twentieth century. It gained considerable visibility during the Great Depression of the 1930s when the League of the Physically Handicapped, a group of young adult New Yorkers, formed to fight for employment. The League, which obtained evidence that the federal agencies created to combat the Depression had a secret policy of not hiring people with impairments, organized picket lines and sit-ins at the Works Progress Administration (WPA) in protest. In response, the WPA ultimately awarded more than five thousand jobs to people with impairments throughout the country. Subsequently, during the 1940s, a group of psychiatric patients formed "We Are Not Alone." The group promoted the idea that people with serious mental illness have the same needs, capabilities, and aspirations as all people. The group supported patients as they transitioned from hospital to community.

In the shadow of the Civil Rights Movement in the early 1960s, the University of California Berkeley accepted Ed Roberts and John Hessler as students. Both men lived with physical impairments and needed to find housing after their acceptance to the university. But university dormitories could not manage Roberts' iron lung, an assistive breathing device for people with polio, or Hessler's physical needs stemming from damage to his spinal cord in a car accident. Instead, these men were forced to live at Cowell Memorial Hospital. But with the help of legal counsel they demanded access to housing at the university and encouraged other students with physical disabilities to apply to UC Berkeley. The university eventually created housing accommodations for these students. Nora Brusuelas, a friend, recalled how Hessler and Roberts... literally turned the university's hallways into their own private speedway. "They'd race up and down in their wheelchairs, scaring nurses and generally raising hell... They were so glad to be out of hospitals, rest homes or back bedrooms" (Campos, 1993). Roberts and Hessler also influenced school architecture and planning to make the whole campus more accessible. They promoted inclusion for all kinds of students on campus. These actions planted the seed of the independent living movement, an effort to affirm that people with impairments can make their own decisions about living, working, and interacting with the surrounding community.

Passage of the 1973 Rehabilitation Act became a focal point for the disability rights struggle. The bill contained specific sections that supported people with impairments in the federal workplace as well as in any organization that received federal tax dollars. It also prohibited discrimination against individuals with impairments in the workplace, and equal or comparable access to technological information and data for people with impairments. While new regulations under the Act were written, they were not implemented by either the Richard Nixon or Gerald Ford administrations. In 1977, the disability rights community grew tired of waiting, and demanded that President Jimmy Carter sign approval of the regulations. Instead, his Department of Health, Education and Welfare Secretary appointed a task force to review the regulation. Worried that the review would water down protections written into the Act, the American Coalition of Citizens with Disabilities insisted the protections be enacted as written by April 5, 1977, or the coalition would take action. When the date came and went and the regulations remained unsigned, disability activists and their allies protested by sitting in at federal offices of the Department of Health, Education and Welfare, including blind people, deaf people, wheelchair users, disabled veterans, people with developmental and psychiatric impairments, and many others. It was most intense in California. In San Francisco, a group of roughly 150 disability rights activists took over the fourth floor of a federal building for 25 days. For activists in the building, the day-to-day experience of the month-long sit-in posed enormous challenges and some literally risked their lives during the protest. Some participants suffered severe, long-term exacerbations of their health problems because of their involvement. Government officials tried to remove the activists by cutting the phone lines and denying them food, water, and medicine. But the protestors were prepared for this response. Deaf and CODA (Child of Deaf Adult) protesters used sign language to communicate through the windows of the building to their allies outside. Help came from the community; the Black Panther Party, for example, provided food throughout the sit-in. Brad Lomax, a Black man with multiple sclerosis, who was a member of the Black Panthers, helped to arrange this support. Other entities that helped meet the needs of the activists included Glide Memorial Church, the Gay Men's Butterfly Brigade, the United Farm Workers Union, the Gray Panthers, and the Salvation Army. On the streets near the building, disability activists and their supporters rallied to declare their support.

Use of the sit-in was chosen because it upended popular notions of people with impairments as weak, incapable of asserting themselves, or as objects of pity. Activist Judith Heumann, who 16 years later would become a US Assistant Secretary for Special Education and Rehabilitative Services, explains: "Through the sit-in, we turned ourselves from being oppressed individuals into being empowered people. We demonstrated to the entire nation that disabled people could take control over our own lives and take leadership in the struggle for equality" (quoted in Grim, 2015). Two weeks into the sit-in, a delegation of activists traveled from San Francisco to Washington DC to intensify their efforts. They organized candlelight vigils outside of the residence of the Secretary of Health, Education, and Welfare, and attempted to gain access to his office building by forcefully pushing their wheelchairs against the doors when their request for entry was turned down. While in the capitol building, Judy Heumann addressed congressional representatives and reporters, saying: "I can tell you that every time you raise issues of 'separate but equal,' the outrage of disabled individuals across this country is going to continue.

It is going to be ignited. There will be more takeovers of buildings until finally maybe you begin to understand our position. We will no longer allow the government to oppress disabled individuals. We want the law enforced" (quoted in Crowley, 2024).

Conceding to protester demands, the regulations were finally signed without changes. According to Kitty Cone, this was the first time that "disability really was looked at as an issue of civil rights rather than an issue of charity and rehabilitation at best, pity at worst" (quoted in Grim, 2015).

In 1988, students at Gallaudet University, the only university specifically for deaf students in the USA, organized the "Deaf President Now" protest. Students called for a deaf president of Gallaudet and a majority of deaf people on the Board of Trustees of their university. The student activists, with support of a number of alumni, faculty, and staff, shut down the campus. They barricaded school gates, burned effigies, and gave interviews to the press. More than a thousand students participated in a rally on Gallaudet's football field. The week-long protest successfully led to the appointment of Dr. I. King Jordan, the first deaf president of Gallaudet.

Two years later in 1990, disability protesters and their allies gathered on the steps of the US Capitol building. They were there to support passage of the Americans with Disabilities Act (ADA), which had stalled in Congress because of issues involving public transportation. Public transit companies vehemently opposed the implementation of strong accessibility regulations, and their lobbying efforts slowed down the entire legislative process. Over 1000 people marched from the White House to the Capitol building. When they got there, about 60 people with impairments led by 8-year-old Jennifer Keelan pushed aside their wheelchairs, walkers, and crutches, and slowly ascended the steps of the Capital, an event known as the "Capitol Crawl." By dragging themselves up the stairs, these protesters publicly expressed their daily struggles with the physical barriers of built environments. Iconic pictures of this event were spread across the country by the mass media. To date, the ADA and the subsequent ADA Amendments Act of 2008 are the disability movement's greatest legal achievements. The ADA prohibits the discrimination of people with disabilities in many aspects of public life.

Despite this tremendous victory, which led to significant improvements in public access for people with impairments, the burden of responsibility still falls on the disability community to bring up the ADA and identify accommodations that do not meet the basic requirements of the law. Moreover, in 2018, the Republican-controlled House of Representatives narrowly voted to weaken the ADA, making people with impairments second-class citizens again, but the bill designed to achieve this backward step failed in the Senate. Says Heumann: "I think we've come a long way in the last 50, 60 years, but we still have so much more to do" (quoted in Rajkumar, 2022).

Breast Cancer Activism

Prior to the 1970s, biomedicine primarily treated breast cancer by performing radical mastectomies. Inspired by ACT UP, in 1991, several activists founded a grassroots organization known as the National Breast Cancer Coalition (NBCC). NBCC describes itself as a collaboration of activists, cancer survivors, researchers, policy makers, grassroots groups, and national organizations that work as disruptive innovators for social change. These breast cancer activists advocated for increased federal funding for research and used an educational approach to help their members achieve social change. Breast cancer activists pursued four core goals: (1) removing the stigma and loss of femininity that had long been culturally linked with breast cancer; (2) empowering women through education and advocacy; (3) increasing women's influence in relevant health policy decisions; and (4) changing medical norms for the treatment of breast cancer. NBCC has trained several thousand advocates who have challenged the status quo and demanded their voices be heard wherever breast cancer decisions are made, from hospital boardrooms to the nation's capital to research laboratories. Driven by a sense of urgency, breast cancer activists have achieved increased consumer awareness of the range of treatment options that are available while increasing the availability of mammography, allowing for earlier diagnosis and less radical treatment approaches. Due in part to NBCC's efforts, federal funding in the USA for breast cancer research increased from $74.5 million in 1989 to $700 million in 2002. Over time, NBCC activism has generated more than $4 billion for breast cancer research. Women advocates now serve on scientific review panels, raise funds for screening and treatment, and link breast cancer to the issue of inadequate social services for women in lower socio-economic brackets, especially the underserved and uninsured.

In *The Breast Cancer Wars*, Barron Lerner (2001) attributes the replacement of radical mastectomies with less disfiguring and less invasive modalities due to the influence of breast cancer activism. This effort also reduced the social stigma attached both to having breast cancer and to having a mastectomy. On December 6, 1994, outside of the San Francisco headquarters of the biotechnology company Genentech, a group of protestors shouted, honked, waved signs, and laid out on the street. Unified by the slogan "access not excuses," they demanded increased access to the then-novel drug, Herceptin. For the protestors at the Genentech and their allies, Herceptin—regardless of the risks it presented—was a symbol of hope. It was a promising treatment for those who had exhausted all other treatment options. In the fall of 1998, breast cancer activists and their allies planned another protest, this time a rally in Washington D.C. intended to convince the FDA to approve Herceptin. Several days before the planned protest, however, activists received word that the FDA approved the drug for treating metastatic breast cancer as a first-line therapy. The planned rally still took place, but was more of a celebration than a protest. In 2017, in London, breast cancer activists, doctors, students, and cancer patients and their family members gathered to protest the high price placed on breast cancer medications, like Herceptin, opening an ongoing struggle with Big Pharma (Epker, 2024).

In 2024, NBCC continues to focus on metastatic breast cancer, which is cancer that has spread from the breast to the bones, lungs, or other parts of the body. Currently, 90% of breast cancer deaths are caused by metastatic disease. The life expectancy of people diagnosed with metastatic disease averages three years. Advocates seek passage of the Metastatic Breast Cancer Access to Care Act, which would provide payment to help ease the pain of sufferers and reduce financial hardship through Medicare.

In terms of cancer science, cancer activists helped to do the following: (1) move medical and social debates about cancer causation "upstream" to consider environmental factors like pollution from toxic chemicals; (2) shifted the emphasis in research from individual patients to societal level factors; (3) accelerate the release of new breast cancer medicines; and (4) push for lay involvement in research as a strategy for raising new questions, critically examining and changing standard research methods, and revising understandings of what counts as proof based on innovative methods of knowledge construction.

Syringe Exchange and Harm Reduction

The community distribution of sterile needles to people who inject drugs (PWID) began in the early 1980s in the era of HIV/AIDS as a small-scale and illegal practice initiated by advocates concerned about drug user health and well-being as highly stigmatized individuals. The goal was harm reduction, a disease prevention strategy used to decrease the negative consequences of illicit drug use and sexual activity (including the spread of HIV/AIDS) without requiring abstinence or enrollment in drug treatment. Harm reduction is predicated on the view that people who are unable or not ready to stop risky behaviors can still make positive changes to protect themselves and others from disease. The earliest efforts were seen as an act of last resort to save lives, as well as outright civil disobedience because of prevailing laws criminalizing outreach efforts that circulated drug use paraphernalia like sterile syringes (McClean, 2022).

Needle distribution emerged in a context in which the label "drug user" had firmly consolidated as a distinct cultural artifact of contemporary society. This view of drug users was produced by government bodies, the mass media, the cultural industries (T.V., movies, theater), policy makers, policy enforcers, and even public health. But the construction of the drug user as a dreaded "social other" and a pariah group is particularly insidious. It causes great harm to many people by perpetuating negative stereotypes and rationalizing mistreatment, criminalization, and the denial of health services (Singer & Page, 2013). In turn, stigmatization and discrimination enhance the guilt many drug users already feel for hurting those around them. As a result, drug users commonly internalize negative attitudes toward themselves. These feelings of shame and isolation may reinforce drug-seeking behavior as an escape from suffering.

The spread of what would later be called AIDS to PWIDs was first reported in the USA in 1981, at the very beginning of the epidemic (Masur et al., 1981). Within a few years, thousands of people who injected drugs were infected. To help PWIDs avoid infection with HIV and to counter the dominant social treatment of drug users, Jon Stuen-Parker and a group of students from the Yale School of Medical began educational outreach on the streets of New Haven in 1983. Their goal was to help PWID avoid infection with HIV. In his self-published autobiography, *Letter To Norman Mailer: From Jail to Yale*, Stuen-Parker (1998) describes his rollercoaster transformation from being a heroin addict who burglarized pharmacies to steal drugs, to a convicted felon, to a Yale medical student. Given his past, Stuen-Parker reports he was spurred to action by the doubting words of a guest speaker at the medical school who told students not to waste their time trying to educate drug users, because they would never change their behavior.

In 1985, Stuen-Parker founded the National AIDS Brigade, a volunteer AIDS prevention initiative targeted at PWIDs. The next year, Stuen-Parker and some of his classmates opened a storefront outreach center for drug users in New Haven. But later that year, he was forced to leave the medical school after failing the first part of his medical board exam three times. He attributed his problem with test taking to dyslexia, but school officials told him he should focus more time on studying and less time on his HIV prevention work. He then switched his major to public health, which he completed in 1992. But he also continued his outreach program.

To make money, Stuen-Parker worked as a Boston cab driver and used some of his earnings to buy syringes legally in Vermont and distribute them in shooting galleries, places where PWIDs gather to inject drugs and often share syringes. The Brigade would eventually offer syringe exchange services in New Haven, Boston, Philadelphia, and New York, although it was illegal to do so. The model for syringe exchange came from Amsterdam. When an inner-city pharmacist there stopped selling syringes, the Junkie Union, a group composed of PWIDs, grew concerned about hepatitis B infection. They successfully organized their own syringe exchange and the idea spread. Participants in the Brigade viewed their efforts as an act of human caring. The objective was to provide PWIDs with sterile syringes while removing potentially infected syringes from the street. Because of this work, during the 1980s and early 1990s, Stuen-Parker was arrested 27 times in seven states, an experience common to the first wave of syringe exchange activists in the USA.

As the HIV epidemic continued to spread, however, local and state governments began to change their policies, legalizing and even funding syringe exchange. Abundant research showed that syringe programs can provide a range of services, including access to and disposal of sterile syringes and other injection equipment (such as drug cookers, tourniquets, alcohol wipes, and sharps waste disposal containers), vaccination for viral hepatitis, disease testing, overdose prevention medications, and linkage to infectious disease care and drug use treatment. This research also shows that these programs are safe and effective tools for the prevention of HIV/AIDS and high-risk behaviors among people who inject drugs (McKnight et al., 2005). Further, harm reduction strategies like syringe exchange have been shown to substantially reduce HIV and hepatitis C infection among PWID, reduce overdose risk, enhance health and safety, and increase by five-fold the likelihood of initiating drug treatment programs (Abdul-Quader et al., 2013; Hagan et al. 2000).

Further, research shows that syringe exchange does not increase crime in areas where programs are based and do not increase illegal drug use (Singer et al., 1997). By 2021, syringe exchange in the USA was legal in 30 states and the District of Columbia, illegal in 11 states, and locally permitted at the city or county level in the remaining states (Legislative Analysis and Public Policy Association, 2023). Over time, the operation of syringe exchange programs has shifted significantly and become institutionalized as a necessary public health measure. Programs that provide sterile syringes to PWIDs operate in 92 countries around the world. Stigma and discrimination, however, continue to hamper equal access to healthcare for people, PWIDs, and other drug users, and women face significantly higher levels of exclusion and barriers to drug treatment.

Reproductive Rights and the Women's Health Movement

Although its roots stretch back in time to the 1830s and Suffragism, the modern women's health movement began in the USA in the 1960s. A primary focus of women activists has been the struggle to gain reproductive rights and to oppose state or medical control of women's bodies. At its most expansive level, the goal has been the restructuring of the total healthcare system and a redefinition of healthcare. This includes a demand for improved service and access for all women and an end to sexism in the health system. In the view of many women health activists, "The oppression of woman is derived from her "womanness": her biologic differences and her ability to bear children. These differences have been used [by men] to build social structures and a supportive ideology of female submissiveness—an ideology so entrenched that [women] came to believe it. Medical science in turn reinforced the ideology" (Marieskind, 1975). A base that helped drive the movement were women's self-help health groups. By 1973, it is estimated that there were more than 1200 women's self-help health groups across the USA (Schneir, 1994).

Abortion, both legal and illegal, has a long history in the USA. The legal status of abortion has varied over time. The practice was generally permitted at the founding of the nation and for several decades afterward. The procedure was made illegal under most circumstances in most states beginning in the mid-1800s. In the 1960s, states began reforming their strict antiabortion laws. Though illegal under most circumstances, abortion was legal in 17 states for a range of conditions beyond those necessary to save a woman's life. While legal therapeutic abortions were relatively few in number, it is estimated that there were more than 1 million illegal abortions occurring annually. About a third of the women who had illegal abortions during those years suffered complications that necessitated hospital admittance and 500–1000 women died each year due to unsafe illegal abortions (Nichols, 2000). Women with the ability to pay had some, if quite limited, access to a legal abortion. For example, in 1967, the UK changed its abortion law to permit any woman to have an abortion with the written consent of two physicians. Over 600 women from the USA traveled to the UK for an abortion during the last three months of 1969 alone. By 1970, costly package deals, which included round-trip airfare, passports, vaccination, transportation to and from the airport, lodging for four days, meals, and the procedure itself, were advertised in the popular media (Gold, 2003).

Poorer women, especially members of ethnic minority groups, had few options outside of a dangerous illegal procedure. Driving the bans on abortion was the concern among white men that increased immigration from countries outside of Western Europe could lead to a decrease in their hold on positions of power. Bans were especially intended to get upper-class white women to have more children (Coates, 2023).

Led by organizations like the National Abortion Rights Action League and Planned Parenthood, activists came together to form a powerful grassroots effort to support women's reproductive rights that culminated in the landmark Supreme Court decision of *Roe v Wade* in 1973. This judicial ruling, based on the 14th Amendment to the Constitution, stated that a woman's choice to have an abortion outweighs the state's concern for prenatal life up until the point of fetal viability (the developmental stage when a fetus can survive outside the womb), which was determined to be 24–28 weeks into the pregnancy. This decision was not made in a vacuum but emerged from several decades of pro-choice grassroots activism and protest by groups across the country. By making abortion legal nationwide, Roe v. Wade had a dramatic effect on the health and well-being of women in the USA. Deaths from abortion fell significantly. Women were able to have abortions earlier in their pregnancies when the procedure is safest. The proportion of abortions obtained early in the first trimester rose from 20% in 1970 to 56% in 1998 (Gold, 2003).

After half a century as the law of the land, on June 24, 2022, a much more conservative Supreme Court overturned *Roe v Wade* arguing in the Dobbs decision that the Constitution does not confer a right to abortion. This enormous step backward for women's reproductive rights unleashed a new wave of pro-choice activism. As Zhu (2023) asserts,

> Community engagement, public activism, and social solidarity represent powerful tools to support people with the capacity for pregnancy [after the fall of *Roe v Wade*]. These strategies have the potential to bridge disparities in access to the full spectrum of reproductive health services amidst the legal barriers newly imposed on clinicians.... [P]ublic activism is no silver bullet to the future of abortion care and rights after *Dobbs v. Jackson*. Nevertheless, it represents a promising solution to bridge gaps in reproductive healthcare access, resources, and infrastructure…

Although reproductive rights continued to be a major focus of grassroots activism after *Roe V Wade*, the woman's health movement also turned its attention to many other issues that affect women's health, including a comprehensive approach to improving healthcare access and demanded an end to sexism in the health system. Even before the Dobbs decision was released, pro-choice advocates throughout the USA began organizing and raising money to help those seeking abortions get to those states where the procedure was less restricted or still legal. The National Network of Abortion Funds began helping to finance transportation, hotel rooms, meals, childcare, and the procedure itself, for people seeking the termination of a pregnancy. Activists also mobilized to enshrine the right to abortion into state constitutions. They hit the streets to gather enough authenticated signatures to put the right to abortion on the ballot in a number of states. As a result, four states, California, Ohio, Michigan, and Vermont, affirmed abortion access. In three others, Kansas, Kentucky, and Montana, voters defeated anti-choice ballot measures. The focus then switched to the 2024 presidential election as a crucial test of abortion access.

Elsewhere in the world the struggle for the right to abortion has traveled a difficult road. Elyse Singer (2022) notes that, "Throughout the twentieth century, governments around the globe intervened in reproductive practices to regulate national birthrates and/or enhance population 'quality.' Draconian measures such as China's one-child policy and Romania's categorical abortion ban, designed to curtail and stimulate population growth respectively, exemplify some of the more extreme means by which states have interceded in the production of individuals and political bodies." In her own ethnography of abortion in Mexico, Singer shows that the legalization of abortion in Mexico City and its incorporation in public hospitals, which was celebrated as a tremendous victory by women's reproductive rights activists, in fact, created a situation in which women seeking abortions commonly are subject to provider lectures about the norms of "good" and "responsible" womanhood. While the legalization and state funding of abortion in the Capital opened up opportunities for women's reproductive choice, it also expanded reproductive governance and the regulation of woman's bodies. Singer (2022) describes how the staff at public clinics do not tend to view abortion as a right available independent of the circumstances surrounding each pregnancy. Rather, for nurses and intake workers in abortion clinics, abortion rights were treated as conditional, contingent, and contextual. During Singer's interviews and observed interaction with clients, almost all staff statements about abortion were tempered by expectations or conditions on the part of women seeking the procedure (e.g., admonishments not to have multiple abortions over time). In 2021, the supreme court of Mexico abolished criminal penalties against women who receive abortions. Two years later, abortion was decriminalized in Mexico at the federal level. As a result, going to Mexico became an alternative for women in the USA unable to seek an abortion at home.

Las Libres, a Mexico-based activist network founded in 2000 by Verónica Cruz Sánchez in Guanajuato, which promotes women's human rights and universal access to abortion in the country, also supports women in the USA who lost their right to choose when *Roe v Wade* was reversed. The organization seeks to do several things: eliminate gender stereotypes and ensure that women are recognized as equals in Mexico; combat violence against women and support women who experience it; provide sexual and reproductive health education; provide trained volunteers to accompany women traveling from other parts of Mexico to seek a legal abortion in the capital; and distribute misoprostol, a WHO-approved abortion pill in Mexico and the USA. After the fall of *Roe v Wade*, Las Libres received a flood of messages from women in the USA asking for help. Las Libres recruited 300 activist volunteers in the USA, who have assisted over 10,000 women. Moreover, thousands of women in Mexico have been charged with the crime of abortion after a miscarriage or some other obstetric emergency. The laws around abortion historically have been so severe in the country that women who lose their pregnancies wind up being accused of doing so on purpose. In 2010, Las Libres secured the freedom of nine women who were imprisoned in Guanajuato for late-term miscarriages and also charged with aggravated homicide of a family member. In the years that followed, Las Libres organized legal defenses that freed more than 100 women from incarceration across Mexico.

Long COVID

Paul Garner, an infectious disease researcher at the Liverpool School of Tropical Medicine, UK, contracted COVID-19 in March 2020. The experience was intense and he thought he was dying. He recalls feeling "absolutely dreadful, sweaty, dizzy… It was very intense fatigue." What most surprised him was oscillating between feeling sick and thinking he had recovered, noting "I would feel better and the illness would come out of nowhere and floor me. It was like being hit over the head with a cricket bat" (Quoted in Joi, 2022). Ultimately Garner realized that he was suffering from a post-COVID condition that in time came to be known as "long COVID." Garner (2020) then started publishing a blog account of his suffering, describing it as:

> a roller coaster of ill health, extreme emotions, and utter exhaustion… The illness ebbs and flows, but never goes away…. The illness went on and on. The symptoms changed, it was like an advent calendar, every day there was a surprise, something new. A muggy head; acutely painful calf; upset stomach; tinnitus; pins and needles; aching all over; breathlessness; dizziness; arthritis in my hands; weird sensation in the skin with synthetic materials…. I joined a Facebook page … full of people with these stories, some from the UK, some from the US. People suffering from the disease, but not believing their symptoms were real; their families thinking the symptoms were anxiety; employers telling people they had to return to work, as the two weeks for the illness was up… I thought I was going crazy for not getting better in their time frame; the doctor said, "there is zero reason to believe it lasts this long". And too, people report[ed] that their families do not believe their ever changing symptoms, that it is psychological, it is the stress.

Garner subsequently reported that patients took his account with them to medical appointments to provide evidence of the authenticity of their prolonged and worrisome symptoms, which continued even after they tested negative for COVID-19 infection.

In time, the condition would be medically defined as a varied set of health problems that persist for three months after a person becomes ill from infection with the SARS-CoV-2 virus. Long COVID is a systemic condition that is manifest in a wide range of respiratory, neurological, psychological, cardiac, or other symptoms that may improve, worsen, resolve and return, or be ongoing. Long COVID can follow an asymptomatic, mild, or severe SARS-CoV-2 infection. As people can be infected by SARS-CoV-2 multiple times, with each new infection they have a risk of developing long COVID (Harvey-Dunstan et al., 2022).

Yet for several years, people were still told by doctors that their array of post-COVID symptoms were "all in your head" (Mendenhall, 2023), what anthropologists call "illness" (experience of feeling sick) without "disease" (a formal and legitimizing medical diagnosis). Sufferers were forced to "confront the stigma caused by its lack of biological verification and societal acceptance, [and they had to] do so in bodies that [were] exhausted" (Rogers, 2022). From the perspective of health activism, medical recognition of the disease, the state of funding, research, and treatment was an uphill grassroots struggle that ultimately culminated in victory. Thus, at a special meeting of the American Medical Association's House of Delegates in June 2021, the powerful medical organization adopted a policy to support the development of an International Classification of Diseases code or family of codes to recognize long COVID and other novel post-viral syndromes as distinct diagnoses and to call for more funding for research, prevention, and treatment. Subsequently, the US National Institutes for Health allocated over $1 billion for research on long COVID and the Department of Health and Human Services accepted long COVID as a recognized disability for government funding and classification purposes. Along with the Department of Justice, it also issued guidance stating that if it substantially limits one or more major life activities long COVID may be a disability under the ADA.

It is important to remember that long COVID is a popularly coined term that grew out of an effort by patients who thought they had weathered a COVID-19 infection only to discover over time that despite their negative COVID-19 test results,] they still suffered from both puzzling and taxing symptoms. The term was first used by Elisa Perego, an archaeologist from Lombardy, Italy. [As she and a group of individuals with similar experiences explain: "The patient-made term 'Long Covid" is, we argue, a helpful and capacious term that is needed to address key medical, epidemiological and socio-political challenges posed by diverse symptoms persisting beyond four weeks after symptom onset suggestive of coronavirus disease 2019 (COVID-19)" (Perego et al., 2020). This effort by an international initiative of patients helped bring long COVID to widespread public and medical visibility. Over time, the term long COVID became increasingly prominent and was complemented by various alternatives (e.g., COVID-19 long haulers) adopted by people with long COVID symptoms, all reflecting a growing need for affirmation of authentic distress and medical attention. As Felicity Callard (a human geology researcher) and Elisa Perego note, "There are strong reasons to argue that Long Covid is the first illness to be made through patients finding one another on Twitter and other social media" (Callard & Perego, 2021). Yet even before COVID-19, several chronic conditions, such as chronic fatigue syndrome and chronic Lyme disease, also had an extensive social media presence among affected persons prior to gaining medical recognition.

In their struggle, by connecting through social media, people with long COVID moved beyond passively enduring their burdensome symptoms and formed online communities that shared experiences and knowledge, and helped participants gain a greater sense of control by becoming health advocates. Online forums allowed people with long COVID to express and share their day-to-day challenges, as seen in the following two testimonials from an online forum social networking site (reddit, 2022):

> I've had the fog and fatigue for well over a year now. It's greatly impacted my ability to think quickly. I'm fluent in 4 languages and have always been sharp as a tack. Now it takes me so much longer to process and problem solve that I no longer feel like the same person. It's as if my fast, modern CPU has been downgraded to a 486dx. In the end, I can still reason and come to the same conclusions it's just much harder. It's causing some serious depression atm [at the moment].
>
> The first time I got it was early April, then late June, then early October. My office was having horrible outbreaks and they still required us to work on site. I can't work. I can't think, and I am a programmer. Simple tasks are impossible, I don't understand documentation anymore, I can hardly read English (the only language I know) anymore. I finally got into a doctor this month and they pretty much told me there isn't much they can do. I can't eat solids, can't have coffee like I used to. Luckily tea is still fine. I eat pretty much only soup as everything else makes me feel sick instantly. Fatigue is so bad.

On these forums, people with long Covid regularly complained that their symptoms were not recognized by public health officials or healthcare providers. They also shared ideas about behavioral or other changes they had made to reduce or control their symptoms. One advocacy group, the COVID-19 Long Haulers Advocacy Project, and began as an online Facebook group and consolidated as a non-profit, patient-led organization with 60 chapters, urged long COVID sufferers to stay current with new research and new research centers, enroll in long COVID research and clinical trials, contact Congressional representatives to advance policy change, and become active in the organization.

Several other advocacy organizations also were founded by people with long COVID. An example is Survivor Corps, started by Diana Berrent while she was attempting unsuccessfully to get medical information and testing for COVID-19. Frustrated, she wrote a letter to her Congressional representative and then posted her letter on Facebook. The post went viral, and she soon was contacted by her congressional representative, who arranged for her to be tested. Afterward, under the banner "Empathize, Organize, Mobilize," she launched Survivor Corps, a grassroots organization committed to educate and mobilize the growing number of people affected by COVID-19 and long COVID (Sellers, 2021).

As Callard and Perego (2021) summarize, long COVID challenged "common assumptions that were in place in the early pandemic and which often persisted despite patient testimony. In the making of Long Covid, conventional hierarchies of evidence, and normative routes for scientific dissemination were frequently disrupted.... Many clinicians and researchers at the forefront of Long Covid research and advocacy ... have had Covid. Others carved out authority by dint of being patients..."

Of note, the Centers for Disease Control and Prevention (2024b) reports that disability, poverty, geographic location, gender, ethnicity, people with other health conditions, and the unvaccinated are more likely to develop long COVID than others. Health inequalities increase both the risk of negative health outcomes and the impact from long COVID. In a study using a nationally representative community-based survey of over 200,000 working-age adults in the UK, Shabnam et al. (2023) found that the risk of long COVID was 46% higher on average for participants from the most deprived areas compared to those in the least deprived areas. They conclude: "Our study demonstrates that people from the most socioeconomically deprived populations have the highest risk of Long COVID, and this inequality is independent of differences in the risk of initial infection. The level of inequality was particularly higher in participants who are female, working in healthcare and in the education sector."

As the USA moves further from the height of the COVID-19 pandemic, the rate of long COVID remains steady. Seven percent of all adults, about 17 million people, reported currently having long COVID in March 2024. Among the 60% of US adults who reported having had COVID, roughly 3 in 10 report suffering from long COVID at some point (Burns, 2024). At a US Senate Committee on Health, Education, Labor and Pensions hearing in January 2024, patients testified about their challenges with long COVID. These witnesses called for additional federal funding to improve the diagnosis and treatment of their condition, signifying that the struggle continues.

ME/CSF and Encumbered Activism

Myalgic encephalomyelitis (ME), also known as chronic fatigue syndrome (CFS), is a complicated and frustrating health condition. It causes extreme fatigue that lasts for months. Other symptoms include memory problems, confusion, dizziness, muscle or joint pain, heightened sensitivity to light, sound, smells, food, and medicines, as well as headaches, sore throats, and tender lymph nodes in the neck or armpits. But symptoms differ from person to person, and the severity of symptoms can fluctuate from day to day. Symptoms increase with physical or mental activity, but do not fully improve with rest. ME/CFS is very debilitating, forcing about one-quarter of its sufferers to be home-bound or even bed-bound. The cause of ME/CSF is still unknown, although many theories have been suggested.

While the disease has been recognized for 40 years, there are no agreed-upon biomarkers for it (that would afform its biological presence). This has led some physicians to conclude the condition is psychogenic, a condition with a psychological origin caused by stress that mimics other disorders. During the 1980s, the derogatory label "shirker syndrome" emerged to express doubt about the biological basis of ME/CSF. A study by Deale and Wessely (2001) of the perceptions of medical care experienced by ME/CFS patients who had been referred to a specialist clinic in the UK found that two-thirds were dissatisfied with the quality of care they received. Dissatisfied patients were significantly more likely to describe delay, dispute, or doctor confusion about their diagnosis, to have received and rejected a psychiatric diagnosis, to perceive their doctors as dismissive or not knowledgeable about ME/CFS, and to feel that the medical advice they were given was inadequate or conflicting. Murray et al. (2019) found a significant gender bias in their analysis of English newspaper articles about patients with ME/CFS. Women sufferers were portrayed as emotionally distressed while their physical symptoms were minimized. The negative impacts of the condition on social and home functioning were emphasized. By contrast, men with ME/CSF were described as action-oriented individuals prior to their illness. In the reporting, men's physical symptoms were prominently discussed and the adverse impacts on their career and involvement in sports were emphasized. As ME/CFS is rarely diagnosed outside the Global North, it is unclear if it is a health issue in the Global South at present.

According to Emily Rogers (2022), who carried out an ethnographic study of ME/CFS activists, people with ME/CFS face a dual-pronged challenge. First, they endure stigmatization as being slackers, pretenders, and lazy by co-workers and employers, and many patients report that their doctors viewed them as hypochondriacs or expressed disbelief. Second, their symptoms make it hard to protest the discrimination they face. The struggle to gain medical legitimation by ME/CFS sufferers is a political one, but the strategies adopted by activists are shaped by their condition. Thus, Rogers describes the unique features of a demonstration at the New York State Psychiatric Institute by ME/CFS activists. It was a cold day and participants were clothed in windbreakers. Under the watchful eye of several police officers, about 15 people walked in a picket line carrying signs that proclaimed their condition was not psychosomatic. Other protesters were lying down on the grass or sitting in folding chairs. Some had to look away as the circling picketers began to make them dizzy. Others wore ear plugs to reduce sensory overstimulation. Collectively, they chanted, "Science not stigma!" A hired film crew transmitted a video of the action to thousands of viewers who streamed it live from their beds, chairs, and couches across the globe. According to Rogers (2022), "The peculiar shape of this protest, complete with its bedbound viewership, typifies the [nature of the] activism surrounding the disease for which they were advocating."

Rogers found that video chats, message boards, and other Internet communication were central to the ME/CFS activists she studied. A common theme of online discussions was what she called "symptom talk," conversations about symptoms and impairment. Symptom talk was central to the social life of the people she studied. Suffering from impairment that was not validated by medical authority motivated sufferers to seek out other forms of support. Shared impairments bound ME/CFS activist groups together. The heterogeneity of symptoms was a regular topic of group conversations, during which participants divulged the most intimate and private aspects of their lives. This practice built trust, camaraderie, and solidarity among virtual strangers. Participants also shared a desire for societal and medical legitimation, more research, and better treatments, the issues that motivated their activism. Their desire for bringing about change, however, was heavily encumbered by their symptoms.

Despite their challenges, ME/CFS activists have had some impact. For example, they supported passage of the Understanding COVID-19 Subsets and ME/CFS Act, to authorize a $60 million program expansion for ME/CFS research. Supporters emailed and called their representatives, and those who could, participated in meetings to ask their representatives to join the call for increased funding for ME/CSF research. The bill was referred to the House Committee on Energy and Commerce for further consideration. In another campaign, activists supported a request by Senator Edward Markey of Massachusetts and 18 other senators from both parties for 1) $9.9 million to fund ME/CFS programs at the Centers for Disease Control and 2) adding ME/CFS patients to the Peer-Reviewed Medical Research Program. ME/CFS was successfully added, resulting in over $500,000 of ME/CFS research funding in 2020. In 2019, following grassroots advocacy, Congress recognized International ME/CFS Awareness Day on May 12th. On a darker note, ME/CFS researchers have complained about being harassed by frustrated sufferers through email and phone messages. While this response has primarily been directed at researchers looking into the psychological aspects of ME/CFS, it has also affected those scientists investigating biological mechanisms of the disease.

Assessing Health Activism

As the discussion above suggests, health-linked social activism entails challenging the existing order whenever it is perceived to lead to suffering, ill health, social injustice, or inequality. It involves going beyond what is conventional or routine in society based on a vision, usually only partially articulated, of a better future. Commonly, it is steered by self-advocacy but often attracts supporters and allies who are not themselves patients. Moreover, the changes that have been won benefit others who have not been involved. Health activism in various places has helped people to redress, to varying degrees, the unequal distribution of power in society and to take more control over their lives (Laverack, 2013). Over time, some of these initiatives have broadened their goals to more universal issues, like healthcare coverage for all.

Based on ethnographic and archival research in Spain, for example, Ker (2023) examines the grassroots struggle to save the nation's national health service, which was universal in terms of access and free at the point of use since Spain's transition from fascism in the 1970s. However, as a result of the global economic crisis of 2008, both healthcare workers and citizens became increasingly alarmed with the deterioration of the healthcare system due to government-imposed austerity policies involving the cutting of public spending on healthcare. This sparked a large-scale movement of healthcare activism, called the 15-M Movement (because it began on May 15, 2011). Activists engaged in a series of massive protests, demonstrations, and occupations. The goals of M-15 were to oppose healthcare cuts, limit healthcare privatization, and safeguard the national health service for all. [Notably, Javier Romañach, a wheelchair-bound Spanish scholar/activist, participated along with other disability activists in the anti-austerity struggle in Madrid. In his writings, Romañach (2009) asserted that disability activism in Spain anticipated the anti-austerity movement. He describes the independent living movement in Spain as a "mini 15-M" that emerged years prior to the anti-austerity movement of 2011–2012. After one year of large marches and rallies, strikes, and legal action, healthcare activists in Spain achieved an important victory when the Madrid Superior Court ruled in favor of a collective legal claim to stop the regional privatization plan.

The privatization of public health services in Spain went hand in hand with austerity cuts in funding, mirroring a much larger neoliberal process of marketization of healthcare that has been imposed by governments around the world. Research shows that such policies lead to an increase in social inequalities and the worsening of various health problems (Castro & Singer, 2004). Such restructuring has been commonly opposed by health activists, whatever their primary health issues. As Laverack (2013) argues, "What is clear is that if we do not challenge top-down programming, individualism, greedy corporations and complacent governments, we will continue to have limited success in improving poor health.... Health activism offers the way forward at a time when difficult political and economic decisions have to be made and when innovative ideas in practice are lacking."

From Love Canal to the Environmental Health Movement

Unlike many sectors of the environmental movement, environmental health focuses on ways toxic chemicals and other anthropogenic hazardous agents in the environment affect human health and well-being. By placing human health at the center of its effort, the movement has sought to show that the quality of the environment concerns everyone. This activist campaign began in 1978 when Lois Gibbs, a 27-year-old homemaker from a working-class family, read a story in her local newspaper and discovered to her horror that her children's elementary school was built on a toxic waste dump. She knew that when they moved to the area located about four miles south of Niagara Falls, both of her children were healthy. After the move they began suffering from some serious health issues, including epilepsy and a low white blood cell count. In the articles she read, Gibbs learned that inexplicable illnesses like epilepsy, asthma, migraines, and kidney damage were being reported by neighborhood residents and abnormally high rates of birth defects and miscarriages were occurring as well. She also knew that there was a noxious smell in the air in and around her home. It permeated her basement and backyard and the blocks around her home. She began to wonder if there was a connection between the illnesses, the odor, and the location of the school her children attended. As a first step, she approached the school board but left without any answers or any acknowledgment that there might be a problem. She recalls, "I always understood that if you had a problem, the government was supposed to help you... They taught you that in school" (quoted in Copeland, 1998). Frustrated, she decided to start a petition to gather signatures from her neighbors demanding answers.

Over the following months, drawing on skills she never knew she had, she organized her neighbors as the Love Canal Parents Movement and took on the State of New York and the Hooker Chemical Company. Hooker had purchased the canal, a trench left over from the unfinished Love Canal hydroelectric power project, and used it, with government sanction, to dump about 20 tons of chemical by-products from the manufacturing of dyes, perfumes, and solvents for rubber and synthetic resins. Included in the toxic soup beneath the school was dioxin, one of the most toxic of manufactured chemicals. In 1953, Hooker capped the 16-acre hazardous waste landfill in clay and sold it to the local school district for $1. The land was used for the site of the 93rd Street School that Gibbs' children attended and homes were built all around the area. Then, unusually heavy rain and snow in 1975 and 1976 raised groundwater levels in the Love Canal area. Basements began to ooze an oily residue.

Under Gibbs' leadership, Love Canal homeowners picketed and rallied, carried empty coffins to the state government offices in Albany, New York, and burned politicians in effigy. After two years of struggle, Gibbs and the other activists won. After the federal government purchased their homes, over 800 families were evacuated from the area and the cleanup of Love Canal began. Their hard work led to the creation of the US EPA's Comprehensive Environmental Response, Compensation and Liability Act, which established an entity called the Superfund, designed to clean up contaminated sites around the country. Occidental Chemical Corporation, which took over Hooker, paid over $230 million in settlements to the state, the federal government, and Love Canal ex-homeowners, although they admitted to no wrongdoing or negligence.

During the crisis, Gibbs received many calls from people across the country who told her they were experiencing similar problems. This made her realize that the problem of toxic waste went far beyond her own backyard. She became determined to support grassroots efforts to fight against this widespread threat. Her husband, who had been supportive of her efforts, balked at the idea of taking on struggles in other places. He urged her to return to her old life as a homemaker. Even her mother told her "you're forgetting you're just a housewife with a high school education" (Fredonia State University of New York, 2010). Gibbs was undeterred. She left Niagara Falls for the Washington, DC, area to establish the Center for Health, Environment and Justice (CHEJ), formerly Citizens Clearinghouse for Hazardous Wastes, to help families living near other contaminated sites like Love Canal. Over time, CHEJ has assisted over 10,000 grassroots groups with organizing training and providing technical and general information nationwide. Through these efforts, a militant environmental health movement spread across the USA and to other parts of the world. Fueling the movement was a mounting frustration with the failure of mainstream environmentalism to address the disproportionate impact of toxic pollution on working-class and minority communities. Working mostly at the state and local levels, environmental health activists organized communities to protest abandoned toxic waste dumps, oppose new hazardous facilities, raise awareness about local disease clusters, and draw attention to cases of environmental injustice. This work continues today.

The movement started by Gibbs attracted an activist/scholar named Kate Davies. In 1965, when Davies was eight years old and living in the UK, her mother was diagnosed with Hodgkin's lymphoma and given less than a year to live by her doctors. Nonetheless, she survived, only to be diagnosed with breast cancer 20 years later. Again, she survived, but in 1995 she developed a rare T-cell lymphoma and died in 2007, ending her 40-year struggle with multiple cancers. Because of her mother's cancer journey, Davies initially wanted to be a doctor, a not uncommon response among children with ill parents. But as she grew up, Davies became more interested in how to prevent cancer from starting in the first place. She committed herself to getting the education she would need to address cancer prevention. She completed a BA in biochemistry, an MA in anthropology, and a PhD in biochemistry. Along the way, she became convinced that toxic chemicals and radiation played important roles in the onset of cancer. When she had her son, she knew that he would be taking in toxic chemicals through her breast milk because she believed everyone had been exposed. This realization led her to join then emergent environmental health movement.

Since that time, Davies has worked with numerous nongovernmental and governmental organizations, including Greenpeace, the Collaborative on Health and the Environment, the Institute for Children's Environmental Health, the International Joint Commission, and the Royal Society of Canada. In her book, *The Rise of the US Environmental Health Movement,* she chronicles the growing concern over chemicals in our air, water, and food, and the efforts being undertaken to address these concerns. Like planetary health advocates, she argues against the notion that humans are separate from or above the environment and that it is our destiny to control nature. She notes, "every breath we take is dependent on the environment, every sip of water, every mouthful of food. If that's the case, we cannot carry on treating the environment the way we have been treating it. We can't carry on dumping our wastes into it, polluting it, contaminating it, because its those very things that we're doing that come back to haunt us through environmentally related diseases" (quoted in Collaboration for Health and Environment, 2013). As an activist, Davies (2013) urges the environmental health movement to follow the example of other social movements, such as the civil rights movement, by considering "collective, peaceful civil disobedience more often."

Like Davies, many of the people who get involved in the environmental health movement know someone with an environmentally related disease or live in a community affected by high levels of pollution. Living with or witnessing an environmental health problem firsthand can motivate activism in a way that hearing about or reading facts and figures alone often does not. Consequently, drawing the public's attention to the health effects of toxic chemicals and other environmental hazards in local settings and the people most immediately impacted is a core strategy of the environmental health initiative. The goal is to put a human face on environmental health. The belief is that the life stories of real people dealing with pressing health issues like cancer make environmental issues much more tangible and immediate.

An example of this work is the Environmental Health Coalition (EHC), which focuses on environmental health and justice in the San Diego/Tijuana corner of North America. Founded in 1980, EHC seeks to reduce pollution and improve health and well-being for people in underserved, low-income communities like Barrios Logan. Founded as residential area by cannery workers, welders, pipefitters, longshoremen, and other laborers and their families migrating from Mexico, after World War II, the City of San Diego rezoned Barrio Logan to allow an influx of polluting industries, junkyards, metal plating shops, and other toxic businesses including those that emit diesel. Diesel emissions are thought to cause 84% of the cancer risk from air pollution in neighborhoods like Barrio Logan, where residents have a higher risk of developing cancer from air toxins than 93% of the country (Environmental Health Coalition, 2024). The family of Maritza Garcia, an ECH activist, has lived in Barrios Logan for two generations. Because of the pollution she grew up around, she witnessed her mother undergo several surgeries due to respiratory illnesses. She also saw many of her friends suffer from breathing and other health complications. Garcia was inspired to get involved with EHC so she could fight against pollution in Barrio Logan. EHC provided her the information she needed to understand what was going on in her community and the skills she needed so that she could speak up to help improve her community. Elizabeth Chavez, another EHC activist from Barrios Logan, proclaims: *"My community is predominantly low-income and people of color families. They deserve a healthy environment in their own homes just like residents up in La Jolla [*a wealthy San Diego neighborhood known for its posh boutiques and seaside restaurants]."

Independent of the environmental health movement in the USA, local grassroots health and environment activist initiatives have sprung up around the world. For example, during the 1970s, a group of women from Iguatemi neighborhood in the district of Sao Mateus, Sao Paulo, Brazil, organized a meeting with the city's water and sewer authority to demand piped potable water be installed in Iguatemi. These woman knew that untreated sewage contaminated the hand-dug wells that residents used for water, causing waves of disease that were especially deadly for vulnerable infants and children. Public health officials, in fact, attributed a decline in life expectancy in the São Paulo to rising infant mortality rates in peripheral neighborhoods like Iguatemi. During the meeting, the women were surprised when the bureaucrat with whom they met told them that they lived in "green area" where there were no residential neighborhoods. In fact, their neighborhood was in a ring of settlements around the city center that was home to migrants from rural areas of Brazil. These migrants lacked legal titles to the land on which their homes were built. In response to the city's stance, the women created a grassroots movement in their neighborhood with help from a local public health worker and the Catholic Archdiocese of São Paulo. Through their efforts, the women were able to secure the construction of sanitary infrastructure as well as a state-run health center in their neighborhood. But these health activists were distressed to learn that the health center lacked adequate staffing, equipment, and medicines. Subsequently, the women began to frame their struggle around the belief that health was the right of every citizen.

Meanwhile, residents in another neighborhood, Jardim Nordeste, created an elected popular health council. The council aspired to co-manage state-run healthcare facilities to guarantee their quality and struggled to win this right, which they achieved in the early 1980s. Grassroots health activists looked to the councils as a way to enshrine health care as a legal right. According to McDonald (2023), "Health emerged as a privileged space for grassroots conceptions of citizenship precisely because it linked broadly held personal experiences to larger emancipatory democratic projects. Participation in social movements offered popular class actors more than simply a means to address material problems; it also provided a space for self-development and self-realization. A focus on the health of infants, moreover, gave their activism a legitimacy and reach greater than they likely would have achieved by focusing on other issues." Significantly, the popular health councils provided a vehicle for grassroots activists to apply pressure on the state. The example of the health councils inspired other experiments in direct democracy and contributed to national democratization and an end of military dictatorship in Brazil in 1985.

Coupling Environmental and Health Activism: From Alberta, Canada to Flint, Michigan to Bergama, Turkey

Historically, environmental and health initiatives have tended to be siloed drives for specific kinds of change. This kind of isolation from potential allies who face a common opposition is not unusual across social movements. According to historian, documentary filmmaker, and activist Jeremy Brecher (2022), "a crucial reason for movements to de-silo, cooperate, and converge stems from a perception of the possibility of gaining power to affect problems through greater cooperation and mutual support." This aspiration for more effective power is illustrated in the movement against the construction of the notorious Keystone XL pipeline, a planned 1200 mile-long project that was intended to convey 800,000 barrels of oil per day from Alberta, Canada, to distant refineries in the USA along the Gulf Coast. The pipeline was fiercely opposed by Indigenous and other groups in both the USA and Canada, including the Dene, Cree, Metis, Oceti Sakowin, and Ponca nations. Indigenous leaders helped build a broad coalition that also involved Nebraska and South Dakota landowners, including conservative ranchers, urban progressives, environmentalists, climate activists, and farm advocacy groups in an intense struggle to oppose the pipeline. "It lasted for more than a decade. The motivation to participate in the struggle varied. For Indigenous people the concern was with possible damage to sacred sites, pollution, and water contamination from leaks and spills that could lead to health risks in adjacent Indigenous communities. Environmentalists saw the pipeline and the dirty tar sand oil—which is three to four times more carbon-intensive than crude oil—it was meant to carry as a damaging source of climate change. For property owners, primarily farmers and ranchers, the threat was that the pipeline would cut across and damage prime agricultural and grazing lands. These varied groups put aside issues that divided them as well as past conflicts, built new trust relationships, and worked together to challenge the forces supporting construction of the pipeline, including oil companies that saw the project as very lucrative.

In addition to regular demonstrations at the pipeline site during a two-week period in 2013, more than 1200 people were arrested for acts of civil disobedience at the White House. In 2014, an improbable coalition calling itself the "Cowboy Indian Alliance" held a five-day "Reject and Protect" encampment in Washington, DC. Art Tanderup, a Nebraska farmer who joined the encampment, explained that the alliance formed because of "common interests between farmers, ranchers and Native Americans in northern Nebraska and southern South Dakota… We've come together as brothers and sisters to fight this Keystone XL pipeline, because of the risk to the Ogallala Aquifer, to the land, to the health of the people" (quoted in

Douglas-Bowers 2014). Mekasi Horine, a member of the Ponca Tribe of Oklahoma and a Native American rights and environmental activist, admitted that at first he was skeptical about the alliance, stating: "I've always been a little bit bitter toward white society… I've experienced a lot of racism—growing up on the res, living on the res. When I went to town I was always treated differently than others. However, Horine eventually was convinced by his mother to join the group opposing the pipeline. She reminded him that cowboys "have that love and respect for the land the same that we do" (quoted in Douglas-Boers, 2014).

After years of struggle, the movement achieved victory when on his first day in office on January 20, 2021, President Joe Biden revoked the permit for the pipeline thereby shutting the project down. As aptly expressed by *climate activist Ashley Lashley, who leads a movement called the HEY (Health and Environment-friendly Youth) Campaign targeted at young people across the Caribbean,* "The health of our people and our environment are all interconnected" (quoted in United Nations, Climate Action, 2022). Building a global planetary health movement, in fact, requires a coupling of environmental and health activism among diverse groups, including grassroots advocates, labor unions, feminist and LGBTQIA+ groups, scholars and researchers, healthcare providers, and faith-based organizations, among others.

The Flint water crisis, a signature environmental disaster in recent times, was a key moment for the convergence of mainstream environmentalism, environmental justice, and health activism. This event began on April 25, 2014, when the postindustrial city of Flint, Michigan, in a cost-saving move at the direction of an emergency manager appointed by Michigan Governor Rick Snyder, changed its drinking water source. Previously, the city used Detroit's system which is connected to Lake Huron, but switched to the Flint River, which flows through the heart of the city. The river served as an unofficial waste disposal site for treated and untreated refuse from the many local industries that were built along its shores, including carriage factories, meatpacking plants, lumber and paper mills, and car manufacturing, with Flint being the birthplace of General Motors. The waterway also has been contaminated with raw sewage from the city's waste treatment plant, agricultural and urban runoff, and toxins from leaching landfill sites. Many residents in this majority-Black city with its high poverty rate (40%), stumbling economy, shuttered auto plants, and laid-off workers immediately noticed a difference in their water quality.

According to Mona Hanna, a pediatrician in Flint who was later named associate dean for Public Health at Michigan State University: "We had greenish and brownish water. It smelled weird. It was giving people rashes and they were losing hair. Patients were asking, "Was it okay to use this tap water to mix their babies' formula?" (quoted in Kwon et al., 2024). Nonetheless, both state and city officials told Flint residents that their water was safe to drink. During a backyard barbeque at Hanna's home, a visiting friend from high school who had worked at the Environmental Protection Agency and had seen a lead crisis unfold in Washington, DC, a decade earlier implored her to look into the issue more closely. Recalls Hanna, "she literally stared me down like, 'Mona, the water doesn't have corrosion control.' That is the moment that I heard about the possibility of lead being in the water. And that's the moment my life changed" (quoted in Kwon et al., 2024). Without that corrosion control, the lead in Flint's pipes could get into the water supply. There is no safe level of lead exposure. Lead toxicity can affect every organ system in the human body, leading to neurological, renal, hematological, endocrine, gastrointestinal, cardiovascular, reproductive, and developmental effects, including mental retardation and growth failure. Children are especially susceptible. At the time, Hanna did not know that lead exposure could come through waterpipes. Yet, the Latin symbol for lead is Pb, which is short for plumbum. This word traces to the Roman Empire which used lead to make waterpipes that carried water into buildings. Hanna realized she had to see if Flint's residents, including her young patients, were being exposed to lead and other toxins through the city's water system.

Hanna led a study that analyzed differences in elevated blood lead level incidence in children younger than five before (2013) and after (2015) Flint introduced a more corrosive water source into its aging water system. These researchers assessed the percentage of elevated blood lead levels in both time periods, and identified geographical location differences through spatial analysis. They found that the incidence of elevated blood lead levels increased from 2.4% to 4.9% after the water source change, and, further, that neighborhoods with the highest water lead levels experienced a 6.6% increase in blood lead levels. Disadvantaged neighborhoods had the highest elevated blood lead level increases. With the study completed and the findings clear, Hanna was faced with a difficult choice. She could go the traditional route and quietly submit a paper to an academic journal, a process that stretches over months during which, every day, children as well as adults in Flint were being exposed to lead, or she could become an activist. She chose the latter path, and sought to meet with city and state officials and show them the unambiguous findings of the study. When they rebuffed her efforts, and she realized the city was in the midst of a public health emergency, she threatened to go public. They were unmoved. Consequently, she went to the press with her findings. The backlash was immediate and intense. Officials accused her of being wrong and causing hysteria, among other accusations. They also ridiculed her, often in a paternalistic tone. She asked herself, "Who am I? I'm barely five feet tall, a brown immigrant woman going up against some of the most powerful forces in the state" (quoted in Institute for Research on Women, 2022). Although briefly devastated by the official response, and suffering from a brief bout of imposter syndrome, she persisted, and won. The story was picked up by the news media locally, nationally, and internationally.

Her efforts helped convince state officials that the city's drinking water was poisoning residents, especially children. She subsequently testified repeatedly before Congressional committees, published her findings in the *American Journal of Public Health* (Hanna-Attisha et al., 2016), and authored the bestselling book entitled *What the Eyes Don't See: A Story of Crisis, Resistance, and Hope in an American City* (Hanna-Attisha, 2018).

At the same time, as Hanna was carrying out her study, awareness of the water crisis prompted many Flint residents and community groups to take action. As soon as they became aware of problems with their drinking water, community organizers began advocating for changes to improve the safety of the city's water supply. The "water warriors," as the activists came to be known, drew on a long history of worker and community organizing in Flint (Lane et al., 2016). The city had been the site of a massive labor struggle in the early twentieth century, as autoworkers pushed for better working conditions. For 44 days in 1936–1937, over 136,000 General Motors workers participated in the sit-down strike in Flint that became known as "the strike heard round the world." Ultimately, the company gave in and the United Auto Workers gained union recognition and a promise the company would not discriminate against workers who had gone on strike. General Motors also raised worker wages though marginally. More recently, Flint activists protested the state government's imposition of an Emergency Manager on the city in 2011.

As many city and state officials continued to ignore the crisis for 18 months, residents took matters into their own hands. Politically engaged groups like the Flint Democracy Defense League and Concerned Pastors for Social Action, as well as individual community activists such as Claire McClinton and Nayyirah Shariff, were joined by newly engaged activists, including a group of women that rapidly became movement leaders, such as LeeAnne Walters and Melissa Mays. Another, Claire McClinton, an auto worker, who had been deeply impacted by the Civil Rights Movement, joined the League of Revolutionary Black Workers because it became clear to her that the union was not doing its part to support Black auto workers. Nayyirah Shariff was one of the co-founders of the Flint Democracy Defense League, a grassroots group organized to challenge Flint's Emergency Manager. LeeAnne Walters, a medical assistant, became involved after she noticed a rash on both of her three-year-old twins. Then her daughter began losing clumps of hair in the shower and her 14-year-old son fell ill. Melissa Mays was one of the first to bring a lawsuit against the State of Michigan for the damage the water crisis caused to her family. These women and many others joined a protracted struggle for a robust governmental response to the water crisis in Flint. They worked with a variety of partners, including academic researchers and private institutions, to analyze tap water in the city, resulting in pivotal studies that changed the trajectory of the crisis.

Hanna's study and resident activism were critical factors in ultimately moving government and regulatory bodies to take the crisis seriously and respond accordingly. The crisis attracted a national outcry focused on the racial inequality that contributed to the environmental catastrophe. Years of sustained advocacy ultimately led to the government replacement of over 10,000 lead pipes and a legal settlement of almost $650 million for city residents.

Dozens of children impacted by the water crisis, and now young adults, have turned their trauma into health and environmental advocacy. They have provided input on public health initiatives, participated in social issue campaigns, distributed filters, and provided free water testing for homeowners. Amariyanna "Mari" Copeny was a 7-year-old beauty pageant winner known as Little Miss Flint when the water crisis began. She and her mother recognized something was wrong with the water when she and her siblings took a bubble bath and found that their eyes and skin burned. Copeny wanted to do something. She decided to make a short video listing facts about her daily life as a resident of Flint without clean drinking water. A screenshot from that video, in which she holds a paper sign that reads, "Flint, MI has been without clean water since April 24, 2014," went viral. She gained national attention in 2016, when at the age of 8, the *Los Angeles Times* published a letter she wrote to President Obama challenging him to visit Flint, Michigan, ultimately leading to meetings with Presidents Obama and Clinton. On January 16, 2016, President Obama declared a state of emergency for the City of Flint and surrounding Genesee County. She also initiated successful crowdfunding campaigns that enabled her to distribute over a million bottles of safe water to Flint residents, distribute thousands of books to children, and give backpacks filled with school supplies to youth. In addition, she has partnered with a water filter company to distribute high-capacity lead removal filters to families and child-focused organizations in Flint.

Copeny, who turned 17 in 2024, calls herself a philanthropist and anti-environmental racism activist. She continues to highlight environmental justice issues to her almost 200,000 Instagram followers and to raise money, including for water filters that she distributes to communities across the USA. She affirms, "I want to keep on using my voice to spread awareness about the Flint water crisis because it's not just Flint that has a water crisis... America has a water crisis" (quoted in CBS News Detroit, 2024). Half joking, Copeny likes to say she will be president of the USA in 2044.

A parallel coupling of environmental and health activism occurred over 5000 miles away from Flint in Bergama, an area in western Turkey. It began in the early 1990s when Eurogold, a multinational corporation comprised of French and Canadian mining companies headquartered in Perth, Australia, conducted test drilling in Bergama searching for gold. During the drilling, poisonous chemical substances contaminated the local water system and caused illness among community children. This experience produced a high level of suspicion about the Eurogold project. The community invited several academics to provide more information about the planned gold mine. People realized that their means of subsistence, their local environment, and various animal species would be destroyed by the mine because many tons of cyanide would be used to leach the gold and other precious metals from the ore. Moreover, tons of heavy metals would be left behind, giving rise to dust that would contaminate the air people breathed and the land where they lived and grew vegetables and fruit for their families. The mining site was surrounded by 17 villages with a total population of 11,000 people. The people of Bergama were acutely aware of their total dependence on the environment. Thus, at one community meeting, a woman who opposed the mine argued that "thousands of people rely on this land that they are going to destroy, and you can see that human beings are somehow rooted in the land like plants" (quoted in Coban, 2004). A farmer emphasized shared concerns about the mine, stating: "our land is very fruitful and more valuable than their gold, but if we do not hinder the poisonous project we all will die because they will turn this land into Arabian deserts" (quoted in Coban, 2004).

Community spokespersons announced at a press conference in 1994 that the mine was a threat to their vineyards, olive trees, children, and the future and that they would not let it operate. Even research carried out for Eurogold showed that more than 90% of the respondents from Bergama opposed the mine. Almost all members of the community, children, women, and men, became active participants in the movement. Villagers who were hired to work on the construction of the mining site were shunned by mine opponents. Early expressions of activism took the form of meetings in village coffee houses, picnics in the fields, and press releases and press conferences. These actions gathered momentum when in 1996 the potential threat became reality and Eurogold commenced construction by cutting down 2500 olive trees to make way for the open pit mine. In response, a crowd of 5000 people blocked the main road for six hours. Over the subsequent weeks, community actions continued in different forms, including demonstrations, marches, sit-ins at the mining site, petitions, lobbying, picnics, festivals, and olive tree plantings. When people blocked the road connecting the mine to the main road, 36 were arrested (Konak, 2011).

Although both men and women were involved in the movement, the most determined participants were women. They organized by visiting their counterparts in nearby villages to urge support for the anti-mine activism. Being the most responsible for the care and welfare of their children, they recognized that any cause of malnutrition (e.g., a decrease in wealth caused by environmental deterioration) or illness (e.g., from contaminated water, poisoned soil) among children adversely and directly affected their lives. Women also raised the issue of an increase in the number of miscarriages caused by the explosions at the mining site. It was usually the women who linked the issues of a clean environment to the future of their children. It was women who emphasized that the destruction of nature would mean the destruction of food sources, livelihood, and health.

In Bergama, linkage with outside environmental organizations helped to make the local conflict a national and ultimately international issue. From the beginning, Bergama's leaders recognized they needed help from beyond their villages and tried to attract public attention to move the issue from the local to the national stage. At one point, over 1000 farmers went to the Turkish capital of Ankara to lobby members of parliament. Additionally, a group of 150 farmers traveled to Istanbul to express their suffering by blocking traffic on the Bosphorus Bridge and chaining themselves to the bridge that connects Europe to Asia. These actions and almost all of the local protests faced strong police response, usually ending in arrests. However, they also attracted the attention of the national media and the public. Collective actions also raised international awareness of the issue in Bergama. Demonstrations by Bergama-born people living in Germany in front of the Berlin branch of Desdner Bank, one of the financial backers of Eurogold's mining operation, also advanced their cause.

As protests mounted, a Turkish court concluded that there was no public interest served by gold mining using cyanide. This ruling successfully led to the cancelation of the environmental permits for the mine in 1998. The ruling power in Turkey at that time, however, proceeded to grant operating permits, but in 2001 these permits also were blocked through the legal struggle led by the Bergama movement. Yet with the support of the central Turkish government, which repressed grassroots mobilizations, the mine continued to operate and to promote opposition for decades.

The spotlight put on Eurogold, however, forced the company to sell the mine to avoid accountability. The mine eventually was purchased by a Turkish gold mining firm that had to end its business activities because of its involvement in a failed coup d'état.

Learning from COVID-19

What does COVID-19 have to teach us about the coupling of the health and environment movements? First, a brief history. In December 2019, a cluster of patients in the city of Wuhan, China, began experiencing symptoms of an atypical pneumonia-like illness, including shortness of breath and fever, which did not respond well to standard pneumonia treatments. At year's end, the World Health Organization announced that all of the initial cases of this disease were connected to the Huanan Seafood Wholesale Market in Wuhan. Of note, in addition to seafood, this market sold wild animals for meat. Reportedly, the market had unsanitary conditions, including livestock of diverse species both wild and domestic kept near animal carcasses, frequent butchering, poor ventilation, and garbage piled on wet floors. These were ideal conditions for interspecies pathogenic transfer. Of note, although some have questioned the Huanan market as the source of human COVID-19 infection, extensive epidemiological evidence supports wildlife trade at the market as the most likely conduit for the origin of the COVID-19 pandemic. This understanding is supported by metagenomic evidence for the plausible intermediate host species, namely raccoon dogs (*Nyctereutes procyonoides*) which were sold at the market and are known to be susceptible to SARS-CoV-2 (Crits-Christoph et al., 2024).

Fearing a repeat of the 2002–2004 SARS (severe acute respiratory syndrome coronavirus or SARS-CoV-1), Chinese authorities closed the market. On January 7, 2020, public health officials in China reported that they had identified a novel coronavirus as the causative agent of the outbreak. Four days later, China reported the first death from the newly identified coronavirus now labeled the SARS-CoV-2 virus. Soon, reports began coming in from other countries of cases of the new disease, beginning with Thailand and followed quickly by Japan and the Republic of Korea. At this point, it became clear the virus was spreading widely, most likely through human-to-human transmission. On January 31, 2020, the US Secretary of the Department of Health and Human Services declared the outbreak a public health emergency. The reported death toll from the disease, eventually called COVID-19, reached more than 1 million worldwide in just 10 months. By May 5, 2022, the global COVID-19 pandemic is estimated to have directly or indirectly caused approximately 15 million deaths, with Southeast Asia, Europe, and the Americas accounting for 84% of this mortality. As this brief (and very partial) review indicates, COVID-19 is a powerful zoonotic disease that had spread from animals to people and proved to be capable of causing enormous loss of life, widespread sickness and suffering, and considerable social and economic disruption. Beyond the mutations that enabled the virus to reproduce inside the human body and transmit from person to person, continued mutations have resulted in multiple waves of different versions of the virus.

Alternatively, some have asserted that human infection with SARS-CoV-2 originated at the Wuhan Institute of Virology and escaped from the lab, whether deliberately or by accident. Actual evidence to support this claim, however, has never been provided. A commentary written by 41 biologists, immunologists, virologists, and physicians (Alwine et al., 2024) affirms: "Neither the scientific community nor multiple western intelligence agencies have found such evidence." Nevertheless, many people, having heard the lab leak narrative so often, believe it is true. One consequence is that scientists, fearing attacks on their integrity (or their lives), have begun steering away from cutting-edge research on emerging infections, downgrading preparedness for the next infectious disease pandemic.

While there has been considerable discussion of the adverse syndemic interaction of COVID-19 and several other diseases (e.g., diabetes, cardiovascular disease), are there anthropogenic environmental factors that contributed to the pandemic? And what might be the implication of environmental interaction with other emergent infectious diseases looming in our future? Epidemiologists, among others, are quite certain that the question is not if there will be another pandemic, but when. In this regard, in May 2024 the Pan American Health Organization (PAHO) issued an epidemiological alert as Latin America began experiencing a rise in cases of the previously obscure oropouche virus disease spread by midges and mosquitoes. This virus was first identified in a 24-year-old forest worker from the community of Vega de Oropouche on the Caribbean island of Trinidad. PAHO also announced the first known human deaths associated with the virus, including cases of fetal deaths in which the virus was transmitted from mother to child during pregnancy. Over 8000 confirmed oropouche cases, including two fatal cases, primarily in Bolivia, Colombia, Cuba, Peru, and Brazil, were reported by PAHO in their alert. The symptoms are similar to those of dengue, including headaches, fever, muscle aches, stiff joints, nausea, vomiting, chills, and sensitivity to light. Will oropouche be the next global pandemic?

If not oropouche perhaps Mpox, the disease previously known as monkeypox because of how it was discovered. This viral disease, related to smallpox, was first identified in 1958 in two outbreaks of a pox-like disease among colonies of monkeys kept for research. The first known human case of mpox was recorded in 1970 in the Democratic Republic of the Congo (DRC). Mpox became a global health concern in 2022 when a type of the virus spread to other countries and led to more than 90,000 cases worldwide, including over 32,000 cases in the USA. The disease spread from person to person through close, skin-to-skin contact. Although it can affect anyone, most Mpox cases during the 2022 outbreak were sexually transmitted and the disease was most common in men who have sex with men. In rare cases, it proved to be fatal. In May 2023, the World Health Organization announced that the global health emergency caused by Mpox had ended based on a decline in new cases. Then, in 2024, a new outbreak began in the DRC caused by a mutated form of the virus. Over 12,000 people in the DRC were diagnosed with the disease, and at least 470 people had died by August 2024. This deadlier variant of Mpox, transmitted by close contact, including among children, soon spread to other countries, leading the World Health Organization to declare Mpox a global health emergency. Notably, an Mpox vaccine has already been made available in more than 70 wealthier countries outside Africa, showing that lessons learned from the COVID-19 pandemic about global healthcare inequities have been slow to produce real change in global prevention practices. Helen Rees, a member of the Africa CDC's Mpox emergency committee, and executive director of the Wits RHI Research Institute in Johannesburg, South Africa, asserted that it was "outrageous" that, after Africa struggled to access vaccines during the COVID pandemic, the region was again left behind (quoted in Rigby, 2024). She added, "This is not equitable, nor does it make public health sense or global health sense, because you can't have an outbreak that's highly infectious in one part of the world and then assume that it won't spread to other regions of the world" (quoted in Saigal & Bojang, 2024).

At this point it is hard to predict if either oropouche or Mpox will become global pandemics, but without doubt there are deadly pandemics in our future and environmental disruption will help drive them.

As the UN Environment Program (Randolf et al., 2020) report titled *Preventing the Next Pandemic: Zoonotic Diseases and How to Break the Chain of Transmission* emphasizes, the rising trend in zoonotic diseases is driven by the degradation of our natural environment. While the report discusses the need to protect the environment to avoid or limit future infectious disease pandemics, it does not specifically address the issue of pollution, which may also turn out to be a key factor in pandemic impact.

As suggested in Chap. 3, air pollution can exacerbate COVID-19 in multiple ways. By increasing oxidative stress and inflammation (i.e., the recruiting of white blood cells and the release of cytokines that initiate tissue swelling at sites of injury or infection, which, if prolonged, cause tissue damage), both acute and long-term exposure to air pollution increases susceptibility to and severity of both respiratory and cardiovascular diseases. Small particulate matter can reach the alveolar sacs in the lungs and travel into the bloodstream, causing an inflammatory response that exacerbates respiratory diseases like COVID-19. Furthermore, other air pollutants such as nitrogen oxides, ground-level ozone, sulfur dioxide, and *carbon monoxide,* create oxidative stress, damage the lungs, and disrupt the endothelial cells that line all blood vessels and regulate exchanges between the circulatory system and other body tissues. Air pollution also disrupts the functioning of the immune system by damaging critical components, including neutrophils, a type of white blood cell, particle-clearing macrophages, and lymphocytes, such as vital T cells and B cells. It also aggravates dendritic cells, which are responsible for coordinating adaptive immune responses. In addition to weakening the respiratory and immune systems, air pollution has been hypothesized to aggravate COVID-19 infection severity through its effect on the ACE-2 receptor, the gateway for the entry of the corona virus inside the body that is found on the surfaces of the respiratory tract.

Indeed, studies of the transmission dynamics of COVID-19 have found that several environmental factors can affect COVID-19 transmission and impact. In particular, very small particulate matter pollution (called $PM_{2.5}$) and other air pollutants have been found to be associated with worse COVID-19 outcomes. Several studies have estimated the linkage of long-term exposure to air pollution and COVID-19 hospitalization and death, and investigation of this connection has become a rapidly expanding area of research. Wu et al. (2020), for example, used data on COVID-19 death counts for more than 3000 counties in the USA (representing 98% of the population) drawn from the Johns Hopkins University Coronavirus Resource Center (which provided information on over 116,000 deaths in the USA). Daily small particle particulate matter concentrations in the air were estimated across the USA using a well-validated atmospheric chemistry and machine learning model. These researchers found that even a small increase in long-term exposure to $PM_{2.5}$ leads to a large increase in the COVID-19 death rate. These results were statistically significant and robust in secondary and sensitivity analyses. Cole et al. (2020) had previously published an ecological regression analysis using data from 355 municipalities in the Netherlands and found results that were similar to those found by Wu and colleagues. These Dutch researchers identified "compelling evidence of a statistically significant positive relationship between air pollution and Covid-19 cases, hospital admissions and deaths" (Cole et al., 2020). This relationship was particularly evident for concentrations of $PM_{2.5}$ and to a lesser extent nitrogen dioxide.

A systematic review of 116 studies conducted in Europe and North America on the impact of air pollution on COVID-19 incidence, severity, and mortality (Hernandez et al., 2022) found that longer term exposure to pollutants appeared more likely to be positively associated with COVID-19 incidence (63.8%). Particulate matter (both $PM_{2.5}$ and PM_{10}), ground-level zone, nitrogen dioxide, and carbon monoxide were most strongly associated with COVID-19 incidence, and $PM_{2.5}$ and nitrogen dioxide with COVID-19 deaths. $PM_{2.5}$ is the most studied air pollutant, and among the 55 studies in the sample, more than half found that higher levels of $PM_{2.5}$ are associated with the increasingly greater spread of COVID-19. The evidence for PM_{10} and ground-level ozone was less consistent than that of $PM_{2.5}$. Long-term exposure to air pollution was more frequently positively associated with increased COVID-19 cases and deaths compared to short-term exposure. While the evidence for North America and Europe is important, a major limitation of this review was its circumscribed regional scope and the fact that most of the countries included are high-income states (except for Mexico). In low- and middle-income countries, the interaction of COVID-19 and air pollution is likely to be significantly greater, given the availability of fewer resources, less healthcare capacity, and higher exposure to outdoor air pollution. Thus, a study of nine Asian cities by Gupta et al. (2021) suggested that "there exists a positive correlation between the level of air pollution of a region and the lethality related to COVID-19, indicating air pollution to be an elemental and concealed factor in aggravating the global burden of deaths related to COVID-19." Past [long-term] exposures to high level of $PM_{2.5}$ were found to significantly correlate with present COVID-19 mortality.

The contribution of air pollution to the COVID-19 pandemic is not unique. Guinto et al. (2022) show that increased air pollution is a pathway that links climate change to HIV/AIDS outcomes. When exposed to high levels of air pollution, HIV/AIDS patients can be more susceptible to acquiring heart disease, asthma exacerbations, COPD, and lung cancer, as well as suffering from more severe outcomes. Air pollution and HIV infection appear to exhibit independent yet synergistic plaque inflammation patterns. When particulate matter is deposited on the epithelial cells that line the respiratory tract, cytokine production is induced, which initiates inflammatory signaling cascades that promote atherosclerosis and thrombosis. Inflammatory responses arise in response to tissues or organs being exposed to harmful stimuli like toxic chemicals. It occurs as a complex cascade that evolved to overcome from acute tissue injury and to initiate the process of healing. Chronic exposure, however, causes prolonged and damaging inflammation. HIV infection also accelerates atherosclerosis, which is the deposit of cholesterol plaque in the walls of arteries causing obstruction of blood flow, magnifying this significant risk to health.

In light of the origin of human exposure to COVID-19, researchers have taken a closer look at points of interaction between humans and wild animals. One of these is the legal and illegal exotic pet trade. In the USA, for example, the high volume of animals sold in this market makes it a uniquely risky context for a future pandemic to develop. The USA is the purchaser of live wildlife in the world, importing an estimated 220 million wild animals per year with a value of $15 billion, with limited health checks or disease testing prior to entry into the country. Some estimates suggest there are as many exotic pets in the USA as there are cats and dogs, with 14% of American households owning one or more exotic animal (Linder et al., 2023). These come from a wide range of species, including primates, birds, reptiles, and fish. It is known that through primates alone, humans can contract up to 200 diseases, many of which can be fatal. The sheer volume of this trade makes it a major vector through which high-risk human–animal interactions can become opportunities for zoonotic disease spillover into human populations. In addition to imports, non-native wild animals are captively bred in the USA in the millions, often in poor and tightly packed conditions that facilitate the spread of disease, before being sold and shipped to customers across the country. For example, a major Mpox outbreak in 2003 originated in one of these large facilities that received a shipment of exotic animals from overseas.

The key lesson the COVID-19 pandemic has to teach us about the critical need for coupling the health and environment movements is this: human-generated damage to the environment, biotic and nonbiotic, has a boomerang effect on health. Fighting for healthier people entails fighting for a healthier environment, and fighting for a healthier environment can be made less abstract and ring closer to home by including human health impacts, including ecosyndemics, as a central concern. Planetary health offers a framework for this needed, unified perspective and hence a way forward in very troubled times.

Solidarity in a Big Tent

As the XL pipeline struggle suggests, achieving planetary health will require the forging of alliances of solidarity across social groups. Andrea Sangiovanni and Juri Viehoff (2023) point out that the term "solidarity" first came into use in the early-to-late nineteenth century as a legal concept in France. Since then, its meaning has changed to refer to a special relationship of unity, bonding, and mutual indebtedness within a group or across groups with common purpose. Solidarity has been invoked increasingly in contemporary social movements like Black Lives Matter, Occupy Wall Street, the MeToo movement, and climate change activism. The term "big tent" commonly is used in reference to a political party having members drawn from a broad spectrum of beliefs, backgrounds, and identities who nonetheless face some common problems. Achieving planetary health will require solidarity, a big tent orientation, and a commitment and capacity for long-term activism.

Taking this idea a step forward, Bruno Latour, an influential French philosopher, anthropologist, and science and technology studies scholar, and Danish sociologist Nikolaj Schultz teamed up to write *On the Emergence of an Ecological Class* (Latour & Schulz, 2022). Their argument is that people of diverse backgrounds and orientations who recognize that the wealthy elite control the forces and relations of environmental destruction must coalesce into a broad-based social class around the imperative to protect the habitability of the Earth. This means developing an explicit political orientation, a class consciousness, and a willingness to engage in class struggle to save the foundations of life on Earth.

Climate activist Greta Thunberg aptly laments, "Our house is on fire. I am here to say, our house is on fire." One thing is clear: those with the most political and economic power; the elites who are the primary benefactors of keeping on our current course; those who deny there is a catastrophe in the making, or say it is too expensive to change, or even that the environment/climate/health crisis can be averted with some technological tinkering, will not "put out the fire." Rather, as Thunberg (Doha Debates, 2021), shown in Fig. 4.3, asserts, "We can no longer let the people in power decide what is politically possible. We can no longer let the people in power decide what hope is. Hope is not passive… Hope is telling the truth. Hope is taking action. And hope always comes from the people".

Fig. 4.3 Greta Thunberg, activist

Discussion Questions

1. What is grassroots activism?
2. What is "solastalgia" and why is it relevant to climate change?
3. What is the differentiation Beatrix Hoffman makes between grassroots health activism and elite health reform?
4. What lessons have been learned from the disability rights movement?
5. How did the cancer patients movement play a role in focusing attention on environmental toxins and cancer?
6. What are some of the key features of the woman's reproductive rights movement?
7. What was the role of Love Canal in the environmental health movement?
8. What lessons have activists learned from Act Up?

Class Projects

1. Pick a current environmental health issue and write an Op Ed for a local newspaper or a blog post.
2. Contact people you know and ask them if they ever participated in a demonstration. If you find one, ask if you can interview them about it. See if you can develop it into a class term paper or writing project.

Conclusion 5

Abstract

The conclusion weaves together the diverse materials presented in the book to affirm the value of a reorientation to health that is informed by a unified syndemics and planetary health framework. Worst-case and best-case scenarios of the year 2050 are visited, followed by a discussion of how we might achieve the later and avoid catastrophe. The chapter argues that we now stand on the precipice and must fight to save and improve life on Earth.

Keywords

Worse case scenario · Best case scenario · Restorative pathway scenario · Equity · Multinational grassroots movements

In the Year 2050

The Future We Choose, a book by Christiana Figueres and Tom Rivett-Carnac (2020), offers two sharply contrasting visions of what the world might be like in 2050. Figueres, who has a master's degree in social anthropology, is a Costa Rican diplomat. She was appointed Executive Secretary of the UN Framework Convention on Climate Change (the Paris Accord that promised net carbon neutrality by 2050). Rivett-Carnac, a British political consultant, worked as a strategist for the Framework Convention. Together, they have played central roles in shaping global climate change policy and, after leaving the UN, co-founded Global Optimism, an organization that seeks to build transformative partnerships that tackle the climate crisis. They also work together on the podcast Outrage + Optimism. Both Figueres and Rivett-Carnac are energetic advocates for environmental and social activism.

The alternative future worlds described by these two climate-focused thinkers constitute worst-case and best-case scenarios of Earth at mid-century.

Worst Case

By 2050, if not sooner, Earth's rapidly mounting crises of mass extinction and climate breakdown will fully merge into a single calamity imperiling all complex life (Crist et al., 2021). In the bleak words of journalist Alfred McCoy (2021), if we do not successfully address the climate/environment crisis, life in 2050 will be "bad, really bad." Getting out of bed in the morning the first thing that will strike you, again, is the air. In many parts of the world it is hot, heavy, and thoroughly polluted. Nor can you just walk out your front door and breathe fresh air. Fewer people can work outdoors, and even indoors the air tastes slightly acidic on especially bad days, making you feel nauseated. The world continues to get hotter, an irreversible process that is beyond our control. Consequently, there are few forests remaining on the planet, most of which have been logged, consumed by wildfire, killed by rampant pests, or dried by the climate. In the Arctic, the permafrost belches methane and carbon dioxide into the already overburdened atmosphere. Ice caps, ice sheets, and glaciers will shrink, pouring vast quantities of water into the ocean. A sea-level rise of as much as 20 inches will occur by 2050. Storm surges will have swept away the coastal barriers that people erected at enormous cost and rising seas will have flooded the downtowns of cities that once were home to more than 100 million people. Coastal villages and towns will be completely washed away. Small island nations will be history. In a decade vast swaths of the planet will be inhospitable to humans and other residents.

With greater moisture in the air and higher sea surface temperatures, extreme hurricanes and tropical storms will be more frequent and damaging to infrastructure, homes, and communities. Storms will bring massive flooding that kills many thousands of people and displaces millions more. In some parts of the world, people will be fleeing to higher ground every day. The news will be filled with accounts of people's homes with water up to their ankles because there is nowhere else to go (as seen in Fig. 5.1). Because of mold, their children will be coughing, wheezing, and always feeling miserable. Drinking water will be contaminated by sea salt intrusions, as will agricultural lands. Because of eco-crisis interaction, it will be difficult to get food and water relief to areas inundated with flood waters. Infectious diseases, like malaria, dengue, and cholera, gastrointestinal and respiratory diseases, and new and emergent diseases will become widespread epidemics. Diseases spread by mosquitoes and ticks will spread to new areas. The public health crisis of antibiotic resistance will intensify as populations grow denser in inhabitable areas and temperatures continue to rise. Child malnutrition will be rampant. Environmental disruption, ecosystem simplification, and loss of biodiversity will lead to overlapping ecosyndemics that will enhance vulnerability and heighten human suffering (Fig. 5.1).

Summer heatwaves will be deadly as temperatures skyrocket to 140 °F (60 °C), a point at which the human body can only remain out of doors for about six hours because it completely loses its ability to cool down. Complicating this threat, there will be diminishing access to drinkable water. Civil unrest and bloodshed over diminished water availability will be normative. Further, food production will drop

In the Year 2050

Fig. 5.1 Environmental injustice

as will the nutrient value of the food that can still be grown. Global trade, and thus access to many goods, will slow down as beleaguered countries move to hold on to their own resources. Food riots, coup attempts, and civil wars will multiply. More powerful nations, using various pretexts, will not hesitate to use their militaries to gain access to the resources of weaker nations.

Rising temperatures will put infrastructure features like rail lines, bridges, roads, and the power grid at risk. Heat causes steel to expand, pushing its molecules farther apart, threatening steel structures with more frequent warping and buckling. Existing infrastructure will become too hot to function, or at a minimum, to function effectively. In prolonged high temperatures, roads will contort due to the thermodynamics of concrete and asphalt (i.e., steel, expansion). Similarly, heat has two negative effects on power transmission. It reduces how much electricity power lines can deliver and it increases demand, further straining an already strained grid, possibly to its breaking point. Infrastructure disruptions and failures quickly become health emergencies.

With the expected rise in population, the total global food demand is expected to increase significantly by 2050. The global food system, which is highly vulnerable to climate change, will falter and be unable to meet the food needs of a growing percent of the world population, with the impacts of malnutrition being most evident among children. Complicating the problem will be a significant loss of fertile topsoil on land and a scarcity of seafood from the oceans. Although adverse impacts will be widespread, Africa is the most threatened continent in terms of severe food insecurity. Other regions with significant increases in severe food insecurity include the Middle East, South Asia, and Central America.

Through a series of extinction cascades, one-third to as many as half of Earth's species will be extinct by 2050. The list includes iconic animals such as lions, elephants, mountain gorillas, rhinos, polar bears, pandas, sea turtles, and bees. Additionally, a large number of plant species will be gone by 2050. This includes many orchids, Bromeliads (including pineapples), black pepper, various crop plants, and potentially, nearly half of all flowering plant species. Helping to drive the loss of species will be coextinctions, the linked extinction of two or more species, a process that is most common when one species is dependent on the other. Often times, coextinction involves a host and its parasites, but can involve a flowering plant and its pollinators or a predator and its primary prey species. As Koh et al. (2004) observed, "Species coextinction is a manifestation of the interconnectedness of organisms in complex ecosystems." As humans are part of this interconnectedness, biodiversity loss will diminish human viability.

Even in wealthier nations, multiple disruptions and threats will exact an enormous psychological toll. As each planetary boundary is significantly exceeded, remaining feelings of hope will slip away. They will be replaced by nostalgia for what once was and the certainty that humanity is slowly but surely heading toward some kind of collapse. Fierce resentment of previous generations that failed to do what was necessary to ward off calamity will be common. When midnight strikes on New Year's Day 2050, for most of humanity there will be little to celebrate. Rather, it will usher in another bleak day of burdensome adversity and a desperate struggle in a chaotic and impoverished world to find food, water, shelter, and safety.

Best Case

Imminent catastrophe need not be our future. Crist et al. (2021) proposed that a viable way to achieve a brighter future is through international action that combines efforts on two fronts: large-scale nature conservation that significantly expands protected natural areas and an equally significant downscaling of human economic, demographic, and food production systems. Yet it cannot be forgotten that such a change will be opposed by those who most benefit from an economic system based on unending profit-driven growth, unlimited natural resource extraction, and stark socioeconomic inequality. Furthermore, "[i]nterventions that exacerbate social injustices, poverty, disempowerment, and alienation, even if they seem viable at the moment, link to historical processes of imperialism that will deepen the metabolic rift and worsen the biodiversity crisis if allowed to continue" (Napoletanoa & Clark, 2020). Because those at the top will not produce meaningful, effective change, and will seek to coopt meek conservation efforts (e.g., so-called green capitalism, green tourism, green industrial products), real change will only come through aggressive mass grassroots activism from below. If this occurs, in the best-case scenario, humans will be in a position to cut greenhouse gas emissions every decade through 2050 and beyond. As a result, the air will get cleaner than it has been since before the Industrial Revolution. Trees, which will be planted and proliferate everywhere, will be celebrated because of the growing abundance of clean air. Enormously expanded tree populations will pull carbon dioxide from the air, release oxygen, and sequester carbon into the soil. This change will contribute to diminishing the climate crisis. Emotionally, the feeling of living on what once more has become a green planet will be transformative, especially in urban settings. Forests once again will cover half of the world and agriculture will become more tree-based, with shady groves of nuts and orchards, timber land interspersed with grazing, and park land areas that spread for miles providing new havens for diverse populations of pollinators and other species. No one will miss the extensive monoculture farms and plantations covered in pesticides, herbicides, and manufactured fossil-based fertilizers.

Fossil fuels will become but a memory. Most energy will be derived from renewable sources such as wind, solar, geothermal, and hydroelectric. Homes and buildings will produce their own electricity: their surfaces will be covered with solar paint containing millions of nanoparticles that harvest energy from the sunlight. Every windy area will have a wind turbine or a whole turbine farm. Excess energy will be routed back to a smart grid. Because there will be no combustion expense, energy will be low cost or even free, and it will be more efficiently used than in the past. Where possible, buildings will collect rainwater and manage their own water use. Renewable sources of electricity will make possible localized ocean desalination, which means clean drinking water will be produced on demand in coastal areas anywhere in the world. Desalinated water will be used in the irrigation of hydroponic gardens, and in flush toilets and showers. Gas and diesel vehicles will only be seen in history museums and in old photographs. Other species also will be benefactors of the transformation. Biodiversity will return across ecosystems, slowing the spread of infectious diseases.

Meat consumption will be less frequent and more expensive, given how much land and water it requires to produce (20 times more land and 20 times greater greenhouse gas emissions per gram of edible protein than common plant proteins). Vegetables will be a staple, and there will be more beans, peas, and legumes on the menu. Given that about 25% of food currently produced goes uneaten, food loss and waste will be diminished through improved food storage and other methods.

While humanity will have successfully reduced new carbon emissions, there still will remain the effects of record levels of carbon dioxide already released into the atmosphere. As a result, glaciers and Arctic ice will still be melting and the sea still rising. Coastal areas around the world will be inundated and people will have to move inland. Growing numbers will live in "ecovillages," intentional communities committed to achieving social, cultural, ecological, and economic sustainability and regenerating social and natural environments. The precise nature of these communities will vary based on local conditions and participatory group decisions but will share the goals of comfortable, low impact lifestyles that restore rather than destroy the environment. These communities, whose numbers are already growing, will stress ecological education and the further expansion of the ecovillage movement.

Severe droughts and desertification will continue to occur in the western USA, the Mediterranean, and parts of China. Ongoing extreme weather and resource degradation will continue to multiply existing disparities in income, public health, food security, and water availability. The struggle to achieve climate and environmental justice will continue but progress will be made year by year. People will know that we dodged a bullet and that we are all in this together. A benchmark of progress will be that some island nations and their populations as well as some populated coastal areas will have been saved.

The popular mood and sense of solidarity will shift profoundly. The world will seem more and more like a friendly and welcoming place. Indeed, even the process of participation in activism will prove to be healing by helping people to better understand themselves and their life experiences, provide a useful coping mechanism in the face of existential threat, offer improved participants self-confidence and interpersonal relationships, allow participants to stand up and speak out against injustices, provide support, validation, and connection to others, and offer a source of meaning and fulfillment in their lives (Swanson & Szymanski, 2020).

A blueprint for getting to the best-case scenario has been offered by William Ripple and his colleagues (Ripple et al., 2024). An ecologist at Oregon State University, in 2019 Ripple led the writing of a scholarly article, co-signed by more than 15,000 scientists from around the world, describing the environmental emergency facing humanity. Five years later, he and co-workers issued a call for the development of what they term a new "restorative pathway scenario." In this roadmap scenario, the goal will be to reduce the consumption of primary resources to keep environmental pressures within planetary boundaries. Further, the restorative pathway envisions a more equitable and resilient world characterized by the preservation of nature, post-growth economics, vastly improved societal well-being and quality of life, higher standards of living, more food production, a diet shift away from meat consumption, and a rapid transition toward renewable energy sources. Recognizing that big problems need big solutions, the pathway, nonetheless, is guided by radical incrementalism, namely achieving massive change by taking a number of small, short-term steps (e.g., protecting stable ecosystems, restoring disrupted ecosystems, addressing local climate risks) that are easier to implement and prevent chaotic disruptions. Unlike other future scenarios, like those used by the United Nations, the restorative pathway does not rely on the development of carbon capture and storage technologies, nor does it assume there will be continued economic growth over time. According to Ripple et al. (2023), "Economic growth, as it is conventionally pursued, is unlikely to allow us to achieve our social, climate, and biodiversity goals. The fundamental challenge lies in the difficulty of decoupling economic growth from harmful environmental impacts." Consequently, the authors conclude that we need to change the globally dominant economy to a system that supports well-being for all people instead of excessive consumption by the very wealthy.

Activist Momentum

Is the best-case scenario possible? Around the world, people are currently taking to the streets to protest at a level that is unprecedented in frequency, scope, and size. Converging and overlapping factors, including climate change, health crises, rising inequality, corporate greed, and oppressive or nonresponsive governments, are fueling social unrest and demands for change. According to the Center for Strategic and International Studies (Brannen et al., 2020), public protests began to ramp up in the aftermath of the 2008 global financial crisis. The frequency of protests increased by an annual average of 11.5% between 2009 and 2019. Further, the size of recent protests surpasses several historical eras of mass unrest, including the late 1960s, late 1980s, and early 1990s. Because the drivers of this social activism are not disappearing, researchers at the Center predict that mass protests are likely to grow over time.

Similarly, researchers at the Initiative for Policy Dialogue/Global Social Justice (Ortiz et al., 2022) documented a growing number of protests globally between 2006 and 2020. After a brief lull in early 2020 due to COVID-19, protests surged again. The study found a greater prevalence of protests in middle-income and high-income countries than in low-income countries. There were also a number of international protests that occurred in multiple countries simultaneously, and the number of these keeps increasing. Key issues propelling social activism were the failure of the political system, economic justice and anti-austerity, civil rights (including ethnic and Indigenous rights), and global justice. Union activist (and anthropologist) Orin Starn (2024), in a commentary on the uptick in labor organizing in the USA in recent years, notes that the struggle often feels like David versus Goliath, that is, workers with limited resources taking on corporate giants with an enormous arsenal of political, psychological, economic, and even physical weapons. Still, he concludes, "We'll continue to fight through moments of doubt and discouragement. Because now and then, a stone can bring the giant down."

Notable in environmental activism initiatives are bottom-up mobilizations for more sustainable and socially just uses of the environment. Environmental defenders frequently are members of vulnerable groups who primarily employ non-violent forms of protest, pictured in Fig. 5.2. These include Indigenous people and small farmers or fisherfolks whose lives and livelihoods are directly threatened by corporate or government-led environmental change or dispossession. Combining strategies of preventive mobilization, use of a diverse set of protest tactics, and litigation has been found to achieve success about 27% of the time. Grassroots campaigns can be powerful forces questioning unsustainable practices and changing minds, even when they do not prevail. Thus, Scheidel et al. (2020) view these movements as "a promising force for global sustainability and just environmental futures." As Nagendra (2018) highlights, "There are hundreds of environmental movements across Asia, Africa and Latin America. Although they are diverse, they have features in common. Such movements emphasize environmental justice and tend to emanate from local cultures. They are often led by women's collectives, and use non-violent means of protest." For example, for over 30 years, the Narmada Bachao Andolan

Fig. 5.2 Indigenous activists

mass social movement in India has organized people to march in protest and brought their cause to court rooms to stall construction of dams across the Narmada River, which runs from Madhya Pradesh in central India to the Arabian Sea. These efforts did not stop the dams, but it did raise worldwide attention about the adverse consequences for people and places caused by big, top-down developmental projects (Fig. 5.2).

With its emphasis on social equality, climate and environmental sustainability, and health, planetary health offers one potential unifying framework for the growing wave of still somewhat siloed grassroots social protests.

Centering Equity and Inclusion

To avoid repeating past offenses of both the environmental and health movements, equity, inclusion, and authority are needed for Indigenous nations, ethnic and sexual minority communities, women, and other marginalized groups. For example, with regard to public health, Peter Sands (2021), the executive director of the Global Fund to fight AIDS, Tuberculosis and Malaria, asks: "What is an equitable definition of what counts as a pandemic? The use of that word isn't just semantics: It's about who we care lives or dies." He argues that once a labeled pandemic is no longer an acute threat to life in high-income countries of the Global North, public health urgency drops, the focus begins to shift, and resource flows start to shrink. This occurred with the pandemics of AIDS and tuberculosis. Decisive global action was organized to contain the threat to life in wealthy countries, but then allowed to linger under the label of local epidemics in poorer, more vulnerable countries, resulting in millions of deaths. Failure to include the voices of the oppressed in decision-making produces biased public health policies and practices. Similarly, activist movements cannot effectively fight anthropogenic climate/environment threats without fighting for climate and environmental justice, fairness, and equity. A growing body of research indicates that real progress on environmental sustainability requires solutions that incorporate social sustainability, and in particular, social and political equity.

Health and Ecological Balance

Anthropological theorist, Claude Levi-Strauss, famously wrote that animals "are good to think" with, meaning we use animals to express metaphorically things we want to communicate to those around us. Thus, in English, we use phrases like "sly as a fox," "strong as an ox," and "quiet as a mouse" to describe human traits. Similarly, in German "stumm wie ein fisch" is used to refer to someone who is mute as a fish, while the expression "affengesicht" is an insult that references the face of a monkey. Looking at the other species in our world, humans generally tend to find their feathered and mostly flighted neighbors (i.e., birds) to be admirable and visually appealing. With their delicate textures, striking color patterns, and whimsical features, the beauty of birds generally delights us. Of course, the real audience of bird appearance is other birds, especially potential mates, but that has not stopped people from communicating information by decorating themselves with bird feathers to enhance our own appeal. Across the globe and for uncounted generations, people have used colorful bird feathers for self-adornment, to display social status and wealth, to exhibit vitality, to express love, and as an act of defiance. By contrast with many other kinds of plumed creatures, people often find vultures to be unattractive, even grotesque. They have hunched shoulders, hooked beaks, and signature featherless heads. Furthermore, they urinate on themselves to cool their bodies on hot days. In short, they are seen as malodorous, bald-headed scavengers with repulsive diets. As eaters of carrion—which they can smell from miles away while they are flying—they push their heads deep into germ-laden rotting animal carcasses. Perhaps most distressing, vast numbers of vultures have been seen on battlefields gorging themselves on the decaying bodies of fallen soldiers. When Charles Darwin observed turkey vultures off the deck of the Beagle in 1832, he wrote in his journal that it was a "disgusting bird" whose head was "formed to wallow in putridity." Even the dictionary does them no favor giving as one definition: a greedy or unscrupulous person.

Whatever humans think about their appearance, the ecological value of vultures has long been known. The baldness of vultures is adaptive; it prevents microorganisms from clinging to their heads as they rid the environment of animal corpses. The stomach acid of these birds is especially potent and corrosive. It allows them to safely digest putrid carcasses infected with deadly pathogens like botulism-causing bacteria, hog cholera bacteria, and anthrax bacteria, removing them from the environment. A decline in vulture populations can lead to increased disease transmission, as other (but less effective) scavengers that are disease vectors, like rats and feral dogs, expand their populations. Vultures, a keystone species, control these threats to health through competition for carcasses.

Vultures were once ubiquitous across India, with a total population of 50 million birds. There are nine different species of vultures in India (of the 23 vulture species on the planet), but most are now, like the Indian Vulture in Fig. 5.3, in danger of extinction following a rapid population collapse in recent decades. With a loss of over 99% of all vultures, the sharpest decline of any animal on the continent, India faces a vulture crisis. At first, the sharp decline of vulture populations was a mystery. Eventually, scientists (Frank & Sudarshan, 2023) realized the birds were being poisoned by a painkiller and anti-inflammatory drugs given to cattle and other livestock beginning in 1994. When vultures swooped in to consume the livestock carcasses that were dumped outside of tanneries in India, they ingested the drug, called diclofenac. It caused their kidneys to fail. As these scientists carried out their research, they heard stories of people being adversely affected by the disappearance of the vultures and they wondered if it was true. So they compared human death rates in India before and after the vultures disappeared. In places that historically had not had many vultures, human death rates remained relatively constant. By contrast, in places that had had large vulture populations in the past, human death rates increased by more than 4%. The change was the most apparent in areas with high livestock numbers (Fig. 5.3).

Frank and Sudarshan (2023) estimated that the loss of the vultures contributed to an extra 104,000 human deaths per year, for a total of more than 500,000 additional deaths between 2000 and 2005. In areas that once had abundant numbers of vultures, they also found that water quality had declined. The extra pollution, it appeared, came from the bacteria and pathogens that proliferated in rotting animal carcasses that formerly would have been picked clean to the bone by vultures, often in less than an hour. Some of the contaminants also came from the chemicals people used to dispose of the carcasses once the birds disappeared.

Fig. 5.3 Indian vulture

As this case indicates, there are real (and grave) human costs of upsetting an ecologically balanced environment and hence real benefits for environmentalists, health advocates, and all people who are put at risk to join in common cause.

On the Precipice

A book that addresses the climactic nature of the current moment is titled *The Precipice: Existential Risk and the Future of Humanity,* by Oxford University-based Australian philosopher Toby Ord (2020). Flowing from the same existential gravity expressed by Christiana Figueres and Tom Rivett-Carnac, Ord argues that safeguarding our future is among the most pressing and long neglected issues we face. Ord's philosophical work, which has been praised as a wake-up call for our species, focuses on big picture questions facing humanity. He asks: how can we best address the most important issues of our times? Ord refers to the times we live in as "the Precipice." He chooses this term because he accepts that we are on the edge. Our current way of life is unsustainable. We are literally playing Russian roulette with our future. Unless we can soon achieve a much higher level of existential safety (best-case scenario), we will destroy ourselves and many other species (worse case scenario). In the book, Ord examines anthropogenic risks like climate change and environmental damage, and ponders the likelihood of catastrophe. He also assesses pandemic risk, viewing the COVID-19 pandemic as a "warning shot." Because Ord believes that humanity is worth saving, he maintains that our first priority is getting off the Precipice. But how?

One pathway, the one presented in the previous chapters, is a mass, multinational grassroots movement, guided by a planetary health 2.0 perspective enhanced by ecosyndemics theory, which joins diverse sectors in demanding far-reaching social changes, sustainable production, and social and environmental justice. Such a movement is possible. As Greta Thunberg (2019) observed at the COP25 climate conference in Madrid: "Well I am telling you there is hope. I have seen it. But it does not come from governments or corporations. It comes from the people…. In fact every great change throughout history has come from the people. We do not have to wait."

Achieving this goal, which is far from guaranteed and would constitute the most sweeping change in human history, will not usher in utopia. Humanity will always face challenges, disease, and conflict. Further, history teaches us that all "solutions" bring on new problems. A change as dramatic as the American Civil War, for example, ended legal slavery (a worthy achievement) but it did not bring social and economic equality. Similarly, World War II, a historic global upheaval, defeated the fascist onslaught but this distinctly hideous ideology still has life, to varying degrees, around the world. Nonetheless, despite the unexpected and undesirable impacts of change, recognizing we are on the precipice is a clarifying experience. It opens the opportunity to be an active choice maker and to ponder the value of advocacy and activism in light of doubts and competing personal commitments. If you accept, like Ord, that humanity is on the precipice and that despite all its faults and foibles is worth saving, the most meaningful thing to do from the perspective of activist Thunberg is to make a commitment to ensure a healthy, biodiverse, equitable future for humans and other life on Earth. In making this commitment, it is important to remember that significant social change rarely happens without ruffling feathers. As noted, elite polluters resist change and thus it will only happen through sustained, unyielding pressure from below. At the same time, as American poet Emily Dickinson (1981) wrote in one of her compositions: "'hope' is a thing with feathers that perches in the soul." Of course, birds and other animals (as well as plants, but also clean water, pollution-free air, and a stable climate) are not just good to think or communicate with; they are vital to our survival, and well worth fighting for.

Class Discussion

1. Contrast best- and worst-case climate scenarios for 2050.
2. Is grassroots activism becoming more or less common why?
3. Why is it critical to grassroots activism to center equity and inclusion?
4. Why are the vultures of India like the canaries miners used to bring into the mines?
5. Are we on the precipice, why or why not?

Class Project

1. Select an issue discussed in this book and organize a debate in class with two groups taking contrastive stances on the issue.

Discussion Questions

1. What are the two sharply contrasting visions of the year 2050 offered by Christiana Figueres and Tom Rivett-Carnac in *The Future We Choose*?
2. What is the biggest hurdle to achieving large-scale nature conservation that significantly expands protected natural areas and an equally significant downscaling of human economic, demographic, and food production systems?
3. What is the current state of grassroots activism?
4. Why is the extinction of vultures an acute human health crisis?
5. What are the implications of Toby Ord's concept of the precipice?

References

Abbasi, K., Ali, P., Barbour, V., Benfield, T., Bibbins-Domingo, K., Hancocks, S., et al. (2023). Time to treat the climate and nature crisis as one indivisible global health emergency. *JAMA Neurology, 80*(12), 1274–1276. https://doi.org/10.1001/jamaneurol.2023.4644

Abdul-Quader, A., Feelemyer, J., Modi, S., & Des Jarlais, D. (2013). Effectiveness of structural level needle/syringe programs to reduce HCV and HIV infection among people who inject drugs: A systematic review. *AIDS Behavior, 17*, 2878–2892. https://doi.org/10.1007/s10461-013-0593-y2

Abdul-Quader, A., McGough, J., Thiede, H., Hopkins, S., Duchin, J., & Alexander, E. (2000). Reduced injection frequency and increased entry and retention in drug treatment associated with needle exchange participation in Seattle drug injectors. *Journal of Substance Abuse Treatment, 19*(3), 247–252. https://doi.org/10.1016/S0740-5472(00)00104-5

Abu-Raddad, L., van der Ventel, B., & Ferguson, N. (2008). Interactions of multiple strain pathogen diseases in the presence of coinfection, cross immunity and arbitrary strain diversity. *Physical Review Letters, 100*, 168102–168104.

Al Mahmeed, W., Al-Rasadi, K., Banerjee, Y., Ceriello, A., Cosentino, F., Galia, M., et al. (2021). Promoting a syndemic approach for cardiometabolic disease management during COVID-19: The CAPISCO international expert panel. *Frontiers in Cardiovascular Medicine, 8*, 787761. https://doi.org/10.3389/fcvm.2021.787761

Albrecht, G. (2005). Solastalgia: A new concept in human health and identity. *PAN: Philosophy Activism Nature, 3*, 44–59.

Alexander, K., Carzolio, M., Goodin, D., & Vance, E. (2013). Climate change is likely to worsen the public health threat of diarrheal disease in Botswana. *International Journal of Environmental Research and Public Health, 10*(4), 1202–1230. https://doi.org/10.3390/ijerph10041202

Allen, S., & Ryan, C. (2016). The decolonizing generation: (Race and) theory in anthropology since the eighties. *Current Anthropology, 57*(2), 129–148.

Alwine, J., Goodrum, F., Banfield, B., Bloom, D., Britt, W., & Broadbent, A. (2024). The harms of promoting the lab leak hypothesis for SARS-CoV-2 origins without evidence. *Journal of Virology, 0*, e01240–e01224. https://doi.org/10.1128/jvi.01240-24

American Nurses Association. (1994). *Nursing: Scope and standards of practice*. ANA.

Askew, D., Brady, K., Mukandi, B., Singh, D., Sinha, T., Brough, M., & Bond, C. (2020). Closing the gap between rhetoric Bryan and practice in strengths-based approaches to Indigenous public health: A qualitative study. *Australian and New Zealand Journal of Public Health, 44*(2), 102–105.

Baer, H. A., & Singer, M. (2024). *Building the critical anthropology of climate change: Towards a socio-ecological revolution*. Taylor & Francis.

Bastian, H. (2019). Consumer-contested evidence: Why the ME/CFS exercise dispute matters so much. *PlosOne*. https://absolutelymaybe.plos.org/2019/02/08/consumer-contested-evidence-why-the-me-cfs-exercise-dispute-matters-so-much/

Bauman, E., & Piper, L. (Eds.). *Holistic health Lifebook: A guide to personal and planetary well-being*. And/Or Press.

Beaudin, P. (2012). *A contemporary socio-cultural exploration of health and healing: Perspectives from members of the Oneida Nation of the Thames (Onyota'a:ka)*. University of Saskatchewan.

Beck, U. (1992). *Risk society: Towards a new modernity*. Sage.

Bentham, J. (1789). *An introduction to the principles of morals and legislation*. Clarenden Press.

Berg, S. (2006). Everyday sexism and posttraumatic stress disorder in women: A correlational study. *Violence Against Women, 12*(10), 970–988. https://doi.org/10.1177/1077801206293082

Berliner, H., & Salmon, W. (1980–81). The holistic alternative to scientific medicine. *International Journal of Health Services, 10*(1), 133–147.

Berry, W. (1969). *The long-legged house*. Harcourt.

Bhatnagar, A. (2017). Environmental determinants of cardiovascular disease. *Circulation Research, 121*(2), 162–180. https://doi.org/10.1161/CIRCRESAHA.117.306458

Bhavnani, D., Goldstick, J. E., Cevallos, W., Trueba, G., & Eisenberg, J. (2012). Synergistic effects between rotavirus and coinfecting pathogens on diarrheal disease: Evidence from a community-based study in northwestern Ecuador. *American Journal of Epidemiology, 176*, 387–395. https://doi.org/10.1093/aje/kws220

Board of Supervisors. (1897). *City of San Francisco to Harvard College*. https://books.google.ca/books?id=yJYz_wheFEIC&pg=PA579#v=onepage&q&f=false

Boillat, S., & Berkes, F. (2013). Perception and interpretation of climate change among Quechua farmers of Bolivia: Indigenous knowledge as a resource for adaptive capacity. *Ecology and Society, 18*(4), 21. https://doi.org/10.5751/ES-05894-180421

Booker, M. (2021). What does 'critical' mean in social science writing, and how can I be critical in my essay? *The Critical Turkey*. https://blogs.ed.ac.uk/criticalturkey/what-does-critical-mean-in-social-science-writing-and-how-can-i-be-critical-in-my-essay/

Bottery, M., Pitchford, J., & Friman, V. (2021). Ecology and evolution of antimicrobial resistance in bacterial communities. *The ISME Journal, 15*, 939–948. https://doi.org/10.1038/s41396-020-00832-7

Boyden, S. (1972). The environment and human health. *Medical Journal of Australia, 1*(24), 1229–1234. https://doi.org/10.5694/j.1326-5377.1972.tb116528.x

Brannen, S., Haig, C., & Schmidt, K. (2020). The age of mass protests: Understanding an escalating global trend. *Center for Strategic and International Studies*. https://csis-website-prod.s3.amazonaws.com/s3fspublic/publication/200303_MassProtests_V2.pdf

Brattland, C., & Mustonen, T. (2018). How traditional knowledge comes to matter in Atlantic salmon governance in Norway and Finland. *Arctic, 71*. 375, 10.14430/arctic4751.

Brecher, J. (2022). How social movements escape silos. *Labor Network for Sustainability*. https://www.labor4sustainability.org/articles/how-social-movements-escape-silos/

Brown, R. (1976). Public health in imperialism: Early Rockefeller programs at home and abroad. *American Journal of Public Health, 66*(9), 897–903.

Brown, Q. (2018). *Indigenous knowledge and ocean science*. TED[x]Brentwood College. https://www.youtube.com/watch?v=0vuZ5Jm67fg

Brown, P., & Stephen, Z. (2004). Social movements in health: An introduction. *Sociology of Health Illness, 26*(6), 679–694. https://doi.org/10.1111/j.0141-9889.2004.00413.x

Bryse, K., Oreskes, N., O'Reilly, J., & Oppenheimer, M. (2013). Climate change prediction: Erring on the side of least drama? *Global Environmental Change, 23*(1), 327–337.

Bullard, R., & Wright, B. (2009). *Race, place, and environmental justice after Hurricane Katrina: Struggles to reclaim, rebuild, and revitalize New Orleans and the Gulf Coast*. Westview Press.

Bulled, N., & Singer, M. (2016). Health and the Anthropocene: Mounting concern about tick-borne disease interactions. In M. Singer (Ed.), *A Companion to the Anthropology of Environmental Health*. Wiley-Blackwell.

Bulled, N., Singer, M., & Dillingham, R. (2014). The syndemics of childhood diarrhea: A biosocial perspective on efforts to combat global inequities in diarrhea-related morbidity and mortality. *Global Public Health, 9*(7), 841–853.

References

Burns, A. (2024). As recommendations for isolation end, how common is Long COVID? KFF Health News. https://www.kff.org/coronavirus-covid-19/issue-brief/as-recommendations-for-isolation-end-how-common-is-long-covid/#:~:text=Since%20December%202022%2C%20 in%20any,adults%20currently%20have%20long%20COVID

Cajete, G. (2020). Indigenous science, climate change, and Indigenous community building: A framework of foundational perspectives for Indigenous community resilience and revitalization. *Sustainability, 12*(22), 9569. https://doi.org/10.3390/su12229569

Callard, F., & Perego, E. (2021). How and why patients made Long Covid. *Social Science and Medicine, 268*, 113426.

Campos, A. (1993). *John Hessler, pioneer in independence for disabled people, dies.* Modesto Bee. https://www.independentliving.org/docs4/campos93.html

Canadian Meteorological and Oceanographic Society. (2008). *The changing atmosphere: Implications for global security conference statement.* https://cmosarchives.ca/History/ChangingAtmosphere1988e.pdf

Carrington, D. (2023). *Rising seas threaten 'mass exodus on a biblical scale', UN chief warns.* The Guardian. https://www.theguardian.com/environment/2023/feb/14/rising-seas-threaten-mass-exodus-on-a-biblical-scale-un-chief-warns#:~:text=Guterres%20said%3A%20 %E2%80%9CLow%2Dlying,homes%20do%2C%E2%80%9D%20he%20said

Carson, R. (1962). *Silent spring.* New York: Houghton Mifflin Company.

Carter, A. (2023). *Voices of the Vezo: Community-led filmmaking in Madagascar.* Seavoice. https://www.seavoice.online/post/voices-of-the-vezo

Casassus, B. (2017). Per Fugelli. *The Lancet, 390*, 2032. https://www.thelancet.com/pdfs/journals/lancet/PIIS0140-6736(17)32737-X.pdf

Castro, A., & Singer, M. (Eds.). (2004). *Unhealthy health policy: A critical anthropological examination.* Rowman.

CBS News Detroit. (2024). *Children of Flint water crisis making a change as environmental and health activists.* https://www.cbsnews.com/detroit/news/children-of-flint-water-crisis-making-a-change-as-environmental-health-activists/

Centers for Disease Control and Prevention. (2024a). *COVID-19 and antimicrobial resistance.* https://www.cdc.gov/antimicrobial-resistance/data-research/threats/COVID-19.html

Centers for Disease Control and Prevention. (2024b). *CDC science and the public health approach to long COVID.* https://www.cdc.gov/covid/php/long-covid/index.html#:~:text=Key%20 findings&text=In%202022%2C%206.9%25%20of%20adults,ever%20reported%20experiencing%20Long%20COVID.&text=While%20Long%20COVID%20can%20occur,risk%20 of%20developing%20Long%20COVID

Chadwick, D. (2003). Pacific Suite. *National Geographic, 203*(2), 104–127.

Charters Erika and Heitman Kristin. (2021). How epidemics end. *Centaurus, 63*(1), 210–224. https://doi.org/10.1111/1600-0498.12370

Cimon, M. (2022). *A tracker for tick-borne illness.* Johns Hopkins Magazine. https://hub.jhu.edu/magazine/2022/spring/lyme-tracker-map/.

Clare, E. (1999). *Exile and pride: Disability, queerness, and liberation.* Duke University Press.

Clearfield, M., Davis, G., Weis, J., Gayer, G., & Shubrook, J. (2018). Cardiovascular disease as a result of the interactions between obesity, climate change, and inflammation: The COCCI syndemic. *The Journal of the American Osteopathic Association, 118*(11), 719–729. https://doi.org/10.7556/jaoa.2018.157

Clearfield, M., Pearce, M., Nibbe, Y., Crotty, D., & Wagner, A. (2014). The "new deadly quartet" for cardiovascular disease in the 21st century: Obesity, metabolic syndrome, inflammation and climate change: How does statin therapy fit into this equation? *Current Atherosclerosis Reports, 16*, 380. https://doi.org/10.1007/s11883-013-0380-2

Coates, R. (2023). *White men have controlled women's reproductive rights throughout American history – the post-Dobbs era is no different.* The Conversation. https://theconversation.com/white-men-have-controlled-womens-reproductive-rights-throughout-american-history-the-post-dobbs-era-is-no-different-206706

Coban, A. (2004). Community-based ecological resistance: The Bergama Movement in Turkey. *Environmental Politics, 13*(2), 438–460. https://doi.org/10.1080/0964401042000209658

Coccia, E. (2018). *The life of plants: A metaphysics of mixture*. Polity Press.

Cole, M., Ozgen, C., & Strobl, E. (2020). Air pollution exposure and COVID-19 in Dutch municipalities. *Environmental and Resource Economics, 76*(4), 581–610. https://doi.org/10.1007/s10640-020-00491-4

Collaboration for Health and Environment. (2013). *The rise of the US Environmental Health Movement: A conversation with Kate Davies*. https://www.healthandenvironment.org/partnership_calls/12257

Cooper, J. (2012). *Surviving sudden environmental climate change: Answers from archaeology*. University Press of Colorado. https://doi.org/10.2307/j.ctt1wn0rbs

Copeland, L. (1998). *Lois Gibb's grass-roots garden*. Washington Post. https://www.washingtonpost.com/wp-srv/style/daily/loisgibbs.htm#:~:text=Harry%20Gibbs%20came%20along%20after,and%20soon%20enough%2C%20daughter%20Melissa

Coté, C. (2016). "Indigenizing" food sovereignty. Revitalizing Indigenous food practices and ecological knowledges in Canada and the United States. *Humanities, 5*, 57. https://doi.org/10.3390/H5030057

Crespo, F. (2021). Reconstructing immune competence in skeletal samples. In C. Cheverko, J. Prince-Buitenhuys, & M. Hubbe (Eds.), *Theoretical approaches in bioarchaeology* (pp. 75–92). Routledge.

Crespo, F. (2022). Leprosy in medieval Europe: An immunological and syndemic approach. In L. Jones & N. Varlik (Eds.), *Death and Disease in the Medieval and Early Modern World* (pp. 295–317). York Midieval Press.

Crist, E., Kopnina, H., Cafaro, P., Gray, J., Ripple, W., Safina, C., et al. (2021). Protecting half the planet and transforming human systems are complementary goals. *Conservation Science, 17*. https://doi.org/10.3389/fcosc.2021.761292

Crits-Christoph, A., Levy, J., Pekar, J., Goldstein, S., Singh, R., & Hensel, Z. (2024). Genetic tracing of market wildlife and viruses at the epicenter of the COVID-19 pandemic. *Cell, 187*(19), 5468–5482.e11. https://doi.org/10.1016/j.cell.2024.08.010

Crosse, A. M., Barry, M., Lavelle, M. J., & Sixsmith, J. (2021). Bridging knowledge systems: A community-participatory approach to EcoHealth. *International Journal of Environmental Research and Public Health, 18*(23), 12437. https://doi.org/10.3390/ijerph182312437

Crowley, M. (2024). *Disability History: The 1977 504 Sit-In*. Disability Rights Florida Blog. https://disabilityrightsflorida.org/blog/entry/504-sit-in-history

Daley, J. (2019). *Syndemic: The little-known buzzword that describes our troubled times*. Smithsonian Magazine. https://www.smithsonianmag.com/smart-news/syndemic-little-known-buzzword-describes-our-troubled-times-180971381/

Davies, K. (2013). *The rise of the US environmental health movement*. Rowman and Littlefield Publishers.

Davis, R., Philip, A., & Mierjeski. (2024). *After Nike leaders promised climate action, their corporate jets kept flying – and polluting*. ProPublica. https://www.propublica.org/article/nike-corporate-jet-travel-carbon-emissions

De La Cadena, M. (1998). Silent racism and intellectual superiority in Peru. *Bulletin of Latin American Research, 17*(2), 143–164.

Deale, A., & Wessely, S. (2001). Patients' perceptions of medical care in chronic fatigue syndrome. *Social Science and Medicine, 52*(12), 1859–1864. https://doi.org/10.1016/s0277-9536(00)00302-6

Demaio, A., & Rockström, J. (2015). Human and planetary health: Towards a common language. *Lancet, 386*(10007), e36–e37. https://doi.org/10.1016/S0140-6736(15)61044-3

Department of Anthropology, University of Pennsylvania. (2021). *Statement on anthropology, colonialism, and racism*. https://anthropology.sas.upenn.edu/news/2021/04/28/statement-anthropology-colonialism-and-racism

Dewitte, S., & Wissler, A. (2022). Demographic and evolutionary consequences of pandemic diseases. *Bioarchaeology International, 6*(1–2). https://doi.org/10.5744/bi.2020.0024

References

Dhimal, M., Bhandari, D., Karki, K., Shrestha, S., Khanal, M., Shrestha, R., et al. (2022). Effects of climatic factors on diarrheal diseases among children below 5 years of age at national and subnational levels in Nepal: An ecological study. *International Journal of Environmental Research and Public Health, 19*(10), 6138. https://doi.org/10.3390/ijerph19106138

Díaz, S., Settele, J., Brondízio, E., Ngo, H., Agard, J., Arneth, A., et al. (2019). Pervasive human-driven decline of life on Earth points to the need for transformative change. *Science, 366*(6471), eaax3100. https://doi.org/10.1126/science.aax3100

Dickinson, E. (1981, original 1862). *The manuscript books of Emily Dickenson*. In R. Franklin (Ed.), Belknap Press of the Harvard University Press.

Doha, D. (2021). *Greta Thunberg's full keynote speech at Youth4Climate Pre-COP26*. You Tube. https://www.youtube.com/watch?v=n2TJMpiG5XQ

Douglas-Boers, D. (2014). *What the Cowboy-Indian Alliance Means for America and the climate movement*. Resilience. https://www.resilience.org/stories/2014-10-29/what-the-cowboy-indianalliance-means-for-america-and-the-climate-movement/ClimateMovement

Drexler, M. (2020). *The cancer miracle isn't a cure*. Harvard Public Health. https://www.hsph.harvard.edu/magazine/magazine_article/the-cancer-miracle-isnt-a-cure-its-prevention/#:~:text=Cell%20division%20is%20an%20imperfect,depressing%20stochastics%20of%20bad%20luck

Dudley, S., & File, A. (2007). Kin recognition in an annual plant. *Biological Letters, 3*(4), 435–438. https://doi.org/10.1098/rsbl.2007.0232

Duffy, A. (2020). Forests worldwide. In R. Duffy & S. Opp (Eds.), *Environmental issues today: Choices and challenges* (Vol. 2, pp. 187–202). ABC-CLIO.

Durie, M. (2004). An Indigenous model of health promotion. *Health Promotion Journal of Australia, 15*, 181–185.

Elling, R. (1988). Worker's health and safety (WHS) in crossnational perspective. *American Journal of Public Health, 78*, 769–771.

Engel, G. (1977). The need for a new medical model: A challenge for biomedicine. *Science, 196*, 129–136. https://doi.org/10.1126/science.847460

Environmental Health Coalition. (2024). https://www.environmentalhealth.org/#

Epker, E. (2024). *A novel drug, a protest, and the fight to prevent breast cancer deaths*. Forbes. https://www.forbes.com/sites/evaepker/2024/03/19/a-novel-drug-a-protest-and-the-fight-to-prevent-breast-cancer-deaths/

Epstein, S. (1998). *Impure science: AIDS, activism, and the politics of knowledge*. University of California Press.

Escalante-de Mattei, S. (2022). *Here's every artwork that climate activists have glued themselves to*. ARTNews. https://www.artnews.com/list/art-news/news/climate-activists-artworks-gluing-protests-1234637104/june-29th-2022/

European Alliance Against Malaria. (2008). *Malaria & poverty*. Belgium.

Fabbri, L., Celli, B., Agustí, A., Criner, G., Dransfield, M., Divo, M., et al. (2023). COPD and multimorbidity: Recognising and addressing a syndemic occurrence. *Lancet Respiratory Medicine, 11*(11), 1020–1034. https://doi.org/10.1016/S2213-2600(23)00261-8

Feng, J., Lin, T., Mihalca, A., Niu, Q., & Oosthuizen, M. (2023). Coinfections of Lyme disease and other tick-borne diseases. *Frontiers in Microbiology, 14*, 1140545. https://doi.org/10.3389/fmicb.2023.1140545

Fernandez, L., Byard, D., Lin, C.-C., Benson, S., & Barbera, J. (2002). Frail elderly as disaster victims: Emergency management strategies. *Prehospital Disaster Medicine, 17*(2), 67–74. https://doi.org/10.1017/s1049023x00000200

Ferrinho, P., Viveiros, M., & Fronteira, I. (2023). Antimicrobial resistance, society and environment: A glocal syndemic. *One Health, 16*, 100512. https://doi.org/10.1016/j.onehlt.2023.100512

Figueres, C., & Rivett-Carnac, T. (2020). *The future we choose: Surviving the climate crisis*. Manilla Press.

Fineberg, H., Brown, L., Worku, T., & Goldowitz, I. (Eds.). (2024). *A long COVID definition. National academies of sciences, engineering, and medicine*. National Academies Press.

Fobar, R. (2024). *Waves of change: A conversation with marine biologist Alex Schnell, who advocates compassion and humane treatment of all animals*. National Geographic, A Fresh Perspective.

Fornace, K., Abidin, T., Alexander, N., Brock, P., Grigg, M., Murphy, A., et al. (2016). Association between landscape factors and spatial patterns of *Plasmodium knowlesi* infections in Sabah, Malaysia. *Emerging Infectious Diseases, 22*(2), 201–209. https://doi.org/10.3201/eid2202.150656

Frank, E. (2024). The economic impacts of ecosystem disruptions: Costs from substituting biological pest control. *Science, 385*(6713). https://doi.org/10.1126/science.adg0344

Frank, E., & Sudarshan, A. (2023). The social costs of keystone species collapse: Evidence from the decline of vultures in India. *American Economic Review*. https://www.anantsudarshan.com/uploads/1/0/2/6/10267789/vultures_manuscript-2023.pdf

Fredonia State University of New York. (2010). *Lois Marie Gibbs biography*. https://www.fredonia.edu/academics/convocation/gibbsbio

Frumkin, H. (2017). What is planetary health? *Planetary Health Alliance*. https://www.google.com/search?q=frumkin+what+is+planetary+health&oq=frumkin+what+is+planetary+health&gs_lcrp=EgZjaHJvbWUyBggAEEUYOTIHCAEQIRigATIHCAIQIRigATIHCAMQIRigATIHCAQQIRigATIHCAUQIRigAdIBCTEzMzAzajBqNKgCALACAQ&sourceid=chrome&ie=UTF-8#fpstate=ive&vld=cid:51e865fd,vid:lw_I7rhn9eY,st:0

Fulton, J. (2022). Trying to save the world is leaving young climate change activists exhausted and frustrated. USA Today. https://www.usatoday.com/story/news/health/2022/09/05/someclimate-organizers-burning-out-after-years-pandemic-work/7893215001/?gnt-cfr=1&gca-cat=p

Gandhi, N., Weissman, D., Moodley, P., Ramathal, M., Elson, I., Kreiswirth, B., et al. (2013). Nosocomial transmission of extensively drug-resistant tuberculosis in a rural hospital in South Africa. *The Journal of Infectious Diseases, 207*(1), 9–17. https://doi.org/10.1093/infdis/jis631

Ganz, M., & Orlovsky, N. (1984). Desertification: A review of the concept. In J. Oliver & R. Fairbridge (Eds.), *Encyclopedia of climatology*. Hutchinson Ross Publishing Company.

Garner, P. (2020). *For 7 weeks I have been through a roller coaster of ill health, extreme emotions, and utter exhaustion*. BMJ Opinion. https://blogs.bmj.com/bmj/2020/05/05/paul-garner-people-who-have-a-more-protracted-illness-need-help-to-understand-and-cope-with-the-constantly-shifting-bizarre-symptoms/

Gartner, D., & Wilbur, R. (2022). Exploring public health's role in addressing historical trauma among U.S. Indigenous populations. In D. Barrett, L. Ortmann, & S. Larson (Eds.), *Narrative ethics in public health: The value of stories. Public Health Ethics Analysis 7*. Springer. https://doi.org/10.1007/978-3-030-92080-7_8

Gary, F. (1995). *Animals, property, and the law*. Temple University Press.

GBD Chronic Respiratory Disease Collaborators. (2020). Prevalence and attributable health burden of chronic respiratory diseases, 1990–2017: A systematic analysis for the Global Burden of Disease Study 2017. *Lancet Respiratory Medicine, 8*(6), 585–596.

Geiger, S. (Ed.). (2021). *Healthcare activism: Markets, morals, and the collective good*. Oxford University Press.

Gensini, V., & Brooks, H. (2018). Spatial trends in United States tornado frequency. *Climate and Atmospheric Science, 1*, 38. https://doi.org/10.1038/s41612-018-0048-2

Ginsburg, F., & Rapp, R. (2013). Disability worlds. *Annual Review of Anthropology, 42*, 53–68.

Global Asthma Network. (2022). The global asthma report 2022. *The International Journal of Tuberculosis and Lung Disease, 26*(Supplement 1), 1–104. https://doi.org/10.5588/ijtld.22.1010

Global Witness. (2019). *Money to burn*. https://www.globalwitness.org/en/campaigns/forests/money-to-burn-how-iconic-banks-and-investors-fund-the-destruction-of-the-worlds-largest-rainforests/

Gold, R. (2003). *Lessons from Before Roe: Will Past be Prologue?* The Guttmacher Report on Public Policy. https://www.guttmacher.org/sites/default/files/article_files/gr060108.pdf

Goldman, M., Turner, M., & Daly, M. (2018). A critical political ecology of human dimensions of climate change: Epistemology, ontology, and ethics. *WIRE's Climate Change, 9*, e526.

References

Goodell, J. (2023). *The heat will kill you first: Life and death on a scorched planet.* Little, Brown and Company.

Goodell, J. (2024). *Opinion: We built our world for a climate that no longer exists.* CNN. https://www.cnn.com/2024/07/12/opinions/climate-crisis-change-extreme-weather-infrastructure/index.html

Greenhalgh, T., Annandale, E., Ashcroft, R., Barlow, J., Black, N., Bleakley, A., et al. (2016). An open letter to The BMJ editors on qualitative research. *British Medical Journal, 352,* i563. https://www.bmj.com/content/352/bmj.i563

Grim, A. (2015). *Sitting-in for disability rights: The Section 504 protests of the 1970s.* National Museum of American History. https://americanhistory.si.edu/explore/stories/sitting-disability-rights-section-504-protests-1970s

Grosso, J. (2008). *Indios muertos, Negros invisibles. La identidad "Santiaguena" en Argentina.* Anthropology Dissertation. University of Brasilia. https://naya.com.ar/tesis/Jose_Luis_Grosso/jose_luis_grosso_index.htm

Guinto, R., Cahatol, J., Lazaro, K., & Salazar, A. (2022). Pathways linking climate change and HIV/AIDS: An updated conceptual framework and implications for the Philippines. *Journal of Climate Change and Health, 6,* 100106. https://doi.org/10.1016/j.joclim.2021.100106

Gupta, A., Bherwani, H., Gautam, S., Anjum, S., Musugu, K., Kumar, N., et al. (2021). Air pollution aggravating COVID-19 lethality? Exploration in Asian cities using statistical models. *Environment, Development and Sustainability, 23*(4), 6408–6417. https://doi.org/10.1007/s10668-020-00878-9

Hahn, R. (2021). What is a social determinant of health? Back to basics. *Journal of Public Health Research, 10*(4), 2324. https://doi.org/10.4081/jphr.2021.2324

Haines, A. (2019). The work of the Rockefeller foundation – Lancet commission on planetary health. *European Healthcare Design Conference.* https://europeanhealthcaredesign.salus.global/journal/view/article/the-work-of-the-rockefeller-foundation-lancet-commission-on-planetary-health-1

Hancock, T. (1985). The mandala of health: A model of the human ecosystem. *Family & Community Health, 11*(1), 1–10.

Hancock, T. (1997). Ecosystem health, ecological iatrogenesis, and sustainable human development. *Ecosystem Health, 3,* 229–234.

Hanna-Attisha, M. (2018). *What the eyes don't see: A story of crisis, resistance, and hope in an American city.* Penguin Random House.

Hanna-Attisha, M., LaChance, J., Sadler, R., & Schnepp, A. (2016). Elevated blood levels in children associated with the Flint drinking water crises: A spatial analysis of risk and public health response. *American Journal of Public Health, 106,* 283–290. https://doi.org/10.2105/AJPH.2015.303003

Harper, T. (2024). *Maybe don't spray-paint Stonehenge.* The Atlantic. https://www.theatlantic.com/ideas/archive/2024/06/stonehenge-spray-paint-climate-protest/678765/

Harrison, L. T. (2024). *Black history month clean water champion: Mari Copeny.* Clean Water Action. https://cleanwater.org/2024/02/02/black-history-month-clean-water-champion-mari-copeny#:~:text=In%20the%20wake%20of%20her,local%20children%2C%20and%20distribute%20backpacks

Hartblay, C. (2020). Disability expertise: Claiming disability anthropology. *Current Anthropology, 61,* S26–S36.

Harvey-Dunstan, T., Jenkins, A., Gupta, A., Hall, I., & Bolton, C. (2022). Patient-related outcomes in patients referred to a respiratory clinic with persisting symptoms following non-hospitalised COVID-19. *Chronic Respiratory Disease, 19.* https://doi.org/10.1177/14799731211069391

Hattenstone, S. (2021). *The transformation of Greta Thunberg.* The Guardian. https://web.archive.org/web/20211030164705/; https://www.theguardian.com/environment/ng-interactive/2021/sep/25/greta-thunberg-i-really-see-the-value-of-friendship-apart-from-the-climate-almost-nothing-else-matters

Hernandez, I., Bakola, M., & Stuckler, D. (2022). The impact of air pollution on COVID-19 incidence, severity, and mortality: A systematic review of studies in Europe and North America. *Environmental Research, 215*(Pt 1), 114155. https://doi.org/10.1016/j.envres.2022.114155

Hillman, M., Fawcett, T., & Rajan, C. (2008). *How We Can Save the Planet*. Thomas Dunne Books.
Hill, C. (2016). Pre-Colonial foodways. In J. Wallach, L. Swindall, & M. Wise (Eds.), *The Routledge history of American foodways* (pp. 9–12). Routledge Press.
Hix, A. (2020). *The most important question facing humanity*. Medium. https://andyhix.medium.com/the-most-important-question-facing-humanity-658ce4848368
Hobson, M. (2024). *Mission blue*. BBC Wildlife. https://apple.news/AVQAvKP6ZS56UVxv1FRV7lA
Hoffman, B. (2008). Health care reform and social movements in the United States. *American Journal of Public Health, 98*(9 Suppl), S69–S79. https://doi.org/10.2105/ajph.98.supplement1.s69
Hogg, R. (1987). Development in Kenya: Drought, desertification and food security. *African Affairs, 86*(342), 47–58.
Horton, R. (2013). Offline: Planetary health—A new vision for the post-2015 era. *Lancet, 382*, 1012.
Horton, R. (2020). Offline: COVID-19 is not a pandemic. *Lancet, 396*(10255), 874. https://doi.org/10.1016/S0140-6736(20)32000-6
Horton, R., Beaglehole, R., Bonita, R., Raeburn, J., McKee, M., & Stig, W. (2014). From public to planetary health: A manifesto. *The Lancet, 384*(9920), 847. https://doi.org/10.1016/S0140-6736(14)60409-8
Hossain, M., Mahbub, S., Nobonita, R., Tahmina, T., Samia, N., Tasmiah, R., et al. (2022). Global research on syndemics: A meta-knowledge analysis (2001–2020). *F1000Res, 11*, c253. https://doi.org/10.12688/f1000research.74190.2
Hunter, R., Garcia, L., Dagless, S., Haines, A., Penney, T., Chloe Clifford, A., et al. (2024). The emerging syndemic of climate change and non-communicable diseases. *The Lancet, Planetary Health, 8*, e430–e431. https://doi.org/10.1016/S2542-5196(24)00112-8
Hutchison, N. (2024). Alex Schnell demystifies what humans know about octopuses. *National Geographic*. https://www.nationalgeographic.com/impact/article/alex-schnell-explorer-story
Institute for Research on Women. (2022). *Dr. Mona Hanna-Attisha: Stories from the frontline of the Flint water crisis*. Anita Ashok Datar Lecture on Women's Global Health. You Tube.
IPCC. (2019). Summary for policymakers. In H.-O. Pörtner, V. Roberts, D. Masson-Delmotte, P. Zhai, M. Tignor, E. Poloczanska, et al. (Eds.), *IPCC special report on the ocean and cryosphere in a changing climate* (pp. 3–35). Cambridge University Press. https://doi.org/10.1017/9781009157964.001
Joi, P. (2022). *The long haulers: What we now know about long COVID*. Vaccine Work. https://www.gavi.org/vaccineswork/long-haulers-what-we-now-know-about-long-covid?gad_source=1&gclid=EAIaIQobChMIsYuiq4zIhwMV_WFIAB2mejkHEAAYAyAAEgLbefD_BwE
Jones, N. (2020). *How native tribes are taking the lead on planning for climate change*. Yale Environment360. https://e360.yale.edu/features/how-native-tribes-are-taking-the-lead-on-planning-for-climate-change
Jones, R., Reid, P., & Macmillan, A. (2022). Navigating fundamental tensions towards a decolonial relational vision of planetary health. *Lancet Planet Health, 6*, e834–e841.
Jore, S., Vanwambke, S., Viljugrein, I., Ketil, K., Anja, W., et al. (2014). Climate and environmental change drives *Ixodes Ricinus* geographical expansion at the northern range margin. *Parasites & Vectors, 7*, 11. https://doi.org/10.1186/1756-3305-7-11
June, L. (2012). *Chonos Pom, dance grounds: Ethnic endemism among the Winnemem Wintu and the cultural impacts of enlarging Shasta Reservoir*. Department of Anthropology, Stanford University, Honors Thesis.
June, L. (2020). *Reclaiming Indigenous wellness and mental health*. Youtube. https://www.youtube.com/watch?v=OhykU0s0mCw
June, L. (2022). *Architects of abundance: Indigenous regenerative food and land management systems and the excavation of hidden history*. Indigenous Studies Program. University of Alaska, Fairbanks.
June, L. (2023). *3000-year-old solutions to modern problems*. TEDxKC. https://www.youtube.com/watch?v=eH5zJxQETl4

References

Kahn, L. (2006). Confronting zoonoses, linking human and veterinary medicine. *Emerging Infectious Diseases, 12*(4), 556–561. https://wwwnc.cdc.gov/eid/article/12/4/05-0956_article

Kanene, K. (2016). Indigenous practices of environmental sustainability in the Tonga community of southern Zambia. *Jàmbá: Journal of Disaster Risk Studies, 8*(1), 331. https://doi.org/10.4102/jamba.v8i1.331

Kater, I. (2022). Natural and Indigenous sciences: Reflections on an attempt to collaborate. *Regional Environmental Change, 22*, 109. https://link.springer.com/article/10.1007/s10113-022-01967-3

Keefe, R., Lane, S., & Swarts, H. (2006). From the bottom up: Tracing the impact of four health-based social movements on health and social policies. *Journal of Health & Social Policy, 21*(3), 55–69. http://www.haworthpress.com/web/JHS

Kenyon, C., Manoharan-Basil, S., & Van Dijck, C. (2020). Gonococcal resistance can be viewed productively as part of a syndemic of antimicrobial resistance: An ecological analysis of European countries. *Antimicrobial Resistance and Infection Control, 9*, 97. https://doi.org/10.1186/s13756-020-00764-z

Ker, J. (2023). The moral economy of universal public healthcare. On healthcare activism in austerity Spain. *Social Science and Medicine, 319*, 115363. https://www.sciencedirect.com/science/article/pii/S0277953622006694#bib28

Keune, H. (2012). Critical complexity in environmental health practice: Simplify and complexify. *Environmental Health, 11*(Suppl 1), S19. https://doi.org/10.1186/1476-069X-11-S1-S19

Khalfan, A., Nilsson, A., Aguilar, C., Persson, J., Lawson, M., Dabi, N., et al. (2023). *Climate equality: A planet for the 99%*. Oxfam GB.

Kirsch, S. (2000). *Reverse anthropology: Indigenous analysis of social and environmental relations in New Guinea*. Stanford University Press.

Klein, N. (2014). *This changes everything: Capitalism vs. the climate*. Simon & Schuster.

Klinenberg, E. (2022a). *Heat wave: A social autopsy in Chicago*. University of Chicago Press.

Klinenberg, E. (2022b). *Dying alone: An interview with Eric Klinenberg*. University of Chicago Press. https://press.uchicago.edu/Misc/Chicago/443213in.html

Koh, L., Dunn, R., Sodhi, N., Colwell, R., Proctor, H., & Smith, V. (2004). Species coextinctions and the biodiversity crisis. *Science, 305*(5690), 1632–1634. https://doi.org/10.1126/science.110110

Konak, N. (2011). *Gold mining and environmental movement: The Case of Bergama, Turkey: Bergama Gold Mining and Environmental Movement in Turkey*. Lambert Academic Publishing.

Kotloff, K., Nataro, J., Blackwelder, W., Nasrin, D., Farag, T., Panchalingam, S., Wu, Y. et al. (2013). Burden and aetiology of diarrhoeal disease in infants and young children in developing countries (the Global Enteric Multicenter Study, GEMS): A prospective, case-control study. *The Lancet, 9888*, 209–222.

Krol, A. (2023). Will climate change drive humans extinct or destroy civilization? *Climate Portal*. https://climate.mit.edu/ask-mit/will-climate-change-drive-humans-extinct-or-destroy-civilization

Kwon, E., Huang, P., Carlson, R., & Ramirez, R. (2024). *10 years after Flint, the fight to replace lead pipes across the U.S. continues*. NPR. https://www.npr.org/2024/04/26/1198909905/flint-water-lead-poisoning-anniversary-chicago#:~:text=The%20lack%20of%20corrosion%20control,impact%20on%20Flint's%20young%20children

Lagunova, E., Liapunova, N., Tuul, D., Otgonsuren, G., Nomin, D., Erdenebat, N., et al. (2022). Co-infections with multiple pathogens in natural populations of *Ixodes persulcatus* ticks in Mongolia. *Parasites and Vectors, 15*, 236. https://doi.org/10.1186/s13071-022-05356-x

Lane, M., Polidori, J., & Hughes, S. (2016). *The Flint water crisis: Could the Flint water crisis happen somewhere else?* Gala. https://www.learngala.com/cases/flint-water-crisis

Lasco, G. (2019). *Why are people who use illegal drugs demonized*. Sapiens. Sapiens.org/culture/drug-users-demonized/

Lasverack, G. (2013). Health activism: The way forward to improve health in difficult times. *Global Health Promotion, 20*(3), 49–52. doi-org.ezproxy.lib.uconn.edu/10.1177/1757975913499038

Latour, B., & Schulz, N. (2022) *On the emergence of an ecological class: A memo*. (Translated by Julie Rose). Polity Press.

Laudisio, A., Marinosci, F., Gemma, A., et al. (2017). The burden of comorbidity is associated with antibiotic resistance among institutionalized elderly with urinary infection: A retrospective cohort study in a single Italian nursing home between 2009 and 2014. *Microbial Drug Resistance, 23*(4), 500–506. https://doi.org/10.1089/mdr.2016.0016

Laverack, G. (2013). *Health activism: Foundations and strategies.* Sage.

Lebreton, L., Slat, B., Ferrari, F., Sainte-Rose, B., Aitken, J., Marthouse, R., et al. (2018). Evidence that the Great Pacific Garbage Patch is rapidly accumulating plastic. *Scientific Reports, 8*, 4666. https://doi.org/10.1038/s41598-018-22939-w

Legislative Analysis and Public Policy Association. (2023). *Syringe services programs: Summary of state laws.* https://legislativeanalysis.org/wp-content/uploads/2023/11/Syringe-Services-Programs-Summary-of-State-Laws.pdf

Lemey, P., Pybus, O., Wang, B., Saksena, N., Salemi, M., & Vandamme, A. (2003). Tracing the origin and history of the HIV-2 epidemic. *Proceedings of the National Academy of Science USA, 100*(11), 6588–6592. https://doi.org/10.1073/pnas.0936469100

Lemke, M., Apostolopoulos, Y., Hege, A., Sönmez, S., & Wideman, L. (2016). Understanding the role of sleep quality and sleep duration in commercial driving safety. *Accident; Analysis and Prevention, 97*, 79–86. https://doi.org/10.1016/j.aap.2016.08.024

Lerner, B. (2001). *The breast cancer wars: Hope, fear, and the pursuit of a cure in twentieth-century America.* Oxford University Press.

Lerner, S. (2024). *How 3M executives convinced a scientist the forever chemicals she found in human blood were safe.* ProPublica. https://www.propublica.org/article/3m-forever-chemicals-pfas-pfos-inside-story

Lewis, M., & Prunuske, A. (2017). The development of an Indigenous health curriculum for medical students. *Academic Medicine, 92*(5), 641–648. https://doi.org/10.1097/ACM.0000000000001482

Li, Y., Wang, S., Toumi, R., Song, X., & Wang, Q. (2023). Recent increases in tropical cyclone rapid intensification events in global offshore regions. *Nature Communications, 14*, 5167. https://www.nature.com/articles/s41467-023-40605-2#Abs1

Lim, X. Z. (2019). Tainted water: The scientists tracing thousands of fluorinated chemicals in our environment. *Nature, 566*(7742), 26–29. https://doi.org/10.1038/d41586-019-00441-1

Lin, W., Weinberg, E., & Chung, R. (2013). Pathogenesis of accelerated fibrosis in HIV/HCV co-infection. *Journal of Infectious Diseases, 207*(Suppl 1), S13–S18. https://doi.org/10.1093/infdis/jis926

Linder, A., McCarthy, V. W., Green, C., Nadzam, B., Jamieson, D., & Stilt, K. (2023). *Animal Markets and Zoonotic Disease in the United States.* Harvard Law School. https://animal.law.harvard.edu/wp-content/uploads/Animal-Markets-and-Zoonotic-Disease-in-the-United-States.pdf

Logan, A., Berman, B., & Prescott, S. (2023). Vitality revisited: The evolving concept of flourishing and its relevance to personal and public health. *International Journal of Environmental Research and Public Health, 20*(6), 5065. https://doi.org/10.3390/ijerph20065065

Lorde, A. (1984). The Master's tools will never dismantle the Master's house. In A. Lorde (Ed.), *Sister outsider: Essays and speeches* (pp. 110–114). Crossing Press.

Lovelock, J. (1991). *Gaia: The practical Science of planetary medicine.* Gaia Books.

Low, P., Panksepp, J., Reiss, D., Edelman, D., Van Swinderen, B., & Koch, C. (2012). Cambridge declaration on consciousness. *Francis Crick Memorial Conference.* https://fcmconference.org/img/CambridgeDeclarationOnConsciousness.pdf

Lowe, D. (2016). Better, faster, more comprehensive manure distribution. *In the Pipeline.* https://www.science.org/content/blog-post/better-faster-more-comprehensive-manure-distribution

Magistretti, C., Sallaway-Costello, J., Fatima, S., & Hartnoll, R. (2021). People-Planet-Health: Promoting grassroots movements through participatory co-production. *Global Health Promotion, 28*(4), 83–87. https://doi.org/10.1177/17579759211044073

Mago, A., Dhali, A., Kumar, H., Maity, R., & Kuma, B. (2024). Planetary health and its relevance in the modern era: A topical review. *Sage Open Medicine, 12*, 20503121241254231. https://doi.org/10.1177/20503121241254231

References

Malle, C. (2019). *Inside the sunrise movement: Six weeks with the young activists defining the climate debate.* Vogue. https://www.vogue.com/article/inside-sunrise-movement-youth-activists-climate-debate

Marcantonio, R., & Fuentes, A. (2023). Environmental violence. *The Lancet Planet Health, 7*(10), e859–e867. https://doi.org/10.1016/S2542-5196(23)00190-0

Marfella, R., Prattichizzo, F., Sardu, C., Fulgenzi, G., Graciti, L., Spadoni, T., et al. (2024). Microplatics and nanoplatics in atheromas and cardiovascular events. *New England Journal of Medicine, 390*(10), 900–910. https://doi.org/10.1056/NEJMoa2309822

Marieskind, H. (1975). The women's health movement. *International Journal of Health Services, 5*(2), 217–223. https://doi.org/10.2190/5XUN-VX3H-KMWM-F17M

Marks, E., Hickman, C., Pihkala, P., Clayton, S., Lewandowski, E., Mayall, E., et al. (2021). *Young people's voices on climate anxiety, government betrayal and moral injury: A global phenomenon.* https://doi.org/10.2139/ssrn.3918955.

Masur, H., Michelis, M., Greene, J., Onorato, I., Vande Stouwe, R., Holzman, R., et al. (1981). An outbreak of community-acquired Pneumoncystis carinii pneumonia: Initial manifestation of cellular immune dysfunction. *New England Journal of Medicine, 305,* 1431–1438.

Mather, M., & Scommegna, P. (2024). *Fact-sheet: Aging in the United States.* PRB. https://www.prb.org/resources/fact-sheet-aging-in-the-united-states/#:~:text=The%20number%20of%20Americans%20ages,than%20it%20has%20ever%20been

Mattijsen, J., van Bree, E., Brakema, E., Huynen, M., Visser, E., Blankestijn, P., et al. (2023). Educational activism for planetary health – A case example from The Netherlands. *Lancet Planet Health, 7*(1), e18–e20. https://doi.org/10.1016/S2542-5196(22)00314-X

McBrien, J. (2019). *This is not the sixth extinction. It's the first extermination event.* Truthout. https://truthout.org/articles/this-is-not-the-sixth-extinction-its-the-first-extermination-event/

McLean, K. (2022). The biopolitics of needle exchange in the United States. *Critical Public Health, 21*(1), 71–79. https://doi.org/10.1080/09581591003653124. PMID: 22389572; PMCID: PMC3291106.

McCoy, A. (2021). *Life circa 2050 will be bad. Really bad.* The Nation. https://www.thenation.com/article/environment/climate-future-disasters/

McDonald, D. (2023). Sao Paulo Rising: Grassroots movements and the right to health in authoritarian Brazil. *Hispanic American Historical Review, 103*(3), 495–526.

McGranahan, C., Roland, K., & Williams, B. (2016). *Decolonizing anthropology: A conversation with Faye V. Harrison, part II.* Savage Minds. https://savageminds.org/2016/05/03/decolonizing-anthropology-a-conversation-with-faye-v-harrison-part-ii/

McKnight, C., Des Jarlais, D., Perlis, T., Eigo, K., Krim, M., Auerbach, J., et al. (2005). Update: Syringe exchange programs – United States, 2002. *MMWR Weekly, 54*(27), 673–676. https://www.cdc.gov/mmwr/preview/mmwrhtml/mm5427a1.htm

McLean, K. (2011). The biopolitics of needle exchange in the United States. *Critical Public Health, 21*(1), 71–79. https://doi.org/10.1080/09581591003653124

McMichael, A. (1993). *Planetary overload: Global environmental change and the health of the human species.* Cambridge University Press.

McMichael, A. (1999). Prisoners of the proximate: Loosening the constraints on epidemiology in an age of change. *American Journal of Epidemiology, 149*(10), 887–897. https://doi.org/10.1093/oxfordjournals.aje.a009732

Mendenhall, E. (2023). *What Tony Fauci says about Long COVID and other postviral illnesses.* Scientific American. https://www.scientificamerican.com/article/what-tony-fauci-says-about-long-covid-and-other-postviral-illnesses1/#:~:text=Fauci%20emphasized%20what%20makes%20long,caused%20a%20person's%20ME%2FCFS

Mendenhall, E., Newfield, T., & Tsai, A. (2022). Syndemic theory, methods, and data. *Social Science & Medicine, 295*(114656), 24. https://doi.org/10.1016/j.socscimed.2021.114656

Mendenhall, E., & Singer, M. (2019). The global syndemic of obesity, undernutrition, and climate change. *The Lancet, 393*(10173), 741.

Mesfin, Y., Hailemariam, D., Biadglign, S., & Kibret, K. (2015). Association between HIV/AIDS and multi-drug resistance Tuberculosis: A systematic review and meta-analysis. *PLoS One, 9*(2), e89709. https://doi.org/10.1371/journal.pone.0082235

Metzner, R. (1992). *Statement of purpose. Green earth foundation catalog.* The Green Earth Foundation.

Mignolo, W. (2009). Epistemic disobedience, independent thought and decolonial freedom. *Theory, Culture and Society, 26*(7–8), 159–181. https://doi.org/10.1177/0263276409349275

Molix, L. (2014). Sex differences in cardiovascular health. *The American Journal of the Medical Science, 348*(2), 153–155. https://doi.org/10.1097/MAJ.0000000000000300

Mora, C., McKenzie, T., Gaw, I., Dean, J., von Hammerstein, H., Knudson, T., et al. (2022). Over half of known human pathogenic diseases can be aggravated by climate change. *Nature Climate Change, 12*, 869–875. https://doi.org/10.1038/s41558-022-01426-1

Munderloh, U., & Kurtti, T. (2011). Emerging and re-emerging tick-borne diseases: New challenges at the interface of human and animal health. In *Critical needs and gaps in understanding prevention, amelioration and resolution of Lyme and other tick-borne diseases: The short-term and long-term outcomes* (pp. A142–A166). The National Academies of Sciences Press.

Murray, R., Day, K., & Tobbell, J. (2019). Duvet woman versus action man: The gendered aetiology of Chronic Fatigue Syndrome according to English newspapers. *Feminist Media Studies, 19*(6), 890–905. https://doi.org/10.1080/14680777.2019

Murray, C., Ikuta, K., Sharara, F., et al. (2022). Global burden of bacterial antimicrobial resistance in 2019: A systematic analysis. *Lancet, 399*, 629–655. https://doi.org/10.1016/s0140-6736(21)02724-0

Murray, C., Poletti, G., Kebadze, T., Morris, J., Woodcock, A., Johnston, S., & Custovic, A. (2006). Study of modifiable risk factors for asthma exacerbations: Virus infection and allergen exposure increase the risk of asthma hospital admissions in children. *Thorax, 6*, 376–382.

Myers, N. (2022). The ecosocial self, place, and well-being: An ethnographic case study with Maasai women from northern Tanzania. *Social Science and Medicine, Mental Health, 2*, 100140. https://doi.org/10.1016/j.ssmmh.2022.100144

Myers, S., & Frumkin, H. (2020). *Planetary health: Protecting nature to protect ourselves.* Island Press.

Myers, S., Potter, T., Wagner, J., & Xie, M. (2020). Clinicians for planetary health. *One Earth, 5*(4), 329–323. https://doi.org/10.1016/j.oneear.2022.03.006

Nagendra, H. (2018). The global south is rich in sustainability lessons that students deserve to hear. *Nature, 557*, 485–488. https://www.nature.com/articles/d41586-018-05210-0

Nakashima, D., Krupnik, I., & Jennifer, R. (2018). *Indigenous knowledge for climate change assessment and adaptation.* Cambridge University Press.

Napoletanoa, B., & Clark, B. (2020). An ecological-Marxist response to the Half-Earth Project. *Conservation and Society, 18*(1), 37–49. https://doi.org/10.4103/cs.cs_19_99

NASA. (2023). *The ocean has a fever.* https://earthobservatory.nasa.gov/images/151743/the-ocean-has-a-fever

NBC Nightly News Kids Edition. (2020). *Sarah Goody.* https://www.youtube.com/watch?v=qarNqQALwdA

Neill, I. (2023). *5 years of strikes for climate: Where is Greta Thunberg now?* The Oxford Student. https://www.oxfordstudent.com/2023/11/20/5-years-of-strikes-for-climate-where-is-greta-thunberg-now/

Newland, B. (2022). *Federal Indian boarding school initiative investigative report.* United States Department of the Interior.

Nichols, F. (2000). History of the women's health movement in the 20th century. *Journal of Obstetrics, Gynecology, and Neonatal Nursing, 29*(1), 56–64. https://doi.org/10.1111/j.1552-6909.2000.tb02756.x

Niering, W. (1998). Postscript on an ecological giant: Frank E. Egler. *Bulletin of the Ecological Society of America, 79*(4), 255–256.

Nixon, R. (1971). *Annual message to the Congress on the State of the Union.* https://www.presidency.ucsb.edu/documents/annual-message-the-congress-the-state-the-union-1

References

Njunda, A., Fon, S., Assob, J., Nsagha, D., Kwenti, T., & Kwenti, T. (2015). Coinfection with malaria and intestinal parasites, and its association with anaemia in children in Cameroon. *Infectious Diseases of Poverty, 4*, 43. https://doi.org/10.1186/s40249-015-0078-5

O'Callaghan-Gordo, C., Moreno, A., Bosque-Prous, M., Castro-Sanchez, E., Dadvand, P., Guzmán, C. A. F., et al. (2022). Responding to the need of postgraduate education for Planetary Health: Development of an online master's degree. *Frontiers in Public Health, 10*, 969065. https://doi.org/10.3389/fpubh.2022.969065

O'Neil, J., Reading, J., & Leader, A. (1998). Changing the relations of surveillance: The development of a discourse of resistance in Aboriginal epidemiology. *Human Organization, 57*(2), 230–237.

Ogden, N., Mechai, S., & Margos, G. (2013). Changing geographic ranges of ticks and tick-borne pathogens: Drivers, mechanisms and consequences for pathogen diversity. *Frontiers in Cellular and Infectious Microbiology, 3*, 46. https://doi.org/10.3389/fcimb.2013.00046

Oliver-Smith, A. (2010). *Haiti and the historical construction of disasters*. Nacla. https://nacla.org/article/haiti-and-historical-construction-disasters

Ord, T. (2020). *The precipice: Existential risk and the future of humanity*. Hachette Books. https://theprecipice.com/

Oreskes, N., & Conway, E. (2010). *Merchants of doubt: How a handful of scientists lbscured the truth on issues from tobacco smoke to global warming*. Bloomsbury Publishing.

Ortiz, I., Burke, S., Berrada, M., & Cortés, H. (2022). *World protests A study of key protest issues in the 21st century*. Initiative for Policy Dialogue/Global Social Justice, https://link.springer.com/content/pdf/10.1007/978-3-030-88513-7.pdf.

Ostfeld, R. (2017). Biodiversity loss and the ecology of infectious disease. *The Lancet, 1*, e2–e3. https://www.thelancet.com/pdfs/journals/lanplh/PIIS2542-5196(17)30010-4.pdf

Otto-Portner, H., Scholes, B., Agard, J., Archer, E., Arneth, A., Bai, X., et al. (2021). *Scientific outcome of the IPBES-IPCC co-sponsored workshop on biodiversity and climate change*. https://files.ipbes.net/ipbes-web-prod-public-files/2021-06/2021_IPCC-IPBES_scientific_outcome_20210612.pdf

Owen, D. (2006). Is Lyme disease always poly microbial?—The jigsaw hypothesis. *Medical Hypothesis, 67*, 860–864.

Pacino, N. (2017). Liberating the people from their 'loathsome practices:' Public health and 'silent racism' in post-revolutionary Bolivia. *História, Ciências, Saúde-Manguinhos, 24*(4), 1107–1124. https://doi.org/10.1590/s0104-59702017000500014

Parker, J. (1993). Toward a nursing ethic for sustainable planetary health. *Proceedings of the First National Nursing the Environment Conference, Melbourne, Australia*, pp. 87–91.

Patel, L., Friedman, E., Stephanie Alexandra, J., Lee, S. S., et al. (2021). Air pollution as a social and structural determinant of health. *The Journal of Climate Change and Health, 3*, 100035. https://doi.org/10.1016/j.joclim.2021.100035

Perego, E., Callard, F., Stras, L., Melville-Jóhannesson, B., Pope, R., & Alwan, N. (2020). Why the patient-made term 'long covid' is needed. *Wellcome Open Research, 39*(1), 73–97. https://doi.org/10.12688/wellcomeopenres.16307.1

Perry, M., & Gowland, R. (2022). Compounding vulnerabilities: Syndemics and the social determinants of disease in the past. *International Journal of Paleopathology, 39*, 35–49. https://doi.org/10.1016/j.ijpp.2022.09.002

Pfenning-Butterworth, A., Buckley, L., Drake, J., Farner, J., Farrell, M., Gehman, A., et al. (2024). Interconnecting global threats: Climate change, biodiversity loss, and infectious diseases. *Lancet Planet Health, 4*, e270–e283. https://doi.org/10.1016/S2542-5196(24)00021-4

Piewnam, P., & Otto, M. (2024). *Staphylococcus aureus* colonisation and strategies for decolonization. *The Lancet Microbe, 5*(6), e606–e618. https://www.thelancet.com/journals/lanmic/article/PIIS2666-5247(24)00040-5/fulltext

Pinchin, K. (2023). *Kings of their own ocean*. Penguin Random House.

Pinkerton, R., Oriá, R., Lima, A., Rogawski, E., Oriá, M., Patrick, P., Moore, S., Wiseman, B., Niehaus, M., & Guerrant, R. (2016). Early childhood diarrhea predicts cognitive delays in later childhood independently of malnutrition. *American Journal of Tropical Medicine and Hygiene, 95*(5), 1004–1010. https://doi.org/10.4269/ajtmh.16-0150

Piqueiras, E. (2021). An emergent Legionnaires' disease syndemic: Water supply systems, infrastructural violence, and afflicted lives in the south Bronx, Ny. *Wayne State University Dissertations*: 3469. https://digitalcommons.wayne.edu/cgi/viewcontent.cgi?article=4468&context=oa_dissertations

Porsanger, J. (2004). An essay about Indigenous methodology. *Nordlit, 8*. https://doi.org/10.7557/13.1910

Prescott, S., & Logan, A. (2019). Planetary health: From the wellspring of holistic medicine to personal and public health imperative. *Explore, 15*(2), 98–106. https://doi.org/10.1016/j.explore.2018.09.002

Rajkumar, S. (2022). *The ADA was a victory for the disabled community, but we need more. My life shows why*. NPR. https://www.npr.org/2022/07/29/1113535976/ada-disabilities-act-activists-more-protections

Ramírez, I., & Lee, J. (2021). COVID-19 and ecosyndemic vulnerability: Implications for El Niño-sensitive countries in Latin America. *International Journal of Disaster Risk Science, 12*, 147–156. https://doi.org/10.1007/s13753-020-00318-2

Ramírez, I., Lee, J., & Grady, S. (2018). Mapping multi-disease risk during El Niño: An ecosyndemic approach. *International Journal of Environmental Research and Public Health, 15*(12), 2639. https://doi.org/10.3390/ijerph15122639

Randolf, D., Refisch, J., MacMillan, S., Wright, C., Bett, B., Robinson, D., et al. (2020). *Preventing the next pandemic: Zoonotic diseases and how to break the chain of transmission*. United Nation Environment Program.

Raynor, J., Grainger, C., & Parker, D. (2021). Wolves make roadways safer, generating large economic returns to predator conservation. *PNAS, 118*(22), e2023251118. https://doi.org/10.1073/pnas.2023251118

reddit. (2022). *R/Coronavirus*. Discussion thread. https://www.reddit.com/r/Coronavirus/?rdt=43673

Redvers, N. (2021). The determinants of planetary health. *Lancet Planet Health, 5*(3), e111–e112. https://doi.org/10.1016/S2542-5196(21)00008-5

Redvers, N., Celidwen, Y., Schultz, C., Horn, O., Githaiga, C., Vera, M., et al. (2022). The determinants of planetary health: An Indigenous consensus perspective. *Lancet Planet Health, 6*(2), e156–e163. https://doi.org/10.1016/S2542-5196(21)00354-

Rehman, Z. (2024). *On the uptick*. Chatelaine blog. https://chatelaine.com/category/health/2/

Rico, M., & Pautass, L. (2023). The right to care at stake: The syndemic emergency in Latin America. In M. Duffy, A. Armenia, & Price-Glynn (Eds.), *From crisis to catastrophe: Care, COVID, and pathways to change*. Rutgers.

Rigby, J. (2024). *Why mpox vaccines are only just arriving in Africa after two years*. Reuters. https://www.reuters.com/business/healthcare-pharmaceuticals/why-mpox-vaccines-are-only-just-arriving-africa-after-two-years-2024-08-24/

Ripple, W., Wolf, C., Gregg, J., Rockström, J., Newsome, T., Law, B., et al. (2023). The 2023 state of the climate report: Entering uncharted territory. *Bioscience, 73*(12), 841–850. https://doi.org/10.1093/biosci/biad080

Ripple, W., Wolf, C., van Vuuren, D., Gregg, J., & Lenzen, M. (2024). An environmental and socially just climate mitigation pathway for a planet in peril. *Environmental Research Letters, 19*, 021001. https://doi.org/10.1088/1748-9326/ad059e

Roberts, D. (2019). Whose conception of human flourishing? In E. Parens & J. Johnston (Eds.), *Human flourishing in an age of gene editing*. Oxford University Press.

Rochlin, I., & Toledo, A. (2020). Emerging tick-borne pathogens of public health importance: A mini-review. *Journal of Medical Microbiology, 69*(6), 781–791. https://doi.org/10.1099/jmm.0.001206

Rockström, J., Steffen, W., Noone, K., Perrson, A., Chapin, E. S., Lambin, E., et al. (2009). A safe operating space for humanity. *Nature, 461*, 472–475. https://doi.org/10.1038/461472a

References

Rodrigo, N., Tavella, M., Fabra, M., & Demarchi, D. (2022). Ancient DNA analysis reveals temporal and geographical patterns of mitochondrial diversity in pre-Hispanic populations from Central Argentina. *American Journal of Human Biology, 34*(7), e23733. https://doi.org/10.1002/ajhb.23733

Rogers, E. (2022). Recursive debility: Symptoms, patient activism, and the incomplete medicalization of ME/CFS. *Medical Anthropology Quarterly, 36*(3), 412–428. https://doi.org/10.1111/maq.12701

Romañach Cabrero, J. (2009). *Bioética al otro lado del espejo: La visión de las personas con diversidad funcional y el respeto a los derechos humanos*. Diversitas, Madrid: Asociación Iniciativas y Estudios Sociales.

Roszak, T. (2001). *Voice of the earth: An exploration of ecopsychology*. Phanes Press.

Rowbotham, T. (1980). Preliminary report on the pathogenicity of Legionella pneumophila for freshwater and soil amoebae. *Journal of Clinical Pathology, 33*, 1179–1183.

Roy, E. (2019). One day we'll disappear': Tuvalu's sinking islands. The Guardian. https://www.theguardian.com/global-development/2019/may/16/one-day-disappear-tuvalu-sinking-islands-rising-seas-climate-change

Ruiz de Castañeda, R., Villers, J., Guzmán, C., Eslanloo, T., de Paula, N., Machalaba, C., Zinsstag, J., Utiziner, J., Flahault, A., & Bolon, I. (2023). One Health and planetary health research: Leveraging differences to grow together. *The Lancet, 7*(2), E109–E111. https://doi.org/10.1016/S2542-5196(23)00002-5

Saigal, K., & Bojang, S. (2024). Top African expert calls for vaccine equity to beat mpox. The African Report. https://www.theafricareport.com/359213/top-african-expert-calls-for-vaccine-equity-to-beat-mpox/

Sandor, J., Norton, J., Homburg, J., Muenchrath, D., White, C., Williams, S., et al. (2007). Biogeochemical studies of a Native American runoff agroecosystem. *Geoarchaeology: An International Journal, 22*(3), 359–386.

Sandström, P., Sandström, C., Svensson, J., Jougda, L., & Baer, K. (2012). Participatory GIS to mitigate conflicts between reindeer husbandry and forestry in Vilhelmina Model Forest, Sweden. *The Forestry Chronicle, 88*(03), 254–260. https://doi.org/10.5558/tfc2012-051

Sangiovanni, A., & Viehoff, J. (2023). Solidarity in social and political philosophy. In E. Zalta, & U. Nodelman (Eds.), *The Stanford encyclopedia of philosophy*. https://plato.stanford.edu/archives/sum2023/entries/solidarity/

Sargent, F. (1972). Man-environment-problems for public health. *American Journal of Public Health, 62*(5), 628–633.

Scheidel, A., Del Bene, D., Liu, J., Navas, G., Mingorría, S., Demaria, F., et al. (2020). Environmental conflicts and defenders: A global overview. *Global Environmental Change, 63*, 102104. https://doi.org/10.1016/j.gloenvcha.2020.102104

Schneir, M. (1994). *Feminism in our time: The essential writings, world war II to the present*. Vintage.

Schumer, L. (2024). How Dr. Fauci Made Peace with Fierce Critics—AIDS Activists—and Befriended a Former 'Nemesis'. People. https://people.com/how-dr-fauci-made-peace-with-some-of-his-fiercest-critics-exclusive-8671230

Schweik, S. (2010). *The ugly laws: Disability in public*. New York University Press.

Sellers, F. (2021). Diana Berrent, founder of Survivor Corp, discusses growing number of long haulers. Washington Post on YouTube. https://www.google.com/search?q=survivors+corps&oq=survivors+corps&gs_lcrp=EgZjaHJvbWUyBggAEEUYOTIICAEQABgWGB4yCAgCE-AAYFhgeMggIAxAAGBYYHjIICAQQABgWGB4yCAgFEAAYFhgeMgsIBhAAGBYYHhj HAzINCAcQABiGAxiABBiKBTINCAgQABiGAxiABBiKBTINCAkQABiGAxiABBiKBd IBCDYxNDRqMGo0qAIAsAIB&sourceid=chrome&ie=UTF-8#fpstate=ive&vld=cid:e50b0 4d3,vid:IsJqlwiYgz0,st:0

Sen, A. (2005). *Forward. Pathologies of power by Paul Farmer*. University of California Press.

Shabnam, S., Razieh, C., Dambha-Miller, H., Yates, T., Gillies, C., Chudasama, Y., et al. (2023). Socioeconomic inequalities of Long COVID: A retrospective population-based cohort study in the United Kingdom. *Journal of the Royal Society of Medicine, 116*(8), 263–273. https://doi.org/10.1177/01410768231168377

Shah, N., Auld, S., Brust, J., Mathema, B., Ismail, N., Moodley, P., et al. (2017). Transmission of extensively drug-resistant tuberculosis in South Africa. *New England Journal of Medicine, 376*(3), 243–253.

Singer, P. (1975). *Animal liberation: A new ethics for our treatment of animals*. HarperCollins.

Singer, M. (1996). A dose of drugs, A touch of violence, A case of AIDS: Conceptualizing the SAVA syndemic. *Free Inquiry in Creative Sociology, 24*(2), 99–110.

Singer, M. (2009a). Doorways in nature: Syndemics, zoonotics, and public health: A commentary on Rock, Buntain, Hatfield & Hallgrímsson. *Social Science and Medicine, 68*(6), 996–999.

Singer, M. (2009b). *Introduction to syndemics: A critical systems approach to public and community health*. Wiley.

Singer, M. (2013). Respiratory health and ecosyndemics in a time of global warming. *Health Sociology Review, 22*(1), 98–111.

Singer, M. (2014). *Climate change and planetary health*. Somatosphere. Sept 8, 2014. http://somatosphere.net/2014/09/climate-change-and-planetary-health.html.it

Singer, M. (2021a). *Ecocrises interaction: Human health and the changing environment*. Wiley.

Singer, M. (2021b). *Ecosystem crises interaction: Human health and the changing environment*. Wiley.

Singer, E. (2022). *Lawful sins: Abortion rights and reproductive governance in Mexico*. Stanford University Press.

Singer, M., & Bulled, N. (2016). Ectoparasitic syndemics: Polymicrobial tick-borne disease interactions in a changing anthropogenic landscape. *Medical Anthropology Quarterly, 30*(4), 442–461.

Singer, M., & Bulled, N. (2024). Long COVID: A syndemics approach to Understanding and response. *Applied Research in Quality of Life, 19*, 811–834. https://link.springer.com/article/10.1007/s11482-023-10266-w

Singer, M., Bulled, N., Ostrach, B., & Ginzburg, S. L. (2021). Syndemics: A cross-disciplinary approach to complex epidemic events like COVID-19. *Annual Review of Anthropology, 50*, 41–58.

Singer, M., Bulled, N., Ostrach, B., & Mendenhall, E. (2017). Syndemics and the biosocial conception of health. *Lancet, 389*, 941–950.

Singer, M., Himmelgreen, D., Weeks, M., Radda, K., & Martinez, R. (1997). Changing the environment of AIDS risk: Findings on syringe exchange and pharmacy sale of syringes in Hartford, CT. *Medical Anthropology, 18*(1), 107–130.

Singer, M., & Page, J. B. (2013). *The social value of drug addicts: The uses of the useless*. Left Coast Press.

Smith, L. (2012). *Decolonizing methodologies: Research and Indigenous peoples* (2nd ed.). Zed Books.

Springborn, M., Weill, J., Karen, L., Ibáñez, R., & Ghosh, A. (2022). Amphibian collapses increased malaria incidence in Central America. *Environmental Research Letters, 17*, 104012. https://doi.org/10.1088/1748-9326/ac8e1d

Sridhar, D. (2020). Covid-19 has shown us that good health is not just down to biology. The Guardian. https://www.theguardian.com/commentisfree/2020/dec/25/covid-19-good-health-biology-pandemic-unequal-effects

Starn, O. (2024). *Inside Amazon's union busting tactics*. Sapiens. https://www.sapiens.org/culture/amazon-union-busting-anthropologist/

Stohl, C. (1991). Planetary health: Are you part of the solution. *Beginnings, 11*, 6.

Stuen-Parker, J. (1998). *Letter to Norman Mailer: From jail to Yale*. National AIDS Brigade.

Supran, G., & Oreskes, N. (2021). *Rhetoric and frame analysis of ExxonMobil's climate change communications*. CellPress. https://www.cell.com/one-earth/pdf/S2590-3322(21)00233-5.pdf

Swanson, C., & Szymanski, D. (2020). From pain to power: An exploration of activism, the #Metoo movement, and healing from sexual assault trauma. *Journal of Counseling Psychology, 67*(6), 653–668. https://doi.org/10.1037/cou0000429

References

Sze, J., Childs, D., Carrasco, R., & Edwards, D. (2022). Report Indigenous lands in protected areas have high forest integrity across the tropics. *Current Biology, 32*, 4949–4956. https://www.cell.com/current-biology/pdf/S0960-9822(22)01540-8.pdf

Tallman, P., Riley-Powell, A., Schwarz, L., Salmón-Mulanovich, G., Southgate, T., Pace, C., et al. (2022). Ecosyndemics: The potential synergistic health impacts of highways and dams in the Amazon. *Social Science & Medicine, 295*, 113037. https://doi.org/10.1016/j.socscimed.2020.113037

Tavella, M. P. (2024). *Can ancient DNA support Indigenous histories?* Sapiens. https://www.sapiens.org/biology/ancient-dna-indigenous-histories-argentina/

Taylor, C. (2024a). *Cosmic connections: Poetry in the age of disenchantment*. Belknap Press.

Taylor, M. (2024b). *Scientists sound alarm after observing worrisome behavior shift in world's most isolated whale species: 'No area of the world's oceans is untouched'*. TDC. https://www.thecooldown.com/outdoors/beaked-whales-study-anthropogenic-impacts/

Thames, A., Irwin, M., Breen, E., & Cole, S. (2019). Experienced discrimination and racial differences in leukocyte gene expression. *Psychoneuroendocrinology, 106*, 277–283. https://doi.org/10.1016/j.psyneuen.2019.04.016

Thiery, W., Lange, S., Rogelj, J., Schleussner, C.-F., Gudmundsson, L., Seneviratne, S., et al. (2021). Intergenerational inequities in exposure to climate extremes. *Science, 374*(6564), 158–160. https://doi.org/10.1126/science.abi7339

Thunberg Greta. (2019) *There is no sense of urgency*. The Real News Network. https://therealnews.com/greta-thunberg-cop25-there-is-no-sense-of-urgency?gad_source=1&gclid=EAIaIQobChMIrOvkzeSciAMV387CBB0vXxi6EAAYASAAEgJ0QfD_BwE

Tiotiu, A., Novakova, P., Nedeva, D., Chong-Neto, H., Novakova, S., Steiropoulos, P., et al. (2020). Impact of air pollution on asthma outcomes. *International Journal of Environmental Research and Public Health, 17*(17), 6212. https://doi.org/10.3390/ijerph17176212

Trewavas, A. (2014). *Plant behaviour and intelligence*. Oxford University Press.

Troeger, C., Colombara, D., Rao, P., Khalil, I., Brown, A., Brewer, T., et al. (2018). Global disability-adjusted life-year estimates of long-term health burden and undernutrition attributable to diarrhoeal diseases in children younger than 5 years. *Lancet Global Health, 6*, e255–e269.

Tsaregorodtsev, G. (1974). Dialectics of interaction of economic and humanistic approaches. *Soviet Studies in Philosophy, 13*(2–3), 100–106.

Tu'itahi, S., Watson, H., Egan, R., Parkes, M., & Hancock, T. (2021). Waiora: The importance of Indigenous worldviews and spirituality to inspire and inform Planetary Health Promotion in the Anthropocene. *Global Health Promotion, 28*(4), 73–82. https://doi.org/10.1177/17579759211062261

Tweed, S., Selbie, D., Tegnell, A., Viso, A.-C., Ahmed, A., Mastov, M., et al. (2023). Syndemic health crises—The growing role of National Public Health Institutes in shaping a coordinated response. *International Journal of Health Planning and Management, 38*(4), 889–897. https://doi.org/10.1002/hpm.3634

UN Secretariat of the Conference on Desertification. (1977). Desertification: An overview. In *Desertification: Its causes and consequences*. Pergamon Press.

United Nations, Climate Action. (2022). *Ashley Lashley: The health of our people and our environment are all interconnected*. https://www.un.org/en/climatechange/voices-of-change-ashley-lashley

US Department of Health and Human Services. (2024). *Tickborne diseases and conditions*. https://www.hhs.gov/climate-change-health-equity-environmental-justice/climate-change-health-equity/climate-health-outlook/tickborne-diseases-conditions/index.html#:~:text=Climate%20change%20is%20one%20of,a%20tick's%20ability%20to%20reproduce

Valentini, D., Vittucci, A. C., Grandin, A., Tozzi, A. E., Russo, C., Onori, M., et al. (2013). Coinfection in acute gastroenteritis predicts a more severe clinical course in children. *European Journal of Clinical Microbiology and Infectious Disease, 3*, 909–915. https://doi.org/10.1007/s10096-013-1825-9

Van Hook, C. (2018). Hantavirus pulmonary syndrome—The 25th anniversary of the Four Corners outbreak. *Emerging Infectious Diseases, 24*(11), 2056–2060. https://doi.org/10.3201/eid2411.180381

Van Westen, R., Kliphuis, M., & Dijkstra, H. (2024). Physics-based early warning signal shows that AMOC is on tipping course. *Science Advances, 10*(6). https://doi.org/10.1126/sciadv.adk1189

Venkatesan, P. (2024). The 2023 WHO world malaria report. *The Lancet Microbe.* https://doi.org/10.1016/S2666-5247(24)00016-8

Ventola, C. L. (2015). The antibiotic resistance crisis: Part 1: Causes and threats. *P&T, 40*(4), 277–283.

Vieira-da-Silva, L. (2018). *O Campo da Saúde Coletiva: Gênese, transformações e aarticulações coma reforma sanitária.* Editora da UFBA, Editora Fiocruz.

Vos, T., Allen, C., & Arora, M. (2015). Global, regional, and national incidence, prevalence, and years lived with disability for 310 diseases and injuries, 1990–2015: A systematic analysis for the Global Burden of Disease Study. *Lancet, 88*, 1545–1602.

Voskoboynik, D. (2018). *The memory we could be.* New Society Publishers.

Wallerstein, N., Duran, B., Oetzel, J., & Minkler, M. (2017). *Community-based participatory research for health: Advancing social and health equity.* Jossey-Bass.

Wang, J., Foxman, B., Mody, L., et al. (2017). Network of microbial and antibiotic interactions drive colonization and infection with multidrug-resistant organisms. *Proceedings of the National Academy of Science USA, 114*(39), 10467–10472. https://doi.org/10.1073/pnas.1710235114

Wark, P., & Gibson, P. (2006). Asthma exacerbations 3: Pathogenesis. *Thorax, 61*(10), 909–915. https://doi.org/10.1136/thx.2005.045187

Webb, J. (2002). Syndemic anemia in British Malaya: An early global health encounter with hookworm and malaria co-infections in plantation workers. *Social Science & Medicine 295*, 113555. https://doi.org/10.1016/j.socscimed.2020.113555

Wehner, M., & Kossin, J. (2023). The growing inadequacy of an open-ended Saffir–Simpson hurricane wind scale in a warming world. *PNAS, 121*(7), e2308901121.

Weingarten, K. (2023). *Eleven tips for sustainable activism without getting overwhelmed.* Migrant Clinician Network. https://www.migrantclinician.org/blog/2021/oct/eleven-tips-sustainable-activism-without-getting-overwhelmed.html

Weintraub, P. (2011). *The human face of human tick-borne infections. Commissioned paper for critical needs and gaps in understanding prevention, amelioration, and resolution of Lyme and other tick-borne diseases: The short-term and long-term outcomes.* Workshop Report: A28–A36. Washington, DC: The National Academy of Medicine.

Welch, B. (2008). *State of confusion: Political manipulation and the assault on the American mind.* Thomas Dunne Books, St. Martin's Press. ISBN978-0-312-37306-1.

West, H. (2020). *No, thank u, next – the Saami are heavily burdened with Western science, so what?* Helga West. Blog. https://helgawest.com/2020/03/06/no-thank-u-next-the-saami-are-heavily-burdened-with-western-science-so-what/

Whitmee, S., Haines, A., Beyrer, C., Boltz, F., Capon, A. G., et al. (2015). Safeguarding human health in the Anthropocene epoch: report of The Rockefeller Planetary Health. https://www.thelancet.com/pdfs/journals/lancet/PIIS0140-6736(15)60901-1.pdf

Whitney, C., Frid, A., Edgar, B., Walkus, J., Siwallace, P., Siwallace, I., et al. (2020). "Like the plains people losing the buffalo": Perceptions of climate change impacts, fisheries management, and adaptation actions by indigenous peoples in coastal British Columbia, Canada. *Ecology & Society, 25*, 33. https://doi.org/10.5751/ES-12027-250433

Wieczorek, A., Morrison, L., Croot, P., Allcock, A., MacLoughlin, E., Savard, O., et al. (2018). Frequency of microplastics in mesopelagic fishes from the Northwest Atlantic. *Frontiers in Marine Science, 5*, 39. https://doi.org/10.3389/fmars.2018.00039

Williams, R. (2017). *A new era in global health: Nursing and the United Nations 2030 agenda for sustainable development.* Springer Publishing Co.

Willen, S., Knipper, M., Abadía-Barrero, C., & Davidovitch, N. (2017). Syndemic vulnerability and the right to health. *The Lancet, 389*, 964–977.

Willen, S., Williamson, A., Walsh, C., Hyman, M., & Tootle, W. (2022). Rethinking flourishing: Critical insights and qualitative perspectives from the U.S. Midwest. *SSM Mental Health*, 100057. https://www.sciencedirect.com/science/article/pii/S2666560321000578?via%3Dihub

References

Winter, D. (2022). *Toxic: 3M knew its chemicals were harmful decades ago, but didn't tell the public, government*. Minnesota Report. https://minnesotareformer.com/2022/12/15/toxic-3m-knew-its-chemicals-were-harmful-decades-ago-but-didnt-tell-the-public-government/

Woodall, T. (2024). *Got food poisoning? One of these 4 bugs is likely the cause*. National Geographic. https://www.nationalgeographic.com/science/article/types-of-food-poisoning-listeria-norovirus-salmonella-ecoli

Wootton, N., Ferreira, M., Reis-Santos, P., & Gillanders, B. (2021). A comparison of microplastic in fish from Australia and Fiji. *Frontiers in Marine Science, 8*, 690991. https://doi.org/10.3389/fmars.2021.690991

World Bank. (2004). *Sri Lanka development policy review*. https://documents1.worldbank.org/curated/ar/669231468164636029/pdf/293960REPLACEM10010BOX066101PUBLIC1.pdf

World Health Organization. (2022). *Global antimicrobial resistance and use surveillance system (GLASS) report, Geneva*. License: CC BY-NC-SA 3.0 IGO.

World Health Organization. (2024a). *Diarrhoeal disease*. https://www.who.int/news-room/fact-sheets/detail/diarrhoeal-disease#:~:text=Diarrhoeal%20disease%20is%20the%20third,aged%205%20to%209%20years

World Health Organization. (2024b). *Gonorrhoea (Neisseria gonorrhoeae infection)*. Fact Sheet. https://www.who.int/news-room/fact-sheets/detail/gonorrhoea-(neisseria-gonorrhoeae-infection)

World Heart Federation. (2023). *Deaths from cardiovascular disease disease surged 60% globally over the last 30 years*. HTTPS://WORLD-HEART-FEDERATION.ORG/NEWS/DEATHS-FROM-CARDIOVASCULAR-DISEASE-SURGED-60-GLOBALLY-OVER-THE-LAST-30-YEARS-REPORT/

Wu, X., Nethery, R., Sabath, M., Braun, D., & Dominic, F. (2020). Air pollution and COVID-19 mortality in the United States: Strengths and limitations of an ecological regression analysis. *Science Advances, 6*, eabd4049. https://doi.org/10.1126/sciadv.abd4049

Wynn, J. (2021). *Human Rights Hero: Dr. Anthony S. Fauci*. American Bar Association. https://www.americanbar.org/groups/crsj/publications/human_rights_magazine_home/the-truth-about-science/human-rights-hero/

Yale Office of Sustainability. (2023). *Yale experts explain climate anxiety*. https://sustainability.yale.edu/explainers/yale-experts-explain-climate-anxiety

Yang, W., Li, Z., Yang, T., Li, Y., Xie, Z., Feng, L., et al. (2024). Experts' consensus on the management of respiratory disease syndemic. *China CDC Weekly, 6*(8), 131–138. https://doi.org/10.46234/ccdcw2024.029

Yoder, K. (2021). *It's not just you: Everyone is Googling "climate anxiety"*. Salon. https://www.salon.com/2021/10/05/its-not-just-you-everyone-is-googling-climate-anxiety_partner/

Young, H., Dirzo, R., Helgen, K., & Dittmar, K. (2014). Declines in large wildlife increase landscape-level prevalence of rodent-borne disease in Africa. *PNAS, 111*(19), 7036–7041. https://doi.org/10.1073/pnas.1404958111

Yu, A. (2023). *IHS awards address HIV syndemic in Indian country*. Indian Health Service. https://www.ihs.gov/newsroom/ihs-blog/november-2023-blogs/ihs-awards-address-hiv-syndemic-in-indian-country/

Zhou, L. (2024). *Something weird is happening with tornadoes*. Vox. https://www.vox.com/climate/24155885/tornado-season-twister-clustering

Zhu, D. (2023). Cross-sectoral community and civic engagement after *Dobbs v. Jackson. The Lancet, Regional Health, 22*, 100514. https://doi.org/10.1016/j.lana.2023.100514

Zikhathile, T., Atagana, H., Bwapwa, J., & Sawtell, D. (2022). A review of the impact that healthcare risk waste treatment technologies have on the environment. *International Journal of Environmental Research and Public Health, 19*(19), 11967. https://doi.org/10.3390/ijerph19191196

Printed in the United States
by Baker & Taylor Publisher Services